RENEWALS 458-4574
DATE DUE

WITHDRAWN
UTSA LIBRARIES

Corporate Social Responsibility and Urban Development

Also by Edmundo Werna

PLURALISM IN HOUSING PROVISION IN DEVELOPING COUNTRIES: Lessons from Brazil (*co-authored*)

COMBATING URBAN INEQUALITIES: Challenges for Managing Cities in the Developing World

IMPLEMENTING THE HABITAT AGENDA: Towards Child-Friendly Cities (*co-authored*)

BUSINESS AS USUAL: Small-Scale Builders and the Production of Low-Income Housing in Developing Countries

URBAN HEALTH RESEARCH: Implications for Policy (*co-edited*)

Also by Ramin Keivani

PLURALISM IN HOUSING PROVISION IN DEVELOPING COUNTRIES: Lessons From Brazil (*co-authored*)

Also by David Murphy

IN THE COMPANY OF PARTNERS: Business, Environmental Groups and Sustainable Development Post-Rio (*co-authored*)

SOMETHING TO BELIEVE IN – CREATING TRUST IN ORGANISATIONS: Stories of Transparency, Accountability and Governance (*co-edited*)

Corporate Social Responsibility and Urban Development

Lessons from the South

Edmundo Werna
International Labour Organization, Switzerland

Ramin Keivani
Oxford Brookes University, UK

David Murphy
The Company of Partners, UK

© E. Werna, R. Keivani and D. Murphy 2009, except Chapter 1 © D. Murphy and A. Ng'ombe 2009 and Chapter 6 © A. Ng'ombe and E. Werna 2009

All rights reserved. No reproduction, copy or transmission of this publication may be made without written permission.

No portion of this publication may be reproduced, copied or transmitted save with written permission or in accordance with the provisions of the Copyright, Designs and Patents Act 1988, or under the terms of any licence permitting limited copying issued by the Copyright Licensing Agency, Saffron House, 6-10 Kirby Street, London EC1N 8TS.

Any person who does any unauthorized act in relation to this publication may be liable to criminal prosecution and civil claims for damages.

The authors have asserted their rights to be identified as the authors of this work in accordance with the Copyright, Designs and Patents Act 1988.

First published 2009 by
PALGRAVE MACMILLAN

Palgrave Macmillan in the UK is an imprint of Macmillan Publishers Limited, registered in England, company number 785998, of Houndmills, Basingstoke, Hampshire RG21 6XS.

Palgrave Macmillan in the US is a division of St Martin's Press LLC, 175 Fifth Avenue, New York, NY 10010.

Palgrave Macmillan is the global academic imprint of the above companies and has companies and representatives throughout the world.

Palgrave® and Macmillan® are registered trademarks in the United States, the United Kingdom, Europe and other countries.

ISBN-13: 978-0-230-52532-0   hardback
ISBN-10: 0-230-52532-6   hardback

This book is printed on paper suitable for recycling and made from fully managed and sustained forest sources. Logging, pulping and manufacturing processes are expected to conform to the environmental regulations of the country of origin.

A catalogue record for this book is available from the British Library.

Library of Congress Cataloging-in-Publication Data

Werna, Edmundo.
  Corporate social responsibility and urban development : lessons from the South / Edmundo Werna, Ramin Keivani, David Murphy.
    p. cm.
  Includes bibliographical references and index.
  ISBN 978-0-230-52532-0 (alk. paper)
  1. Industries—Social aspects. 2. City planning. I. Keivani, Ramin, 1963– II. Murphy, David, 1956– III. Title.
HD60.W47 2009
307.1'416–dc22   2008030681

10 9 8 7 6 5 4 3 2 1
18 17 16 15 14 13 12 11 10 09

Printed and bound in Great Britain by
CPI Antony Rowe, Chippenham and Eastbourne

Contents

List of Figures and Tables   vi

Preface   vii

Introduction   1
  Edmundo Werna, Ramin Keivani and David Murphy

Chapter 1   Corporate Social Responsibility   7
  David Murphy and Austine Ng'ombe

Chapter 2   Urban Development   34
  Edmundo Werna

Chapter 3   Citywide Interventions   52
  Ramin Keivani

Chapter 4   Construction   106
  Ramin Keivani

Chapter 5   Utilities   143
  Ramin Keivani

Chapter 6   Social Development   180
  Austine Ng'ombe and Edmundo Werna

Chapter 7   Conclusion   204
  Edmundo Werna, Ramin Keivani and David Murphy

Bibliography   216

Author Index   231

Subject Index   235

List of Figures and Tables

Figures

Figure 1.1	Carroll's CSR pyramid	15
Figure 1.2	Global CSR report output by year	15
Figure 1.3	Global CSR report output by region	28
Figure 3.1	'Three Pillars' model of sustainable development	54
Figure 3.2	Relative importance of main pillars of sustainable development through time	56
Figure 3.3	Trends of population growth and decline of agricultural land in China	80
Figure 4.1	The Pearce schema: construction industry and its relationship with other sectors of the economy	108
Figure 4.2	Construction of healthy and sustainable districts and condominiums	123
Figure 4.3	Team Living Waters – helping to build houses in Brazil	124
Figure 5.1	Overall access to improved sanitation by category of service in 2000	155
Figure 5.2	Continuum of utility/service provision	161
Figure 5.3	1.5 million people on 1 May 2001	171
Figure 6.1	Number of people living with HIV by region	191

Tables

Table 3.1	Key organisations in OSC Viva Guarulhos	93
Table 4.1	Summary of the main modes of housing provision in developing countries	113
Table 5.1	Per capita water use in Asian and Latin American cities	149
Table 5.2	Percentage coverage of water and sanitation in selected regions and countries in 2000	153
Table 5.3	Performance indicators in water utilities in ten African cities	163
Table 5.4	Community involvement	169
Table 5.5	Water volunteers	170
Table 6.1	The Copenhagen commitments	183
Table 7.1	Types of CSR elements/practices per case study	205

Preface

The idea for this book originated from an action research project on corporate social responsibility (CSR) in developing countries carried out by United Nations Volunteers and the New Academy of Business from 2001 to 2004. Edmundo Werna was the research manager for United Nations Volunteers (UNV) with David Murphy assuming this role for the New Academy. The research was not urban-specific, as it analysed CSR in general and business-community relations more specifically. However, this research, combined with parallel work of the authors of the present book on urban development, showed that there is a gap in the CSR literature within the specific urban context. This was defined as an important gap, and led to the idea of producing this book. Writing the book entailed revisiting the original research with a fresh perspective to identify appropriate urban based case studies, developing important points of debate and relevant theoretical and policy discourses that would allow fresh adaptation of the material to make a contribution to the specific role of CSR in urban areas in developing countries. Ramin Keivani came on board at the onset of the idea of the book, and worked throughout the whole process together with Edmundo Werna and David Murphy. Austine Ng'ombe worked on Chapters 1 and 6 of the book and is co-author of these two chapters.

The specific presentation of the case studies in this book draws heavily on the work of a number of the researchers from the UNV-New Academy research project. Therefore, their contribution is fully acknowledged here. The research team included: Roberto Felicio (case studies from Brazil), Joseph Boateng (Ghana), Lubna Forzley (Lebanon), Leonard Okafor (Nigeria), Charmaine Nuguid-Anden (Philippines), and Jean Niyonzima (South Africa). The specific section analysing CSR practices in Chapter 7 is informed by the work of Rupesh A. Shah on the UNV-New Academy project and his contribution is also fully acknowledged with warm thanks.

The authors of the book also thank both UNV and the New Academy for the research which, as noted, became the catalyst for the book.

The authors would like to pay homage to Sharon Capeling-Alakija (*in memoriam*), the Executive-Coordinator of United Nations Volunteers during 1998–2003, for all her support and inspiration related to the project with the New Academy of Business, and beyond. Homage is also paid to Anita Roddick (*in memoriam*), the founder and chair of the New Academy of Business as well as founder of The Body Shop, for all her relentless work in promoting CSR.

Edmundo Werna dedicates his work on the book to his late father-in-law George Ishihata, at the very least for the privilege of enjoying his contagious joy of living. Also, Ishihata, who worked for most of his life for the government of the state of Sao Paulo in Brazil and many times in close relationship with private companies, contributed to promote corporate social responsibility long before such a term even existed in the literature.

Ramin Keivani would like to dedicate his work on the book to his late father Manzar Moatazed-Keivani for his unwavering support all through out his life, his thirst for knowledge, his belief in goodness of human beings and resolute determination in the face of adversity.

David Murphy would like to dedicate his contribution to the book to his father Frank who worked for many years as a business manager and who introduced David to the private sector with his first full-time summer job with Pepsi-Cola in the mid-1970s.

Introduction
Edmundo Werna, Ramin Keivani and David Murphy

In 2003, the United Nations Volunteers (UNV) launched an initiative called 'Building Solidarity' as part of its urban agenda. The objective was to stimulate private construction companies to support the upgrading of urban low-income settlements in developing countries via corporate social responsibility (CSR). While a few initial attempts were made to link some companies and low-income settlements on an individual basis, it was felt that 'Building Solidarity' could only reach scale with the involvement of international organisations representing the relevant stakeholders. Therefore, UNV approached SDI (Slum/Shacks Dwellers International), representing low-income communities, and a construction industry association.

UNV's effort was a failure. The construction industry association declined the proposal, explaining that its agenda was already too busy and it could not take up a new initiative at the moment. The also negative reaction of SDI was surprising, considering that its constituents were meant to be beneficiaries of the upgrading projects. SDI appeared to be suspicious about a possible hidden agenda of private companies helping poor settlements without a direct commercial profit. What does this failed experience tell us? Is there, or not, a future for CSR in urban development? Can CSR provide a value added for cities and towns in developing countries? If yes, how?

This book will show that there is room for optimism, although CSR should not be taken as a panacea either. For a number of reasons, the aforementioned experience of UNV should not be taken as definitive proof of 'no-go'. First, organisations do change their views and policies over time; therefore this situation could alter. Second, individual construction companies and low-income communities still have the autonomy to engage in individual CSR projects. UNV ultimately succeeded in promoting a number of CSR projects pairing individual companies and low-income settlements. This book will also present further evidence. While at the time SDI was the largest international organisation representing low-income communities, a major limitation was that its constituents still came from a small number of countries, which means that a large number of communities did not belong to the organisation. SDI's leadership also includes a number of NGOs, which influence the decision-making process. And recently another, broader, organization representing low-income communities has been created, the International Alliance of Inhabitants, which could be an alternative to promote CSR with urban communities. In sum, there is scope for greater global action on CSR, perhaps under the future facilitation or leadership of international organisations, or at least at the local level. Nevertheless, the UNV experience does show that there is still much work to be done for CSR to be recognised as a valuable instrument to promote urban development, and the present book aims at contributing to this process.

This introduction prepares the ground for the whole book. It includes the following: (i) the importance and objective of the book, (ii) the countries and the themes of urban development to be studied, (iii) the overall structure of the book, and (iv) the audience of the book.

The importance and objective of the book

The book explores the growing role and importance of business-community relations in the field of international development, particularly in urban settings. While the role of the private sector in development has been the subject of great attention, the focus to date has been primarily on the contribution of its commercial activities and investments. However, more recently, the private sector's social role has also become a subject of attention. Within this context, there is a particular emphasis on business-community relations, which can be defined as the support of private enterprises to local communities via non-commercial means, an important dimension of CSR.

The role of business-community relations in development assistance is becoming more prominent. A growing number of private companies have established their own individual community development or social investment programmes. In addition, many agencies of the United Nations system have sought partnerships with the private sector to support local communities. Other development stakeholders, such as government agencies and NGOs, have also pursued new partnerships with business. Despite such progress to date, the contribution of CSR to development could be considerably larger. There is a great untapped potential, and the issue still needs to be better understood. Business-community relations are fundamentally different from commercial transactions, and are still largely neglected in the business and development literature, with the specific theme of urban development a notable gap.

As this book will show, cities and towns are pivotal for development. At the same time, urban poverty is on the increase and is already half of the total poverty in developing countries. For these reasons, assistance to urban populations is crucial to development. There is a need to discuss innovative solutions to urban problems, and business-community relations have an important role to play. However, the literature on the role of the private sector in urban development has largely focused on its commercial aspects. In parallel, the literature on urban volunteerism does not place much emphasis on CSR (although volunteerism and CSR are clearly connected).

Considering the above, this book seeks to raise the awareness of academics and practitioners about the value of CSR as a tool in development assistance. The book provides an overview on the themes of CSR and business-community relations, explaining their importance for development in general and for urban settings in particular. It illustrates the argument with rich evidence (case studies) from a wide geographical spread of developing countries, leading to recommendations for both further research and practice.

The countries and themes of urban development studied

The case study chapters of this book encompass four themes of urban development in urban areas of six developing countries, with complementary data from other countries. The case studies have been derived from an international action research project on CSR carried out by the New Academy of Business[1] and UNV (2004), which included 70 case studies in seven developing countries. The vast majority of these case

---

[1] The New Academy of Business was founded in 1995 by Anita Roddick as a business education and research organization that focused on the promotion of responsible and sustainable business practice. Its flagship programme was the MSc in Responsibility and Business Practice which was launched in 1997 in partnership with the University of Bath's School of Management. In 2005, the New Academy was transformed into the Association of Sustainability Practitioners, a membership network that seeks to promote learning that transforms behaviour from unsustainable to sustainable practices.

studies are not urban-related, and therefore the findings and conclusions of the aforementioned research are also not specific to urban development. The present book has selected information from the research which is specific to cities and towns, and it provides specific analysis within such a context. Therefore, the book builds on the research of the New Academy of Business and UNV, by providing a fresh perspective to the overall theoretical analysis of CSR and it application to urban development.

There are many other examples of private companies that engage with urban communities, individually or in association with other actors. However, the purpose of the book is not to be exhaustive, but to provide an analysis of selected cases and wider literature.

The countries of the case studies included in this book cover all the regions of the developing world. Their inclusion in the book is not intended to be representative of the developing world as a whole. The case studies nonetheless demonstrate that the argument of the book is pertinent to places as distant and different to each other as Philippines (Asia), Ghana, Nigeria and South Africa (Africa), Brazil (Latin America) and Lebanon (Middle East).

It is also important to note that the analysis of selected cities and towns does not aim to make statistical generalisations, but to demonstrate general principles. This is a valid procedure based on a case studies methodology (e.g. Paredes *et al.*, 2007; Wallman, 1984; Werna, 1996; Yin, 1989).

The four urban development themes included in the case study chapters are namely city-wide interventions, the construction industry, utilities and social issues (such as education and health). While this set of themes provides a broad picture of urban development, it should be noted that their choice follows a similar rationale to the choice of cities/ towns and countries. The idea is not to include absolutely everything nor to extract statistical generalisations, but to demonstrate general principles.

The book's structure

The ideas and argument introduced here will be developed in the book in seven chapters.

The two basic subjects of the book, CSR and urban development, are subsequently analysed in the first two chapters.

- **Chapter 1** focuses on CSR, introducing the concept and later deepening the analysis with attention to developing countries. It also

shows that urban development is still a gap within this body of literature.
- **Chapter 2** analyses the literature on urban development, noting the gap regarding CSR. The chapter concludes by affirming the importance of CSR in urban settings, preparing the ground for the remainder of the book.
- **Chapters 3 to 6** are based on a series of case studies. Each chapter focuses on a specific theme of urban development, noted in a previous section of the present chapter (3: city-wide interventions, 4: construction, 5: utilities, and 6: social development). The chapters include major experiences from six developing countries, complemented by summarised data from other countries in this part of the world.
- **Chapter 7** is the conclusion, drawing together evidence and common lessons from the case studies particularly from the standpoint of the different elements and practices of CSR. It also makes appropriate recommendations for the benefit of the research community and practitioners in the context of development assistance. One of the key arguments is that CSR should not be taken as a panacea, and there are indeed difficulties, noted in the book and concluded in Chapter 7. Despite these challenges, CSR initiatives can add value for urban development if appropriately designed and implemented with communities and other relevant stakeholders. This represents a major theme of the book as a whole.

The book's audience

The main audience of this book can be divided into two broad groups of practitioners and academics: those with a major interest in role of business in development and/or the broader concept of CSR, and those with a major interest in urban development.

Each group has its specific know-how and at the same time specific knowledge gaps. While the former group may be familiar with the issues included in Chapter 1, which covers CSR, such a chapter is necessary as background for the latter group. Given that to date the bulk of the CSR literature has focused on developed countries, and at the same time considering that the book has a focus on developing countries, many CSR experts may also find the aforementioned background useful.

Conversely, while the readers who are urban experts may be familiar with the issues included in Chapter 2, which covers urban development, this chapter is important to the other group of readers.

Together the first two chapters provide a necessary background for the understanding of the remainder (and bulk) of the book – which, it is anticipated, will bring new knowledge and added value to both groups of readers.

The book may also be of interest to many practitioners and academics specialized in one of the different disciplines within the overall umbrella of social sciences – thus constituting a third group of readers lacking specific knowledge on business/CSR or on urban development. Therefore, the background chapters (as well as the remainder of the book) will also be useful for this more general audience.

1
Corporate Social Responsibility

David Murphy and Austine Ng'ombe

The idea of Corporate Social Responsibility (CSR) has gained unprecedented international influence and attention in recent years within both business and development circles. In addition to its growing integration into business strategy, CSR is becoming as a key public policy concern from the local to the global level. Although the theory and practice of CSR have deep historical roots, the current CSR agenda is much more diverse and complex, and remains contested. Increasing numbers of companies are being challenged to express forms of social and environmental responsibility in their business practice. Local, regional and national governments and international organisations are facing growing pressure from various non-state actors to develop different and sometimes contradictory responses such as voluntary codes of conduct, social and environmental auditing and reporting guidelines, cross-sector partnerships, formal legislative/regulatory measures and sometimes merely maintaining the status quo.

This chapter provides a broad overview of the theory and practice of Corporate Social Responsibility, highlighting growing academic and practitioner interest in CSR and related concepts as instruments for development. The chapter explores the evolution of CSR thought and action with greater emphasis on more recent trends and developments.

The chapter provides both historical context and a selected review of a burgeoning set of CSR literature. This includes a discussion of the virtues and criticisms of CSR as well as the practical application of the concept in a number of key CSR practice areas. The chapter also includes a particular focus on the place of CSR in the work of the United Nations and more broadly in the field of development.

One of the key conclusions of the chapter is that the geographical balance of the CSR literature is predominantly based on the experience of Western Europe and North America much to the neglect of developing countries and other parts of the world. The specific relationship between CSR and urban development will be explored in Chapter 2.

1.1 CSR origins

The history of CSR dates back at least 5,000 years (Conroy, 2007), however the social responsibility of business did not begin to be recognised as a distinct area of academic inquiry until the 1950s. One of the first books in the business management literature, Howard Bowen's (1953) *Social Responsibilities of the Businessman*, described what we now call CSR as the "obligations of businessmen to pursue those policies, to make those decisions, or to follow those lines of actions which are desirable in terms of the objectives and values of society" (p. 6).

CSR practice in the 'modern' era can be traced to the 'enlightened self interest' of 19th-century industrial philanthropists who introduced various social initiatives. In the Victorian period, businesses such as Cadburys, Rowntrees and Hersheys sought to improve living standards of their employees (Clement-Jones, 2005). British entrepreneurs including Robert Owen, Titus Salt, George Wilson, the Clark family and the Cadbury brothers wanted healthy, contented workers in their factories and saw a need for various social welfare schemes to alleviate the adverse living and working conditions of the time. In addition to providing worker housing, their philanthropy extended to a range of public and social buildings such as churches, shops, parks and hospitals. The German industrialist Robert Bosch introduced equivalent schemes for his workers and their communities. Similar examples of corporate provision of worker housing and social facilities can be found in the 19th-century workers colonies in France, Austria, Italy, Holland and Germany, and in early company towns such as Pullman in America (Cherry, 1972). The establishment of foundations such as those of Rockefeller and Carnegie represent early examples of CSR in the United States.

In late 19th-century Japan, factory employers provided welfare benefits in an effort to entice and retain workers (Hall, 1988). While in some Western countries the early business welfare schemes could be linked to the Protestant work ethic, industrial philanthropists also understood the relationship between long-term profitability and the health and welfare of the local communities where their businesses were located (Barrett, 1997).

Not all of this enlightened self-interest was voluntary. Social critics such as novelist Charles Dickens and utopian socialist William Morris challenged irresponsible industrialists by arguing that the harsh working and living conditions of British cities desperately needed improvement. Morris's 1891 novel *News From Nowhere* imagined a future society where exploitative and physically harmful factory work was transformed into a cooperative, sustainable model where small was indeed beautiful. Other socialist writers such as Frederick Engels and Karl Marx insisted that the careless nature of capitalism would eventually lead to its demise (Murphy and Bendell, 1997).

1.2 The evolution of CSR

By the late 1960s, CSR had begun to move beyond Bowen's and others focus on the responsibilities of the individual business owner/manager towards the social and environmental accountability of the company as an entity (Davis, 1967; Falck and Heblich, 2007). Growing public environmental awareness and the emergence of environmental movements in many Western countries were key drivers that prompted various companies and industries to begin to respond to environmental challenges (Murphy and Bendell, 1997).

The Royal Dutch Shell Group was one of the first major companies to introduce formal CSR policies and procedures. An internal Shell management information brief dated September 1969 demonstrates that the company recognised early on the growing significance of the environment as a social responsibility issue for large corporations:

> The size and wide range of Group companies' activities make the problem of environmental conservation a matter of close concern. The efforts and resources devoted to its solution ... are part of the pattern of doing business in a way that is responsible and socially acceptable. (Shell Briefing Service, 1969: 8)

In order to formalise the company's commitment to environmental issues, Shell introduced its first official policy on environmental conservation in December 1969 (Murphy and Bendell, 1997).

Around this time, the social dimensions of CSR tended to focus on business ethics in both the workplace and in commercial transactions, and on corporate philanthropy in the form of donations and endowments for various local community causes. Supply chain issues related to human rights violations, child labour and forced labour had yet to gain prominence on the CSR agenda.

1.2.1 Three waves of CSR

Some writers have attempted to document the history of CSR in chronological order such as one offered by John Elkington (2004) that describes three historical pressure waves through which CSR has evolved – *limits, green* and *global*.

- **CSR Pressure Wave 1: 'Limits'** covers the period of 1960–1978 when Western governments sought to limit environmental impacts and natural resource exploitation through legislation and regulation. Businesses were expected to meet minimum environmental standards. This was made easier partly by the founding in the early 1960s of Amnesty International and Worldwide Fund for Nature (WWF), which were committed to the realisation of global social and environmental standards respectively. This wave reached its peak in the early 1970s during which major global summits were held and more global organisations with an interest in the environment were founded. For instance, *Friends of the Earth* and *Greenpeace* were founded in 1969 and 1971 respectively. Earth Day was launched in 1970 and the Stockholm UN Conference on the Human Environment took place in mid-1972. A few months earlier the Club of Rome published the seminal report *Limits to Growth*. Wave 1 underwent a downfall during the late 1970s, perhaps as global attention shifted from the natural environment to the catastrophic oil price shocks of 1978.
- **CSR Pressure Wave 2: 'Green'** was initiated in the early 1980s with the focus of environmentalists shifting from 'limits' to 'green'. That is, the focus shifted from imposing limits on exploitation of the environment, to the production of 'green' products, thus, moving towards sustainable utilisation of natural resources. The concept of sustainable development was coined during this period. Accordingly, and among other things, this wave saw the publication of the popular Brundtland's Report in 1987. The green consumer movement began to emerge in many Northern countries in the late 1980s, and the UN Earth Summit was held in Rio de Janeiro, Brazil in 1992. All of these represented major efforts by the international community to address critical issues that posed danger not only to the environment but to business as well.

- **CSR Pressure Wave 3: 'Global'** began in 1999 when protests erupted against international institutions such as the World Bank and various global corporations, typified by the 'Battle of Seattle' and numerous others sites of protest coinciding with major international summits around the turn of the century. Such protests raised concerns about global capitalism but also emphasised the crucial role that business could play in fostering sustainable development. The Global wave has been characterised by rapid developments in information and communication technology (ICTs), which have subsequently subjected global corporations to intense public scrutiny, making it possible for stakeholders to access and share information about business (mis)deeds at a rate faster than ever before. Issues of corporate governance and strategic competitive advantage of businesses have more recently characterised the wave. The prominence of globalisation on the current development agenda has increased the level of complexity surrounding the concept of CSR. Over the past decade, the list of business responsibilities for social and environmental matters has continued to grow with human rights, climate change and poverty issues featuring prominently on the CSR agenda in recent years.

1.3 Recent thinking and action on CSR

As noted above, the need for businesses to be CSR-compliant can be linked to the growing prominence of issues of globalisation and advancements in technology. The CSR arguments and counter-arguments generally revolve around the broad theme of the role of direct business involvement in tackling socio-economic problems of the world. However, despite the increasing awareness of CSR, the concept still remains one of the most confusing and misunderstood notions in the modern corporate world (Sexty, 2004; 2008). Despite the lack of clarity of what constitutes CSR, one of the most recent additions to the literature is a CSR encyclopaedia (Visser et al., 2007).

So, what then is CSR in the 21st century and why do so many international businesses and their stakeholders appear to be increasingly obsessed with the concept? The starting point is an attempt at providing a current working definition of CSR.

One of the widely quoted business practitioner definitions of CSR is by the World Business Council for Sustainable Development (WBCSD) which states that "corporate social responsibility is the continuing commitment by business to behave ethically and contribute to economic development while improving the quality of life of the workforce and their families as well as of the local community and society at large" (WBCSD, 1999: 3). CSR is a concept that frequently overlaps with similar approaches such as corporate sustainability, corporate responsibility, and corporate citizenship. While the concept may not have a universal definition, it is increasingly seen as the integration of wider economic, social, and environmental imperatives into the core strategies and activities of business entities. At the heart of this holistic definition is the challenge to the business community to go beyond the profit motive and assume a certain measure of social and environmental responsibility beyond mere legal compliance.

Despite the rise of CSR in recent years, it remains an elusive and highly contested concept. There are so many competing definitions (Visser, 2006a; Wanderley, 2002; Sexty, 2004; Moon, 2002 in Visser, 2006a) that the most prominent feature that emerges from them is the vagueness associated with the concept and a lack of effective proposals to be suggested and implemented (Wanderley, 2002). The elusiveness of the term can perhaps be attributed to its multidimensional nature. There are also claims that if correctly defined, CSR cannot be achieved. This is the sceptical thesis to which scholars like Gray and Milne (2002: 73) prescribe when they note that "If it is defined in a way that suits business... [CSR] ends up fairly trivial or tautological. If it is defined as an individual would understand it, the concept is clearly unachievable by a financially successful organization because responsibility runs against the principles of self-interest upon which most notions of business are predicated."

Indeed CSR has been called many different things depending on one's perspective. CSR-related concepts and terms include: business ethics, corporate citizenship, business sustainability, business and society, corporate governance, socially responsible investment (SRI), ethical entrepreneurship, corporate environmental management, eco-efficiency, and product stewardship, to name a few (Habisch and Jonker, 2005; Visser, 2006a; Baker, 2007). Research on education on CSR conducted in Europe in 2003 confirms the multiplicity of concepts synonymous with CSR (Visser, 2006a; Matten and Moon, 2004). In that survey only 16% of business schools in Europe were found to be using the term CSR. The research also found 40 different labels for CSR programmes, 50 different labels for modules on CSR and a host of synonyms for the concept.

Holme and Watts (2000: 7) define CSR as "the commitment of business to contribute to sustainable development, working with employees, their families, the local community and society at large to improve their quality of life" (quoted by Wanderley, 2002). This sounds a good candidate definition but it contains an assumption that the reader already knows what 'sustainable development' is. A good CSR definition should explicitly spell out issues of how to deal with impacts on environment, economic prosperity and social justice.

For Mallen Baker (Baker, 2007), the Development Director for the UK-based corporate-membership organisation Business in the Community, "CSR is about how companies manage the business processes to produce an overall positive impact on society." Again, the weakness in this definition lies in its inability to plainly bring out the element of environmental preservation. Construction Excellence (2007), a UK organisation that aims to promote excellence in the design of the urban environment, defines CSR as "the commitment to integrate socially responsible values and concerns of stakeholders into their operations in a manner that fulfils and exceeds current legal and commercial expectations." What tends to be the norm in the efforts to clarify CSR is that each authority defines the term according to their area of expertise (Baker, 2007). As a result the definitions are either ambiguous or have one of the key dimensions of CSR implied in the definitions.

According to Visser (2006b), Carroll's CSR Pyramid (1991) is probably the most well known model of corporate social responsibility. Unlike many other advocates of CSR who consider economic, environmental and social issues to be the key dimensions in CSR, Carroll considers four – economic, legal, ethical, and philanthropic. The four are presented in a pyramid (Figure 1.1) with economic responsibility occupying the more important position at the base of the pyramid. Legal responsibility occupies the second position, followed by ethical and then philanthropic responsibility at the top of the pyramid. Carroll argues that all of these responsibilities have always existed to some degree, but ethical and philanthropic responsibilities have only become significant in recent years (Sexty, 2004).

The argument behind Carroll's pyramid is that economic responsibility is the first priority for companies. Businesses are expected to provide goods and services as reflected in their business case. However, corporations should make profits within the framework of national and international legal systems. Ethical responsibilities include issues that communities do not usually expect companies to address such as support for human rights or social justice. Companies are also not always under legal obligations to meet these kinds of ethical responsibilities. Lack of proper understanding of ethical business responsibilities has attracted considerable debate. Such responsibilities that are not required by law will always be difficult to observe. Philanthropic responsibility entails being a good corporate citizen. It may take the form of charitable giving, cause-related marketing, etc. Philanthropy tends to be more of a discretionary or voluntary activity on the part of business; however, communities may expect larger businesses to carry out such activities. In summary, Carroll contends that the cumulative responsibility of companies involves a simultaneous fulfilment of economic, legal, ethical and philantropic responsibility. The model has however not escaped criticism. Visser (2006b) for instance, questions its universality, arguing that CSR defies universal modelling. The concept of CSR is highly location-specific, meaning that the ordering of the blocks of responsibilities as indicated in the pyramid may change depending on the country or locality concerned.

Beyond the plethora of CSR definitions and frameworks, there are three generally accepted dimensions that are fundamental to CSR. Elkington's (2004) popular idea of Triple Bottom Line (TBL) is perhaps the best proposition to elaborate the three key constituents of CSR. The three elements embedded in the TBL concept are economic prosperity, environmental quality and social equity. TBL is a strategy that evaluates the performance of a company based on its economic, social and environmental contributions. From the time it was coined, TBL has received wider acceptance among the research community, politicians, policy makers and many other CSR experts. It has become a widely accepted tool for reporting businesses' performance against economic, social and environmental indicators. Perhaps it is because of the introduction of the proposition that TBL reporting has increased in the last decade. A check on Corporateregister.com, a database of company CSR reports, reveals that the number of CSR company reports has been rising since 1992, rising from only 22 in 1992 to 2240 in 2006 (Figure 1.2).

CSR is ultimately about promoting sustainability through business action in three areas: economic, environmental and social. For this reason we prefer the more holistic and easy-to-understand definition of the UK's Department of Trade and Industry (United Kingdom Government, 2007) which states that CSR "is about how business takes account of its economic, social and environmental impacts in the way it operates – maximising the benefits and minimising the downsides."

Figure 1.1 Carroll's CSR pyramid
Source: Visser, 2006b.

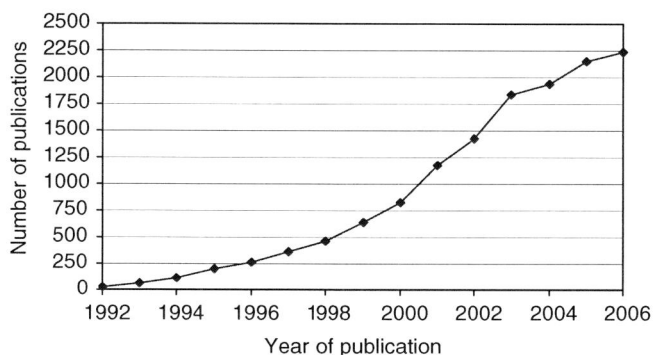

Figure 1.2 Global CSR report output by year
Source: Corporateregister.com, 2007.

Prime Minister Gordon Brown elaborates the UK's position on CSR in the UK Government's (2004) CSR report:

> Today, corporate social responsibility goes far beyond the old philanthropy of the past – donating money to good causes at the end of the financial year – and is instead an all year round responsibility that companies accept for the environment around them, for the best working practices, for their engagement in their local communities and for their recognition that brand names depend not only on quality, price and uniqueness but on how, cumulatively, they interact with companies' workforce, community and environment. Now we need to move towards a challenging measure of corporate responsibility, where we judge results not just by the input but by its outcomes: the difference we make to the world in which we live, and the contribution we make to poverty reduction.

CSR is about how businesses align their values and behaviour with the expectations and needs of stakeholders (not just shareholders and customers, but also employees, suppliers, communities, regulators, special interest groups and society as a whole). There are other concepts that describe the role of the business community in the search for solutions to socio-economic problems. These are outlined below.

1.4 CSR-related concepts

There are numerous other terms that are frequently used in place of CSR. Key among them are the following examples: Business-Community Relations, Corporate Citizenship and Corporate Governance. These need to be clearly understood in order to ascertain the global position of CSR.

1.4.1 Business-Community Relations

The definition of Business-Community Relations (BCR) is not as contested as the broader concept of CSR. In 2004, United Nations Volunteers (UNV) and New Academy of Business published a joint global report on *Enhancing Business-Community Relations: The role of volunteers in promoting global corporate citizenship*. They define BCR as "the ways in which communities and businesses interact with one another" (New Academy of Business and UNV, 2004: 13). This interaction ranges from philanthropy to social investment, including strategic business involvement in local communities such as employee volunteering and stakeholder accountability. Here, the community could include a local village in which the business is located, employees of the business or an international coalition of activists. BCR activities would include renovating community buildings, providing poles for rural electrification projects, sinking boreholes, providing scholarships to deserving pupils and paying royalties (New Academy of Business/UNV, 2004). These activities are done in exchange for a sustained license to operate. It therefore follows that BCR is only a component of CSR.

1.4.2 Corporate Citizenship

According to McAlister *et al.* (2005: xi), Corporate Citizenship (CC) is "the extent to which a business adopts a strategic focus for fulfilling the economic, legal, ethical, and philanthropic social responsibilities expected by all stakeholders." The concept of CC borrows its tenets from, and is a metaphor of the idea of a 'good citizen'. Responsible citizens dispose of their garbage in designated areas instead of dumping it on high streets, for example. This is because dumping garbage in designated areas is considered to be more socially acceptable (McIntosh *et al.*, 1998). Thus, citizenship is a notion that implies a two-way relationship anchored around the 'scratch my back, I scratch yours' metaphor. Companies that nurture this mutually reinforcing relationship are more likely to flourish because they are expected (and actually aim) to do 'the right thing'.

Proponents of this more strategic relationship between corporations and the host societies include Michael Porter and Mark Kramer of Harvard University (Porter and Kramer, 2006). The authors argue that citizenship initiatives, which are anchored on non-reciprocal relationships between company and society – i.e. where the company is seen as the sole provider – are doomed to fail. Meaningful CC initiatives can be achieved if the business adopts a competitive strategy where it understands the importance of the interdependence that exists between the company and the society. The citizenship policy therefore needs to be anchored in the strategies of the business. This enhances the corporation's competitive advantage whilst uplifting the living standards of the society. A business decision to support a community health project, for example, would not be a blind donation by the company but a CSR activity decided on the basis of competitive strategy to enable the business to strengthen its competitive advantage.

The relationship between CC and CSR is very difficult to spell out. The most visible distinction between the two is that CC is a form of CSR that emphasises the notion of social contract. The two concepts are nonetheless often used interchangeably (Habisch and Jonker, 2005).

1.4.3 Corporate governance

Corporate governance can be defined as "the implementation of policies, procedures and reporting arrangements to ensure a company understands and manages its risks effectively" (Llewellyn, 2005: 111).

The existing framework of structures and mechanisms for corporate governance (CG) can be traced back to the establishment of the modern corporation as a distinct legal entity in the early 20th century. This framework has been based on three main principles:

(i)   the legal concept of ownership as property rights; with the residual claims of ownership vested in stock/shareholders;
(ii) the separation of ownership and control under company law: i.e. recognising the impracticality of a diverse body of shareowners exercising day to day control of company operations;
(iii) the elaboration of structures of CG through Articles of Association under company law whereby the power of control is divided between directors and shareholders.

The legal and regulatory framework thus establishes an agency contract between 'owners' and 'managers', which means that directors are formally in the position of trustees, vested with the responsibility to ensure that the company is managed in the owners' interests. In order to limit the managerial discretion arising from the separation of ownership and control, the basic agency contract is supplemented by further rules and fiduciary duties regulating the behaviour of directors as trustees.

In practice, large publicly owned companies are not run solely by directors, but through executive management bodies reporting to boards of directors. Directors monitor the managerial performance of executives who effectively assume the statuatory and fiduciary responsibilities of their directors.

Some scholars like Kuhndt *et al.* (2004: 2) have clarified the concept as Responsible Corporate Governance (RCG), which they define as "a stakeholder-based policy instrument, which aims at allocating responsibilities to societal actors aiming at corporate accountability". The authors go further to outline guidelines that CEOs should follow in order to observe RCG. These are reproduced hereunder:

- assume societal leadership for responsibility;
- identify clearly and specifically their social, environmental and economic values in accordance with the demands of their stakeholders;
- define their social, environmental and economic priority areas for action;
- adopt specific management practices to integrate these values into their operations and take measurable action;
- disclose comprehensive data on their social, environmental and economic impacts;
- undertake a comprehensive review of their activities; and
- strive for continuous learning.

On this basis it therefore follows that, simply put, Corporate Governance is the way company managers strategically design and implement CSR initiatives. It is a management tool and can provide a framework for CSR initiatives.

Despite the diversity of concepts related to CSR, there is a common denominator that seems to unite them. The key concept behind community relations, citizenship and governance (and other CSR-related concepts) is the idea that companies should not account for their financial performance only. They should also endeavour to audit, account for and report their social and environmental impacts and make positive contributions to the communities in which their businesses operate. After all, products and brands are judged not only on the basis of their quality and price but also on the basis of the reputation of the manufacturers of those products (Employer Supported Volunteering, 2007).

Although there is clearly growing public awareness and academic interest in the topic, CSR remains a much contested concept. There continue to be both a lack of agreement on a coherent, consistent definition, coupled with disagreements about the actual benefits of CSR practices for both business and society. A detailed analysis of academic debates about the potential and limits of CSR are beyond the scope of this book. For readers wishing to explore these debates further, Clement-Jones (2005) explores the ongoing tensions between CSR utopians, sceptics and realists. The often-quoted adage of "the business of business is business" (Friedman, 1962) lies at the heart of debates between these three groups and others. The following section touches on some of these tensions in the context of the work of the United Nations on CSR in recent years.

1.5 CSR, partnership and the United Nations

While the role of businesses in international development has been the subject of great attention for many years, this has primarily been understood from the perspective of a strong faith in the multiplier effects and spillover benefits of commercial business activities. However, more recently, the role of businesses in (direct) development assistance is becoming more pronounced. A growing number of private companies have gone as far as establishing their own individual community development assistance programmes. In addition, many multinational development agencies such as the World Bank, the International Monetary Fund, the Organisation for Economic Co-operation and Development (OECD), and the United Nations system have sought partnerships with the private sector to support local communities. Equally, other development stakeholders, such as government agencies and Non-Governmental Organisations (NGOs), are pursuing new partnerships with businesses in an effort to foster development.

Although partnership has been recognised as a key component of international development policy for more than three decades, the active participation of business as a development partner is a more recent phenomenon and one that is still not universally embraced by all development actors. Businesses have had relationships with the United Nations since its inception in 1945. At its most simple level, the private sector has historically met, and continues to meet, the procurement needs of an organisation as large as the UN. Business has also taken an active interest in the UN's political, economic and social debates from the outset. The International Chamber of Commerce and other business interests were represented at the founding United Nations Conference on International Organisation in San Francisco. Business and industry widely endorsed the new UN Charter, as exemplified by the "earnest and enthusiastic support" of General Electric (cited in Tessner, 2000: xix).

Early on the pattern of UN-business relations took on a regulatory flavour with proposals from 1945 onwards for international action on restrictive business practices. This pattern intensified and continued as UN membership expanded in the 1950s and 1960s with former colonies in Asia and Africa gaining independence and advocating international regulation of commodity prices.

This was complemented by the Commission on Transnational Corporations (TNCs) in 1974, which constructed the approach of the UN towards the private sector as having a strong multi-lateral and regulatory element. However, by the mid-1980s, efforts to draw up a UN Code of Conduct for TNCs had been more or less abandoned. In March 1991, the US government requested all its foreign embassies to lobby their host governments to "quietly build a consensus against further negotiations" on the UN Code. The Code's official demise came in 1992, when the president of the UN General Assembly reported that "delegations felt that the changed international environment and the importance attached to encouraging foreign investment required a fresh approach."

Following the first regulatory moves of the 1970s and 1980s, the early 1990s saw the relationship between the UN and the private sector become infused with the flavours of collaboration, partnership and voluntary action. This reconsideration towards collaboration has emerged alongside the growing impact and reach of business activities globally and a new rationale, promoted by Kofi Annan, for closer cooperation and partnership between the United Nations and non-state actors, including the business community. The rethink has also developed at a time when the business community is increasingly appreciative of the role of the United Nations, which helps to provide a stable and favourable framework for business and development. A third driver in this move towards a more collaborative stance towards business has been the rise of sustainable development as a locus for action.

The high-profile 1992 UN Conference on Environment and Development in Rio de Janeiro offered an inclusive vision of partnership. The global partnership called for at Rio grew out of recognition that international co-operation needed more than traditional forms of foreign aid. A key point was the assertion that global partnership would only be effective if based on new levels of co-operation between all key sectors of society and government. One of the major achievements of the UN system both at Rio and beyond has been the integration of global partnership principles into international policy processes. Representatives of all of the major groups identified in Agenda 21 at Rio – business and employers' organisations, trade unions and workers, NGOs, indigenous peoples, local authorities, youth groups, women's organisations, farmers and the scientific community – are now actively engaged in the development and implementation of policy frameworks for sustainable development and other global issues.

Following the appointment of Kofi Annan as Secretary-General in 1996, the role of business as both a development actor and UN partner gained further momentum. The launch of the UN Global Compact in 2000 brought strategic leadership to UN-business-civil society engagement and a supportive value-based platform for both responsible business practice and UN institutional learning.

The Global Compact aims to promote responsible corporate citizenship to enable business to be part of the solution to the challenges of globalisation. It is a voluntary initiative based upon ten principles in the areas of human rights, labour standards, environment and anti-corruption (see p. 23).

The Global Compact is formed as a network with its core comprising the Global Compact Office within the UN Secretary-General's Office and six UN agencies – the Office of the High Commissioner for Human Rights (OHCHR); the United Nations Environment Programme (UNEP); the International Labour Organization (ILO); the United Nations Development Programme (UNDP); the United Nations Industrial Development Organization (UNIDO); and the UN Office on Drugs and Crime (UNODC). The Global Compact was not designed to be a prescriptive or regulatory instrument, but the UN rather aims to provide a framework to promote good corporate citizenship through committed and creative leadership and a strong focus on learning. The six UN partner agencies work individually and sometimes together to promote the Global Compact principles at global, regional, national and local levels. Much of this work has focused on the development of tools and training materials to assist companies to integrate the principles into their business practice.

The strategic partnership value of the Global Compact, according to Georg Kell and David Levin (Kell and Levin, 2002: 2), is that it makes "the UN relevant by leveraging its authority and convening powers in ways that will actually produce the positive social change it aspires to create." With more than 4,000 participants, including over 3,000 businesses in 90 countries around the world, the Global Compact has become the world's largest corporate citizenship initiative.

Other private-sector-related work within the UN varies considerably in form and structure. For example, various UN entities conduct research and organise events on the role of business in development. Other organisations within the UN system act more directly on the ground with businesses, sometimes involving employee volunteers. For example, United Nations Volunteers (UNV) offers business people opportunities to share their skills and experience with UNV's development partners and beneficiaries throughout the world, whereas the ILO promotes social marketing approaches to improve job quality in micro-

The UN Global Compact Principles

The Global Compact's ten principles in the areas of human rights, labour, the environment and anti-corruption enjoy universal consensus and are derived from:

- The Universal Declaration of Human Rights
- The International Labour Organization's Declaration on Fundamental Principles and Rights at Work
- The Rio Declaration on Environment and Development
- The United Nations Convention Against Corruption

The Global Compact asks companies to embrace, support and enact, within their sphere of influence, a set of core values in the areas of human rights, labour standards, the environment, and anti-corruption:

Human Rights

- **Principle 1:** Businesses should support and respect the protection of internationally proclaimed human rights; and
- **Principle 2:** make sure that they are not complicit in human rights abuses.

Labour Standards

- **Principle 3:** Businesses should uphold the freedom of association and the effective recognition of the right to collective bargaining;
- **Principle 4:** the elimination of all forms of forced and compulsory labour;
- **Principle 5:** the effective abolition of child labour; and
- **Principle 6:** the elimination of discrimination in respect of employment and occupation.

Environment

- **Principle 7:** Businesses should support a precautionary approach to environmental challenges;
- **Principle 8:** undertake initiatives to promote greater environmental responsibility; and
- **Principle 9:** encourage the development and diffusion of environmentally friendly technologies.

Anti-Corruption

- **Principle 10:** Businesses should work against corruption in all its forms, including extortion and bribery.

and small enterprises in countries such as Ghana, India and Vietnam, in addition to its work on the Global Compact as well as many other CSR-related initiatives.

UN-private sector engagement on CSR-related initiatives is growing. Recent research by Bull *et al.* (2004), Witte and Reinicke (2005) and Sørensen and Petersen (2006) reveals a wide range of UN-business collaboration in the following areas:

- **Policy dialogue:** encompassing both formal and informal engagement in intergovernmental processes including the development of norms and standards
- **Global advocacy:** organising joint campaigns to raise public awareness about the UN and its goals, targets and programmes
- **Resource mobilisation:** sharing and coordinating resources for development projects and humanitarian assistance including technical advice, funding, employee volunteering and in-kind support
- **Information and learning:** facilitating the exchange and sharing of knowledge, research and collaborative learning
- **Operational delivery:** cooperating on the design and implementation of on-the-ground projects
- **Investment and market mechanisms:** securing private investment for development (e.g. job creation, provision of services, infrastructure) and supporting sustainable markets for socio-economic empowerment

The expansion of the UN Global Compact and other forms of UN-business partnership activity demonstrates that the UN system is increasingly leveraging the knowledge, expertise and other resources of the private sector to support the achievement of UN goals and targets. Despite this enthusiasm and momentum, many partnership sceptics remain in the wider UN stakeholder community and indeed within the UN itself.

Although the language of partnership and cooperation increasingly infuse the UN's work with the private sector, the collaborative approach is not without its critics. For example, Judith Richter, who has worked as a consultant for UNICEF and WHO, expresses concern over the influence of large corporations upon the UN system (Richter, 2002) Kenny Bruno of CorpWatch.com uses the term 'bluewash' in his report Greenwash+10 and raises questions about the motives and actual practices of companies that are "wrapping themselves in the UN flag and claiming to be champions of UN values such as human rights and poverty elimination, as well as environmental protection" (Bruno, 2002: 6). A significant issue that emerges from these critiques is that the engagement of individual companies in order to voluntarily improve their performance on any number of issues can be a distraction from a wider set of changes that need to be enacted within the global economic system for more environmentally sustainable, people-centred forms of development and targets such as the Millennium Development Goals (MDGs) to be achieved. Ann Zammit (2003: 8) of the UN Research Institute for Social Development (UNRISD) suggests:

> While many see TNCs as unquestioned purveyors of development and progress, for others TNCs will not further development in the South unless these firms operate within an internationally agreed framework of ground-rules. This view is espoused not only by those protesting against the current form of globalisation: the work of many scholars demonstrates that neoliberal economic policies...do much to inhibit economic and social development in many parts of the world. This poses an important challenge to the UN partnership approach.

The implication arising from such critiques is that UN-business partnerships should not supplant the development and enforcement of legal and regulatory mechanisms to promote more responsible business globally. Given the above, it is not surprising that the 2005 UN General Assembly resolution on global partnerships encouraged "further efforts by...the private sector, to engage as reliable and consistent partners in the development process" and challenged the UN's business partners to bring "social values and responsibilities to bear on a conduct and policy premised on profit incentives, in conformity with national laws and regulations".[1]

Two years earlier at a 2003 UNRISD conference on 'CSR and Development', some of the participants highlighted a number of ways for UN agencies to promote CSR and enhanced business contribution to development:

- **Setting norms:** The UN should adopt a regulatory role. Examples of such formal accountability mechanisms exist in a spectrum from

---

[1] United Nations General Assembly (2005) p. 2.

harder mechanisms such as the Framework Convention on Tobacco Control and the draft Norms on the Responsibility of Transnational Corporations and other Business Entities with regard to Human Rights to softer approaches such as the Global Compact.
- **Promoting policy dialogue:** The UN should engage Member States in an exploration of policy options. Building upon an idea expressed by UNEP's Cornelis van der Lugt that the UN has "never been given a mandate by governments to take one particular position", there is possibly a significant role for UN agencies in examining different approaches, developing benchmarks and indicators, promoting independent verification, and building capacity to advance implementation.
- **Follow-up by UN Secretariats:** The UN agencies and officials should remind Member States of their commitments under international law.
- **Using the UN's procurement and investigative power:** The UN should use its procurement system to influence business behaviour. This could also include the development of whistle-blower system encompassing investigative procedures related to malpractice.
- **Putting information in the public domain:** The UN should increase transparency by making information on standards and practices of individuals companies publicly available.
- **Best practice learning:** The UN should develop understanding about practices of companies operating in different geographic, socio-economic and sector contexts.

The Millennium Declaration and the MDGs demonstrate that there is international consensus on the key challenges that have to be addressed in order to meet the needs and hopes of people everywhere. There is also growing recognition that the cause of 'larger freedom' can only be advanced by broad, deep and sustained global cooperation among States and non-state actors. Effective and accountable partnerships between strong and capable states, private sector businesses, civil society organisations and the UN system may actually be the only way to achieve wide ranging UN reforms as well as the MDGs.

There is also clear UN leadership and policy commitment to reforms that reshape the organisation dramatically with unprecedented boldness and speed. Global partnership between the UN and business should also be seen as one of cornerstones of the UN reform process. Both parties have much to learn from each other about how best to respond to complex global challenges, and how to reform their own organisations and to ensure that they are accountable to their respective stakeholders.

1.6 CSR and development

As noted in the previous section, Corporate Social Responsibility is a concept with growing prominence in the field of international development, particularly related to the work of the United Nations. Its importance as an instrument for tackling poverty and other social problems associated with underdevelopment has been recognised by agencies at many levels of governance such as the global, regional, national, and local levels.

As demonstrated throughout this chapter, CSR is multidimensional in nature. The diversity and dynamics of CSR issues, many of which are encapsulated in the MDGs, add to the complexity of finding the best ways for businesses to respond to these multi-faceted challenges. The interlocked issues of poverty, disease, climate change, corruption, human rights, and related concerns are extremely difficult to harmonise into a solid body of theory and practice. These challenges are exacerbated by the attendant emerging dynamics of global political and economic governance in the context of globalisation, regional integration and technological advancements. Despite the scale and urgency of development needs, determining the best ways for private enterprises to respond to poverty, for example, remains extremely complex (Bendell and Visser, 2004). The localised nature of development needs and aspirations implies that global corporations wishing to invest in social concerns have to familiarise themselves with the differing socio-cultural environment of the areas that they operate in. Dealing with a wide variety of political regimes around the world adds to the difficulty of advocating CSR best practice principles to guide the business community. Moreover, the opportunities for corporate contributions to the MDGs often lack comprehensive understanding of processes of development, especially in the developing world (*ibid*). Many businesses operating in low-income countries produce products that are beyond meeting basic needs and their social investments do not necessarily address the real issues affecting communities. Moreover, academic interest in CSR generally appears to have had a bias towards industrialised countries and their large corporations, with limited attention to the social responsibilities of local or national companies in developing countries.

The general picture that emerges from the CSR literature is that the concept is gaining increasing levels of global popularity among researchers and practitioners in their diversity. With the rising threats to human survival and development coming from multiple sources such as climate change, disease, and poverty, it is anticipated that this global interest in the role of the private sector in the achievement of MDGs will continue to grow. There is however, enough evidence to suggest that despite its growing popularity, CSR is still predominantly a subject focused on Northern industrialised countries. The North-South divide on CSR is evident in a number of ways. In Africa, for example, only 53 CSR-related journal articles were published between 1995 and 2005. Even then South Africa was dominant in these publications (Visser, 2006a). Out of the few articles published over the reference period, three-quarters of them related to the two powerful nations of South Africa and Nigeria with only 25% being attributed to the remainder of the continent. A similar trend is discernible from CSR reports worldwide as Figure 1.3 suggests below.

The graph suggests that out of the total stock of global CSR reports issued between 1992 and 2006, only 3% (represented by corporations in South Africa and Brazil) were issued by corporations in the developing world. Countries with a cumulative total of less than 60 reports were however excluded from the data. In contrast, Europe and North America had the largest proportion of reports, with approximately 85% of the reports. Outside Europe and North America, Japan, Hong Kong, the Republic of Korea and New Zealand, together had 12% of the reports attributed to them over the reference period.

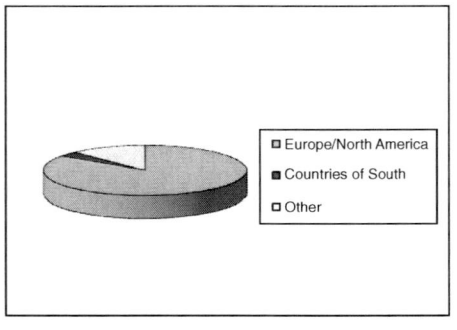

Figure 1.3 Global CSR report output by region

Source: Adapted from Corporateregister.com, 2007.

Promotion of CSR in developing countries demands a multidimensional approach that reflects the social, economic, environmental, and political issues that are relevant locally. Such an approach needs to address a diversity of issues including: government and politics; universal application of models of development; the role of small, medium and micro enterprises (SMMEs); the role of NGOs and the civil society; and technological capacity.

1.6.1 Government intervention and political will

The lack of government capacity (and political will) to initiate and monitor CSR in countries of the South is often cited as one of the factors that hinder progress in CSR initiatives (Lund-Thomsen et al., 2006; Doane and Holder, 2007). Furthermore, unlike their Northern counterparts, governments of the South usually lower their social (e.g. labour costs) and environmental standards in order to speed up industrialisation. Companies of the South are also unable to regulate themselves (Jeppesen, 2006; UNIDO, 2002); enforcement of CSR codes is weak. Weak enforcement potentially leads to child labour, corruption and sometimes even complete disregard of CSR (Doane and Holder, 2007). This hugely affects CSR performance as the concept relies heavily on self regulation and enforcement. But why have governments of the South assumed a lax stance towards CSR agenda? The key may be the issue of prioritisation. While CSR may be seen to be important at the global level, governments in countries of the South are more preoccupied with hunger, unemployment, poverty, HIV/AIDS, malaria, water & sanitation problems, waste management, environmental pollution, corruption and many other challenges (Kumar et al., 2001). With limited state welfare and infrastructure, governments and companies concentrate on more pressing problems of which top of the agenda are the provision of adequate housing, healthcare and education. It is not surprising that in the quest to reduce the impacts of these problems, some private sector organisations have taken the leading role in initiating some CSR-related projects in the South. However, in many cases, CSR is usually nothing more than an ad-hoc philanthropic activity (UNIDO, 2002; Chahoud et al., 2007).

1.6.2 Universal application of CSR models

There seems to be general agreement among writers that one of the major reasons why CSR efforts fail in the South is the adoption and application of generalised/universal approaches, coupled with a bias in analytical frameworks (Jeppesen, 2006; Vogel, 2005; Visser, 2003; Karnan, 2006; Blowfield and Frynas, 2005). These global CSR models and standards as reflected in the UN conventions are not only imposed on countries of the South by governments and companies of the North; they are also initiated without consulting the South. The standards are designed within the best business practice of the North. Requirements of the South are usually neglected. It thus becomes very difficult for companies of the South to embrace such standards because the environments within which the Northern and Southern companies operate are very different. According to the UN (2007: 8), "The governments and citizens of low and middle income countries would do well to set the CSR agenda for themselves, taking the best of what has evolved to date and of what their business communities already have to offer." Some countries in the South have started adopting this approach by designing their own country-specific CSR standards. In China, for instance, a textile industry standard (CSC9000T) was designed and adopted in 2005. The standard is based on the Chinese legislation and it provides a framework for Chinese textile firms wishing to operate socially responsibly.

With regards to adoption of universal models, Visser (2003) cites an example of Carroll's CSR pyramid (see Figure 1.1 above) which according to Carroll and many others consider to be a universal model. According to Visser, Carroll's pyramid cannot be applicable to developing countries because the economic, cultural/social, environmental and political landscapes in these regions differ from those of the North. Visser further suggests that Carroll's model can be applicable to developing countries but only if the order of the blocks in the pyramid is reshuffled from economic – legal – ethical – philanthropic, to economic – philanthropic – legal – ethical responsibilities. Even other models such as Prahalad and Hart's (2002) bottom of the pyramid (BOP) is also criticised. The BOP model proposes that the poor 4 billion people at the bottom of the pyramid (UNDP, 2004) should be encouraged to buy from those at the summit of the pyramid, the rich. Prahalad and Hart argue that this is one way by which poverty can be alleviated. But critics like Karnan (2006) argue that buying from, and not selling to the poor is what may ultimately alleviate poverty.

1.6.3 The role of small, medium and micro enterprises

SMMEs play a vital role in the economic development of the countries of the South. SMMEs are known to be the vehicle for poverty alleviation in developing countries. According to Jeppesen (2006) SMMEs constitute about 90% of registered private sector in the South. Because of their ability to provide intensive labour, SMMEs are important providers of employment and producers of total industrial output. They also contribute hugely towards innovation, growth and development. For this reason, it is wise that any efforts to drive CSR in countries of the South should be targeted at SMMEs. Many more reasons to target SMMEs in any CSR agenda exist. Unlike large companies, SMMEs have more links with the local civil and cultural environments and are in most cases more aware of the local conditions that may be prerequisites for the success of CSR projects (UNIDO, 2002).

Visser (2003) also notes that in countries of the South, the cumulative social and/or environmental impacts caused by smaller and medium companies far exceed those caused by high profile multinational companies (MNCs). But most of the smaller companies operate out of the provision of law (UNDP, 2004) and usually off the radar of the media (Visser, 2003; Hopkins, 2006). And unlike the MNCs, SMMEs are less likely to adopt CSR initiatives (Hopkins, 2006). This was challenged by Kumar *et al.* (2001) in their 2001 poll in India where among other things, they found that MNCs were not demonstrating the same social and environmental commitment as they do in the North. However, MNCs are not the worst CSR offenders in the South. It is the labour intensive SMMEs which matter more in these regions. SMMEs are also better placed to understand, effect and interpret local economic development. But the problem is that SMMEs are neglected in the CSR literature (Visser, 2003). In countries of the South, the dimensions of the triple-bottom line are inseparable: economic development inevitably leads to social and environmental improvements. "One inherent strength in many developing countries is the level of public participation and stakeholder engagement that takes place, particularly at a community level. Yet, ironically, this is seldom recognised and the emerging global models for stakeholder engagement are being driven by the developed world" (Visser, 2003: 4).

1.6.4 The role of NGOs and civil society organisations

Non-governmental organisations (NGOs) and other civil society organisations play a crucial role in the emerging CSR movement in the South. They often assume the role of spokespersons or representatives of the voiceless stakeholders. With particular reference to labour issues, for example, many workers in developing countries work without representation of trade unions. It is therefore of paramount importance in such cases to think of how best workers can participate in a CSR agenda. Although a public opinion poll in India by Kumar *et al.* (2001) reveals that members of the general public trust NGOs, the general picture is that NGOs and other civil society organisations in countries of the South are not always trusted. They are under growing suspicion that they exist simply for economic gains (Chahoud *et al.*, 2007). The organisations tend to prioritise issues that are a subject of international campaign pressure (UN, 2007). Blowfield and Frynas (2005) pose a seemingly simple but challenging question: can representatives like NGOs afford to draw a clear line between serving the interests of the voiceless poor communities or serve those of their funders? It is most likely that in such cases NGOs will not press companies for improved working conditions of employees, let alone the livelihoods of society as a whole. The reason is simple: the NGOs/Civil society organisations are under contract with their funders in the same way companies are under contract with company shareholders. In times of conflict, it only makes sense to serve the 'master' and not the 'servant'. The situation is even worse for groups that are not represented, like the house maids. These are mostly ignored in CSR programmes because, as Blowfield and Frynas (2005) put it, "the groups are not primary stakeholders and they rarely present any threats to the productivity of business. Besides, businesses do not depend on them very much." Chahoud et al. (2007) present a case in India where a local CSR national network, the Global Compact Society (GCS) has been accused of being too business-centred and of failing to open its doors wider to its stakeholder organisations. The GCS was founded following the launch of the UN Global Compact in India. Another Indian network, the India Partnership Forum (IPF) that was founded in 2001 presents similar and worrying low levels of its awareness from among its member stakeholders. This is despite IPF being a 'Multi-stakeholder Dialogue for Promoting Corporate Social Responsibility' in the country. This suggests that while they may be crucially needed, representative NGOs and other civil society organisations need to act honestly if CSR initiatives are to be of any benefit to the poor majority of stakeholders in the South.

1.6.5 Technological capacity

Literature informs us that the success of CSR hinges around technological progress, particularly ICT ranging from satellite TV to high speed internet. Technology enables stakeholders to compare and rank performances of businesses against competitors. This is in line with the Global Reporting Initiative (GRI) which encourages companies to report on their CSR performance (Elkington, 2004). Such models and tools may not work well in countries of the South where there is a relative lack of information and environmental technologies. Furthermore, CSR certification systems are only beginning to emerge. If not done in-house, such services are very expensive and beyond the reach of many SMMEs to whom monitoring and auditing may be a burden (UNIDO, 2002). With high poverty and illiteracy levels, limited access to credit facilities, financial inputs, information and training on social and environmental management systems, countries of the South still face many obstacles in their efforts to implement strategic, comprehensive CSR programmes. As Visser (2003) asks, "What good does it do to produce a truckload of glossy sustainability reports posted online if most of the business' immediate stakeholders (the community around the business) are illiterate, have no electricity, no telephone, let alone access to internet?" Indeed this is the situation common in many countries of the South. In India alone, for instance, 300 million people belong to this category, living on less than $1 a day (Bendell and Shah, 2006).

1.7 Conclusion

This chapter has analysed key contributions to the academic and practitioner literature on CSR, noting the evolution of thinking and action on this emergent concept. The chapter has also reviewed more recent efforts to link CSR and development, and highlighted the role of the United Nations and the particular CSR challenges facing developing countries. Despite the numerous obstacles identified above, CSR represents a potential development opportunity for countries in the South. The particular concerns and needs of different contexts should be taken into account when designing regional and national CSR models. This should be done with caution because wholesale copy and paste approaches are likely to fail due to social, cultural, economic and environmental incompatibilities. Appropriate models for the developing countries are needed if CSR is to be tapped as a tool for poverty alleviation and fostering sustainable development, particularly in urban settings. The following chapter will focus on urban development and will revisit the role of CSR in this particular context as we expand our exploration of the linkage between CSR and urban development.

2
Urban Development

Edmundo Werna

Having analysed corporate social responsibility (CSR) in general in Chapter 1, it is important now to understand why the book focuses on urban settings. The first two sections of Chapter 2 provide background data and an analysis to explain why one should pay attention to urban development: the first section focuses on the importance of cities and towns to development, and the second on the problems and challenges of urban poverty. Following, in section three, the chapter analyses the gap on CSR in the urban development literature.

2.1 The importance of cities and towns

Urbanisation is a global phenomenon. The 21st century has been called the urban century. The urban population of the world has been drastically expanding, both in absolute and in relative terms, especially in the developing world, which is the focus of this book. According to data compiled by UNDP (1999), in 1970 the ratio of city dwellers in developing as opposed to industrialised countries was one to one. Today this ratio is nearly two to one. It will be three to one by the year 2015, and will approach four to one by 2025. Since 1970, 1.23 billion urban residents have been added to the world population, of which 84% have been in less-developed regions. In the words of a report of the World Bank (1999: 1):

> At the threshold of the 21st century, cities and towns are forming the front line in the development campaign. Within a generation, the majority of the developing world's population will live in urban areas. The number of residents in developing countries will increase by 2.5 billion – the current urban population of the entire world.

While in the past the rural population throughout the world was larger than the urban, according to UN-Habitat (2006a) the year 2007 marks the point in which both populations are even. The tendency is that urban populations will continue to outgrow their rural counterparts in the years to come.

Moreover, other international predictions estimated that by 2008 world urban population will exceed the rural (UNFPA, 2007; WUP, 2005). It seems, however, that this milestone was in fact reached rather early in 2007 (People and Planet, 2007) with some reports pinpointing May 23 as the day when the world became officially majority urbanised (NC State University, 2007). What is significant for us, however, is not so much the exact date of this demographic shift but rather its symbolic significance in terms of growth of cities and implications for urban development and citywide interventions.

It is also worth noting that available data suggests that in developing countries as a whole the demographic shift to a majority urbanised state has some way to go yet and is expected to be reached around 2020. In Africa this will be even later and beyond 2030 (WUP, 2005). It is, nevertheless, sobering to consider that in the next two decades cities in the developing world will absorb 95% of urban growth (UN-Habitat, 2006a) and in the next 25 years 97% of the total population growth (Ricz, 2007). Moreover, the rapid rates of urbanisation have already led to growth of mega-cities of over 10 million in developing countries. In 1975 there were three mega-cities in the world, namely Tokyo, New York and Mexico City (WUP, 2005). In 2005 there were 20 such cities in the world. More importantly for our purpose 16 were located in the developing world (WUP, 2005).

Cities and towns are pivotal for development. They are the engines of economic growth. There is a growing amount of evidence about their role in the emerging era of globalisation and land markets (McGreal *et al.*, 2002; Parsa *et al.*, 2004; Keivani *et al.*, 2001): they serve as centres for finance and producer services; are areas of production of innovation; and are the powerhouses of manufacturing and consumer markets. Thus cities play a crucial role in the global, national and regional economies.

In its recent *State of the World's Cities 2006/7*, UN-Habitat (2006a: 46–47) notes:

> The link between urbanisation and socio-economic development cannot be disputed. Countries that are highly urbanized have higher incomes, more stable economies, stronger institutions and

are able to withstand the volatility of the global economy than those with less urbanized populations. The experiences of developed and developing countries also indicate that urbanisation levels are closely related to levels of income and performance on human development indicators... In both developed and developing countries, cities generate a disproportionate share of gross domestic product (GDP) and provide huge opportunities for investment and employment.

Urban-based economic activities account for up to 55 per cent of gross national product (GNP) in low-income countries, 73 per cent in middle-income countries and 85 per cent in high-income countries... Cities also generate a disproportionate amount of revenue for governments. (pages 46–47).

UN-Habitat (2006a) also explains that infrastructure development in urban areas is cost-effective, because the concentration of population and enterprises greatly reduces the unit costs of piped water, sewers, drains, roads, electricity, garbage collection, transport, health care, schools, etc.

It is also important to note that the wealth generated in urban areas – noted above in terms of both GNP and GDP – has an impact that extends well beyond the administrative limits of the cities and towns where they are located, many times benefiting the whole country. The same is true for facilities and institutions which are eminently based in urban areas – such as international ports and airports, primary hospitals, universities, central governments – which benefit region- or nation-wide populations.

In sum, there is a rationale for investing in urban development, with special attention to developing countries. This is reinforced by the fact that a significant share of the urban population in the developing world still live in poverty, an issue which will be analysed next.

2.2 Urban poverty

The fact that cities and towns generate significant wealth does not mean that they are devoid of poverty. There are still huge intra-urban socio-economic differentials, as analysed in detail for instance by UN-Habitat (2006b) and Werna (2000). While a small proportion of urban dwellers in developing countries live in comfort, large numbers still find themselves in poverty. One strong indicator is that there are some 998 million people living in slums in cities throughout the world – one out of every three city dwellers (UN-Habitat, 2006b). In sum, we are witnessing what Nicholas You (2007) describes as the urbanisation of poverty. Citing the UN-Habitat 2006/7 report on the State of World Cities he argues:

> ... living conditions in [urban] slums are as bad if not worse than living conditions in the poorest rural areas. Slum dwellers are just as likely to suffer from hunger, malnutrition and disease as their rural counterparts (You, 2007: 215).

To this we must add highest prevalence of HIV among women, high infant mortality rates, lack of utilities, sexual and general violence and crime, etc. Overall, You (2007) argues that end result is such that the rate of growth of urban population in the world estimated at 2.24% is roughly equal to the rate of growth of slums estimated at 2.22%. The same figures for sub-Saharan Africa are 4.58% and 4.53%.

The absolute numbers of urban poor may suffice to demonstrate the existence and magnitude of the problem, hence the importance of combating it. This can be reinforced by comparisons with rural poverty. There is an argument among some development academics and practitioners that poverty in rural areas is more prominent – and therefore deserves more resources – than poverty in urban areas. However, such relative prominence has often been overestimated. The following points summarised in Werna (2000) illustrate the relative importance of urban poverty:

- *Higher living costs.* In most developing countries urban residents face higher living costs, because many items that have to be bought in urban areas are free or cheaper in rural areas as they grow or are produced locally – e.g. fuel, food, fresh water, traditional building materials, and housing itself.
- *New/extra needs.* In addition to the higher costs of basic needs, urban living also entails new or additional needs, a fact which requires extra expenditure. For example, long distance daily commuting is an ordinary feature of urban living, which means that public transport (and associated costs) becomes an indispensable need. Also, urban living generally involves more complex and costly recreational habits (cinemas, shows, night life), which are important in a milieu that lacks the appropriate space, time and cultural bonds often necessary for rural types of recreation (encountered in nature, in extensive village celebrations, etc.). There is also a much higher pressure for consumption in general (of non-basic goods) in urban areas, due

to a much more aggressive marketing milieu, and to the constant day-to-day exposure of the poor to people who ostentatiously show their expensive goods. (It is often argued that access to a wider range of goods and services constitutes an advantage of urban settlements over rural areas. While this may be true for those who can actually purchase such goods and services, the reality for the masses of urban poor is different – they often sacrifice basic needs in order to be able to purchase non-basic goods and services).

- *Greater vulnerability to changes in income.* Urban dwellers often have a greater dependence on cash incomes, which means greater vulnerability to price rises and falls in income. This problem is minimised in rural areas due to subsistence production and foraging.
- *Socio-cultural bonds.* Support networks based on family, kinship and/or ethnic-cultural background are generally stronger in rural areas, and prove to be fundamental in many episodes of crisis and emergency. Socio-cultural bonds and derived support networks tend to be weaker in urban areas, due to the pressures of urban living, associated psycho-social stresses, and ethnic-cultural mixtures. For instance, the widespread phenomenon of street children is a clear and sad evidence of this problem.
- *Greater health risks.* The urban poor face the 'worst of both worlds': while they still suffer problems common to rural areas (such as infectious diseases and malnutrition), they also suffer problems which are particular to urban areas (chronic and psycho-social diseases), This was first highlighted in the 1980s by Harpham *et al.* (1988) and later adopted by the Healthy Cities Project of the World Health Organisation, which is still running.

There is a widespread belief among many development thinkers and practitioners that urban poverty will 'naturally' disappear solely by combating rural poverty. They believe that the urban poor are basically rural migrants running away from poverty in their regions of origin (thus ignoring the significant percentage of poor who are born in urban areas). Therefore, the argument goes, if rural poverty is removed, no more poor people would migrate to cities and towns, and the poor who are already living in such urban settlements would migrate back to the (now economically better) rural areas.

Removal of poverty and the creation of opportunities in rural areas might perhaps attract a number of urban dwellers. Yet, there is no evidence whatsoever that it would constitute a comprehensive solution to urban poverty. The example of many Western European countries reinforces this point. Rural poverty in absolute terms (i.e. acute deficiency or deprivation of basic needs) in this region of the world is rare. Yet, many dwellers of Western European cities still face harsh living conditions, such as homelessness, crime, pollution, unemployment, overcrowding (squatters), and psycho-social conditions. The majority of urban dwellers just do not want to move to rural areas. They prefer to work in typically urban occupations (e.g. services) rather than in farming, or they may prefer urban socio-cultural habits to rural ones (Werna, 2000).

So far, the present chapter has firstly shown the importance of cities and towns, and therefore the importance of investing in them. Following, it has noted that urban poverty is still widespread, therefore there is a need to address it. It is true that there have been many international and national actors involved in combating urban poverty. Yet, as the data provided above illustrates, it is necessary to do much more. Therefore, there is a need to discuss innovative solutions to urban problems, and CSR has a role to play. However, the urban development literature on the role of the private sector so far has focused on its commercial role, with no proper analysis of CSR. Other actors have been extensively analysed, i.e. the government (both central and local), NGOs and communities – but their connection to the private sector via CSR has yet to be adequately analysed. This will be covered in the next section.

2.3 CSR: a gap in the urban development literature

There are two sub-sets of the urban development literature, which are important for the purpose of CSR. First, the broader role of the private sector in urban development will be examined – to see if/how CSR appears. Secondly, considering that CSR is related to private sector volunteerism, the sub-set of the literature on urban volunteerism in general will also be examined – to see if/how the private sector appears. Considering that the case studies of this book are largely about business-community relations, the present section will also make explicit references to this dimension of CSR.

2.3.1 The role of the private sector in urban development

This literature focuses overwhelmingly on the debate about the relative importance of the public *vis-à-vis* the private sector, and whether the latter should expand its role, and how. The book by Werna *et al.* (2004) carried out a major review of such literature, and it is built on the overall debate on the role of the private sector in development as a whole. This analysis remains prevalent, as recent publications evidence – e.g. Keivani *et al.* (2005), Meng (2006), Mukhija (2004). Therefore, Werna *et al.* (2004) will be used as a basis for the forthcoming analysis.

The goods (or services) provided to a given population can be divided into three sets:

- public,
- private, and
- merit.

The first set, as the name indicates, are those to be provided directly by the public sector, by and large including 'soft' goods (or services) such as public health, education and other welfare areas. This includes those goods/services for collective consumption, which cannot exclude individuals who do not pay for their use (e.g. street lighting, police), therefore making it difficult for private provision, which entails profit. It also includes goods/services in places whose provision by the private sector entails monopoly. In addition, it includes private goods/services in places where the private sector is not capable of providing them.

The second set, as the respective name indicates, are those goods/services provided by the private sector (either directly or via government contracts), normally including 'hard' infrastructure such as electricity, water, and telecommunications.

Merit goods, in turn, are seen to be essential for the well being of individuals or society as a whole and governments may decide to supply them, or provide subsidies for their consumption, whether or not they can be supplied as pure private goods, and may overlap with public goods, such as for example education, public health and sometimes low-income housing.

Despite of the aforementioned basic classifications, there is a heated debate about redefining the boundaries of the three sets of goods/services, which is centred on the discussion on diminishing the role of the government and expanding the role of the private sector.

The central argument of the privatisation thesis is that the public sector is wasteful, inefficient, and unproductive. Nationalised industries and public welfare agencies are seen as stifling individual initiative and responsibility. In addition, it is argued that with a few exceptions the private sector is inherently a much more efficient production and allocation mechanism since it abides by the rules of the market. This means that its survival depends on its work and as a result it will use all its initiative and ingenuity to optimise production and increase profits.

Such an incentive is lacking in public industries. Finally, public sector control of the economy and its agencies and industries are seen as preventing the growth of a viable private sector alternative.

Possible arguments favourable to participation of the private sector in the production of urban services are (Werna *et al.*, 2004, based on David, 1992):

- Merit inherent to private enterprise, in terms of promoting and breaking power concentration;
- Possibility of mobilising extra capital or know-how resources;
- Superior efficiency due to competition and greater freedom or tendency to reduce losses and unproductive work, to reward performance, etc.;
- Not being attached to strict bureaucratic procedures; and
- The ability to carry out scale economies, mainly for acting in several jurisdictions.

Private provision is always possible, and usually preferable when consumers could be charged for it, and where there are no obstacles, such as technological or investment scales, to run parallel services bringing competition.

Private sector solutions also occur when the public sector is incapable of meeting local demand. In other cases, the public sector hires the private sector to supply a certain service instead of providing it directly. In some cities the private sector has developed an important role in supplying a variety of basic services and infrastructure to low-income communities. Batley (1996) for example notes that in several cities such as Recife (Brazil), Hermosillo (Mexico), Ahmedabad and Calcutta (India), Penang (Malaysia), the private sector has undertaken various forms of service provision. Depending on the city concerned, such services have included management of public parks, public transport, electricity generation and supply as well as education. Depending on city and type of service, the institutional mechanism for private sector provision has included various forms: contracting out, lease/franchise, public regulation of private competition and joint ventures.

The private sector has been pushing up against the boundaries of traditional public goods/services, such as those for collective consumption, finding ways of charging everybody who use them. One example is the management of roads, many of which have been privatised and now have barriers with tolls. A striking example in cities particularly in developing countries is policing, where, due to the upsurge of urban violence, there has been a dramatic increase in private security.

There is the case of goods/services that are 'natural monopolies', such as water supply systems or electric power distribution networks, since they are built and become the responsibility of a sole company. It is virtually impossible for another company to build another water supply system or electricity distribution network in order to compete if quality is not good or if price is too high (UNCHS, 1996a). However, this problem can be overcome by breaking up large scale national utility services into smaller units that could compete with each other.[1]

In sum, the 'neoliberal' pro-privatisation perspective in development argues that even if the private sector is not present or prominent in a given city or specific good/service, it should be encouraged and supported. And the direct participation of the government in provision is seen as unfair competition to the private sector, and should be discouraged.

But there are also counter-arguments. During the 1990s a number of authors such as Davey (1992), were cautious about the privatisation thesis arguing that there is little supportive evidence that basic assumptions in favour of private sector provision actually do exist in developing countries. These primarily relate to the capacity of private organisations to meet the financial and human resources required for the task and the market conditions which would support an efficient and competitive market, particularly lack of adequate suppliers and information to allow for informed, free and honest choice and decisions. Thereby, not ensuring efficient private market production. Many countries that have chosen to privatise their services seem to have made this decision based not on concrete evidence, but on political and pragmatic reasons, such as lack of resources or difficulties in extending services (Batley, 1996).

It is also known that there are several difficulties inherent to service privatisation in developing countries, such as money collection; how to establish correct price levels; importance of evaluating demand; lack of credit for investments and lack of incentives to make long-term investments. It has also been argued that the actual sale of public firms to the private sector is mainly suitable for those areas of the economy where the markets are already working very well, or would do so if they could do so – i.e. where the government enterprises are competitive

---

[1] The reader is also referred to Chapter 5 for a detailed discussion on urban water utilities in developing countries.

with private business or where this could easily be created. However, in areas of partial or complete market failure they place considerable doubt on the success of straightforward privatisation.

The debate on privatisation becomes even more complex when supply of several components of goods or services, such as planning, financing, execution and evaluation is broken down. Each component may be controlled by a certain agent, regardless of the other components. For instance, a public agency would plan a certain service, whereas a private company would account for its financing. This is commonly known as a public-private partnership (PPP), which has been seen as a solution for using the respective attributes of the public and the private sector. PPPs have been widely promoted in international cooperation, with one example being UNDP's Public Private Partnerships Programme for the Urban Environment (PPP-UE) which is now known as PPPs for Service Delivery (PPP-SD).

The success of such programmes, however, is contingent on the existence of a good institutional capacity within both the public and private sectors. The former must be able to prepare the goods or services for privatisation and regulate the activities thereafter. The latter, on the other hand, must have both the financial and human resource capacity and run the service efficiently and competitively.

The basic arguments in favor and against privatisation have been summarised above. While the debate continues, the point to be made here is that the focus in the literature is on the *commercial* aspects of the private sector, rather than its possible contribution via CSR.

The debate on privatisation includes a specific sub-set on goods and services for low-income communities. The arguments in favour of privatisation follow the general ones explained before. The counter-arguments note that a privatised good or service makes no difference between rich or poor clients. In developing countries this means that the poor cannot afford to use a very expensive privatised service, unless someone else, usually the government, pays for the difference between the real cost and the price the user can pay which then takes us back to subsidised state provision. Despite the recent attention to Bottom of the Pyramid markets by some global and national companies (Prahalad and Hart, 2002), the private sector has also tended to have fewer incentives to make a permanent investment in low-income areas, since there are no guarantees that demand for their products will continue. Apart from this, if the area is illegally occupied or subdivided, there is also the risk of companies having to evict settlement dwellers in order to follow through with commercial investments.

A notable exception regarding CSR in the literature on the role of the private sector in urban development is a recent publication by UN-Habitat, the UN agency that covers urban development in general (UN-Habitat, 2007a). This publication focuses precisely on the role of "business for sustainable urbanisation", and promotes the idea of CSR, including the presentation of a set of case studies. While this is an important publication for the purposes of CSR in urban development, it does not offset the need and value-added of the present book, due to the reasons explained below.

First, UN-Habitat (2007a) does not include a detailed investigation or conceptualisation of CSR nor a conclusion which draws together possible findings and lessons. Also, while the case studies do include relations between companies and communities, the publication does not mention the concept of business-community relations, let alone analyse it.

Second, the UN-Habitat publication mentions CSR within the context of opportunities for private businesses in low-income settlements. While this is an important point, the publication does not discuss how this can be carried out – i.e. mainstreaming CSR within the overall commercial activities (and ethics) of a given private company, or, particularly, within its relations with low-income communities.

Third, the publication provides only brief information on each case study. This does not include a full account of the CSR experience, let alone the positive lessons and indeed possible negative ones. Also, while some of the cases seem to be related to CSR (or business-community relations in particular), others are not, including for example one case of a private company which engages with a local government through what seems to be a commercial activity (there is no detailed information) through a public-private partnership, and one case of a regional development bank which promotes small enterprises in low-income communities, among others. This further blurs the understanding of the specific value-added of business-community relations or CSR more generally, leaving mainly the idea that the actions of the private sector are generally beneficial to low-income urban communities.

Finally, the publication is part of the so-called 'grey literature' – produced by a given organisation about itself (in this case it is UN-Habitat's promotion of businesses for sustainable development). In many cases such types of publication do not find their way into the mainstream academic literature.

2.3.2 Volunteerism in urban development

The literature on the role of the volunteer sector in urban development primarily focuses on Non-governmental Organisations (NGOs) and Community-based Organisations (CBOs). A notable exception providing a broader framework and analysis is UNV (2001), which will be analysed afterward.

The analysis of the role of NGOs in low-income urban communities is often associated with the lack of capacity of the public and private sectors, although it has also been argued that they have a value of their own. As reviewed by Werna *et al.* (2004), the NGOs are non-profit foundations and civil associations. When recognised as being of public interest, these legal entities may receive budget resources and other contributions, which may be deducted from the income tax of the donor. In parallel, many NGOs have been supported by some Northern hemisphere governments, as well as some foundations which were not willing to help authoritarian governments and political parties in the Southern hemisphere.

In a number of developing countries NGOs helped to maintain political pluralism giving support to community entities of the civil society; in other countries they assisted local communities to remain politically active in order to maintain authoritarian governments under popular pressure. In the latter, the importance of NGO activities in the organised communities increased significantly with democracy.

The total number of NGOs in the world is unknown. Anheier *et al.* (2001) estimated the number of NGOs operating at the international level to be around 40,000. At the national level, estimates in India alone put the number of NGOs at between one and two million.[2] This growth, both in number and importance, mainly in the developing world is partly related to a deterioration of the socioeconomic situation and political crises that took place in many countries, as well as to the lack of ability by the governments to find feasible alternatives for development.

Another reason for the greater number of NGOs, particularly in Latin America in past decades, is the lack of representativeness of the governments. In many cases military governments forced many professionals and lecturers to leave the government and the universities. Some of

---

[2]http://www.indianngos.com/ngosection/newcomers/whatisanngo.htm "What is an NGO?" 5 January 2007.

these professionals found new jobs in NGOs, where their skills were recognised. With the renewal of democracy many of these professionals returned to the civil service and brought their experience of work developed in NGOs.

A further reason is the increasing and maturing process of awareness of social issues by professional and non-professional staff who have found in their NGO work the necessary means to improve knowledge.

The role played by NGOs in rendering services in low-income urban areas must be stressed, considering the prevalence of urban poverty (noted in the previous section). Besides, in many cases city governments invest more in richer areas than in districts where low-income populations prevail, and these populations receive little or no investment in services.

However, although the work of NGOs has been established in many developing countries, and has been internationally recognised, rarely are the NGOs able to work on a scale that leads to a considerable impact on poverty reduction. The need to change this impact scale is one of the major current challenges faced by those who try to develop programmes for a large number of people, without losing the inherent qualities of a small scale project.

Two objections often raised to NGOs must be pointed out. First, their administrative costs may be too high. This criticism, however, is not accepted as holding universally true and much may depend on the particular circumstances of the NGO concerned. Indeed, there is evidence to suggest that in some cases the opposite may be true.

In some countries, for instance, Bangladesh, the role of NGOs has been assessed negatively. Criticisms mainly concern excessive individual bureaucracy, corrupt political practice and excessive intellectualism of their members. It is also argued, at the institutional level, that there is duplication of roles, overlapping, lack of coordination, etc. Some of these criticisms are known to be true, but others are improperly generalised and without substance (Karim, 1996).

Until recently, there was a large gap between NGOs and the public and private sectors, since NGOs tended to operate autonomously from the other sectors. This may have been because NGOs believed that public and private groups or institutions were not committed to urban development. This was a great mistake on the part of NGOs and it led not only to confusion and suspicion about their activities, but also to more negative comments that damaged their image. For instance, one of the arguments against NGOs is that they are involved in financing political groups and parties with no representativeness. Nevertheless, this criticism clearly indicates lack of information. In the 1990s, with the revival of democratic movements in many developing countries, these issues were considerably clarified.

Another criticism concerns legitimacy and responsibility. These criticisms make NGOs vulnerable because they depend on external funds and are not able to mobilise or develop an internal/alternative resource base (Hall *et al.*, 1996). Research suggests that over-dependence on external donors who often require short term measurable results is less likely to be effective in promoting and supporting long term social and institutional changes which are necessary for sustainable development (Edwards and Hulme, 1992). However, should legitimacy and responsibility of NGOs be questioned only due to their financing context, without taking into account their commitment and services rendered to the population?

Indeed, not. Even the above authors do not negate the legitimacy of the NGOs due to their reliance on external donors. Rather it is the funding arrangements and conditions imposed on their operations, particularly short specifications of outputs and targets, that is the focus of their criticism. Therefore, they emphasise the need for a partnership approach with enhanced participation, learning, reciprocity and transparency, perhaps through independent third parties and longer term objectives for NGO activity in terms of institutional developments and advancement in social organisation rather than quick material results. At the same time, NGOs are advised to expand their source of fund raising particularly in terms of local funding sources to ensure their long-term independence and legitimacy. As part of civil society, NGOs should develop strategies and goals together with civil society groups struggling for democratisation and development of the society as a whole. NGOs should certainly strive for greater acceptance and a more positive image.

Finally, it is worth noting that in some developing countries the increasing number of NGOs is encouraged by local governments. One of the reasons is the recognition of the growing financial resources offered by international development agencies to NGOs or to partnerships between governments and NGOs.

In sum, fundamental arguments pro and counter NGOs have been shown above, and note that there is a balance in favour of NGOs. But the question to be asked by this book is about the possible role of CSR in the NGO context. While, as already noted, some NGOs are supported by foundations, the possible role of foundations set up by private companies (which would be within the CSR framework) is overlooked. Also, the above analysis has noted the traditional resistance of many developing countries to NGOs working with the private (and the public) sector. While this may be changing, again there is no emphasis on their role for facilitating and channelling CSR of private firms and individuals.

The urban volunteer sector also includes grass-roots communities, mainly Community-based Organisations (CBOs). Similar to the literature on NGOs, the one on grass-roots organisations is associated with the lack of capacity of the public and private sectors, although, also equally to the case of NGOs, it has also been argued that grass-roots organisations have a value of their own.

John Turner was a pioneer in highlighting the importance of urban grass-roots communities since the 1960s (e.g. Turner, 1967, 1968, 1977; Turner and Fichter, 1972). Since then, a large literature on the subject has developed, and is still being produced (e.g. Viloria-Williams, 2006).

In general, it has been argued that public and private services in most developing countries hardly cover all areas necessary to include all the households in their stated jurisdictions. Thus, families and communities are forced to take their own measures to obtain water supply, sewerage collection, garbage disposal and other services in regions where cities grow fast.

Possibly the main advantage of community involvement in supplying their own services is their in-depth knowledge of local characteristics and needs. Therefore, even if a public agency, private company or NGO already provides some kind of service, it is advisable to have community recommendations and participation. The direct involvement of the community in part or the whole supply of a determined service is beneficial because it guarantees its supply, mainly when there are no other options for provision. Also, grass-roots participation strengthens low-income communities institutionally/politically, as they have to organise themselves to provide the necessary goods or services.

There are also arguments against community participation. For instance, that such communities have the right to have essential urban services provided by the government, therefore their direct involvement in provision constitutes a kind of exploitation. Also, it has been argued that CBOs sometimes may be controlled by a minority, therefore leading to inequalities within a given low-income community. Despite such arguments, the overall balance of the literature is in favour of community participation, and also encourages partnerships with other actors. But the focus of such partnerships is mainly with the public and the private *commercial* sectors, for instance through community contracts – when the local government or/and a private enterprise provides the equipment and technical assistance, and a CBO is hired to provide the labour from the local community. The possible association with private companies through CSR has been overlooked.

As already noted, while the bulk of the literature on urban volunteerism concentrates specifically on NGOs and community organisations (analysed above), a publication by UNV (2001) provides a broad analysis, therefore it will be reviewed here.

This publication defines volunteerism based in five key elements:

(i) the notion of reward (mainly altruistic behaviour but also noting that volunteering contains an element of exchange and reciprocity),
(ii) free will (thus excluding compulsory labour),
(iii) the nature of the benefit (to differentiate volunteering from a purely leisure activity, as the former requires there to be a beneficiary other than/in addition to the volunteer),
(iv) the organisational setting (a broad framework allows for both formal [organised] and informal [one-to-one] volunteering to be included), and
(v) the level of commitment (some definitions allow for one-off voluntary activities to be included; others demand a certain level of commitment and exclude occasional acts).

Corporate volunteerism appears as one type of organisational setting, in parallel to other modalities such as non-profit or voluntary organisations, public sector volunteering and one-to-one volunteering.

UNV (2001) also defines four different types of volunteer activity, delineated according to a final outcome or final purpose criterion:

(i) mutual aid or self-help,
(ii) philanthropy or service to others,
(iii) participation and
(iv) advocacy or campaigning.

The analysis of the second type notes that it takes place within voluntary or community organisations, although in certain countries there is a strong tradition within the public sector and interest is growing in the corporate sector.

After a theoretical analysis of urban volunteerism, UNV (2001) presents the specific role of this UN programme as a partner in international assistance for urban development. Within such a context, it notes the importance of promoting corporate volunteerism.

While the references about corporate volunteerism in UNV's publication are indeed important, they are embryonic, and note that CSR was still mainly circumscribed to companies in developed countries. Such a publication calls for private companies to work with low-income urban communities in developing countries *via* corporate volunteerism, but it does not include an analysis of possible existing experiences or potential.

As noted in the introduction of this book, UNV also produced another publication (New Academy of Business and UNV, 2004), this time specific to CSR. However, as also explained before, this publication does not explore urban development per se.

Within the United Nations, there are two agencies whose mandates entail an expected stake in CSR in urban settings i.e. UN-Habitat and UNV. Both have been analysed in the present chapter. There are accounts of further engagement with private companies through CSR in urban settings within the UN system, notably UNDP. However, we do not know specific analyses of such cases.

A number of private companies working on aspects of urban development through CSR programmes have produced their own publications (e.g. Suez, which works in water, electricity, sewerage and garbage collection; Lafarge, on building materials, among others). Yet, these are essentially corporate booklets or leaflets. They provide no substantial analysis of the whole of CSR in urban settings, and so far have had no known impact on mainstream and academic literature.

Such experiences of private companies engaging with communities on their own or in association with a third party are commendable. This is why their references are given here. They are not analysed in-depth because, as noted in the introduction, the purpose of the present book is not to be exhaustive, but to provide some in-depth cases plus general analysis.

2.4 Conclusion

Chapter 1 introduced CSR and its importance, at the same time evidencing that urban development is still a gap within such a body of literature. Conversely, Chapter 2 has shown why it is important to focus on urban settings, and also that CSR is still a notable gap in the urban development literature.

In short, the present chapter has illustrated that there is a justification for supporting urban development due to the economic importance of cities and towns and due to the extent of urban poverty. While many stakeholders have indeed been fighting urban problems in general and urban poverty in particular, it is necessary to do much more. It is important to think about new ways to address urban problems, and CSR can play a role in such a context.

However, the literature on urban development has largely ignored CSR. The analysis of the private sector has been preponderantly about its commercial and investment roles, and this chapter has shown that the discussion of CSR in such a context has been at best superficial. Equally, the analysis of the role of other stakeholders in urban development (governments, NGOs, community-based organisations) does not throw much light on their possible connections with the private sector via CSR. Therefore, there is a need to better understand the role of CSR in urban development. The following chapters will provide concrete examples by linking CSR and specific themes of urban development.

3
Citywide Interventions
Ramin Keivani

This is the first of the case study chapters. It deals with broader interventions related to city regeneration, neighbourhood upgrading and community development. The other case study chapters focus on more specific interventions, necessary for housing and other buildings, for roads, utilities and social services such as health and education. In all cases, it is important that the interventions are seen as part of a broad framework of sustainable urban development. Therefore, this chapter begins with a section on such a framework, which serves as a background for the other sections as well as for the following chapters. Next, the present chapter looks at what types of citywide interventions are needed in order to achieve sustainability objectives. In particular we shall focus on interventions in terms of urban regeneration aimed at economic and physical redevelopment of cities before addressing more briefly interventions for social development and environmental protection. The chapter will then proceed to examine the potential role of CSR for citywide and community level interventions before providing an overall conclusion to the debate as a whole.

3.1 Sustainable urban development

The use of the term sustainability has now become so ubiquitous in both public and private policy discourse that it can sometimes be viewed as becoming almost meaningless in practical terms due to the many different interpretations and definitions of the term and/or its adoption as politically expedient gestures. Indeed, it has been noted that there are over 200 different definitions of the term (Parkin, 2000). Consequently, there is a serious concern that the issue has become so vague, contested and indeterminate a concept that it is open to wide spread abuse by politicians and business people alike (Porritt 2005; Warner and Negrete, 2005). Often the term is used more as a rhetorical charade to justify *status quo* or absolute minimum measures that may be required by law rather than a real intention of changing their ways.

In fact the phrase "sustainable development" first came to notice in the "World Conservation Strategy: Living Resource Conservation for Sustainable Development" published in 1980 (Lee, 1994). It was, however, propelled to the front of the international policy agenda in 1987 following the publication of the report of the World Commission on Environment and Development "Our Common Future" otherwise known as the Brundtland report (WCED, 1987). However, it was five years later at the 1992 Rio Earth Summit that more than 170 countries ratified the Brundtland report and offered a more refined definition that has become the main currency in terms of sustainable development until today:

> To equitably meet developmental and environmental needs of present and future generations (United Nations, 1992).

This definition provides direction for the subsequent inclusion of environmental considerations into broader areas of policy decision-making.

Perhaps one of the more useful and holistic definitions of sustainability is that of 'triple bottom line', a phrase that was first coined by Elkington (1998) and can be defined conceptually as economic prosperity, environmental quality and social justice. While the triple bottom line was originally proposed as a form of institutionalising reporting of wider impacts of corporate activity it has proved a useful concept for examining sustainable development policy and practice at the wider societal level. This is represented in Figure 3.1.

An important question to ask, however, is who benefits from sustainable development? The social sustainability pillar specifically points to social justice and urban equity as an important principle of sustainable development. In practice, however, social sustainability has received least attention both in the development of the conceptual discourse and praxis. Colantonio (2007) argues this is due both to the origins of the sustainability debate arising from ecological concerns of economic activities and difficulties in accurate measurement of what social sustainability actually means. As such Colantonio brings evidence from Organisation for Economic Co-operation and Development (OECD) (2001) to show that up to early 2000 social sustainability was largely a

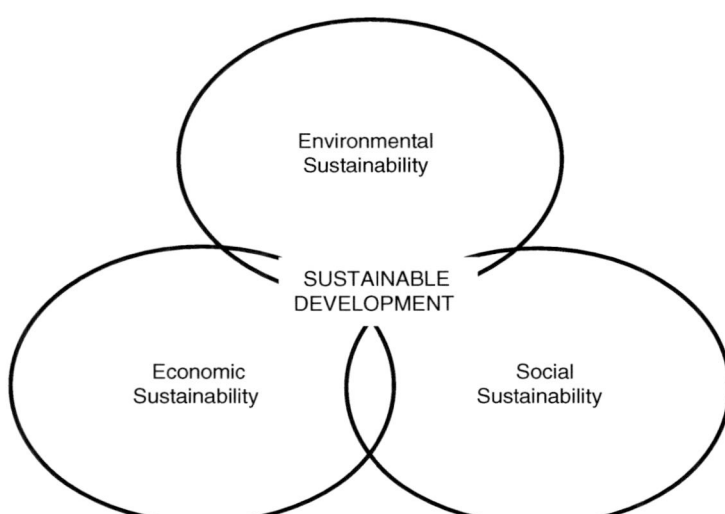

Figure 3.1 'Three Pillars' model of sustainable development

peripheral adjunct as social implications of environmental politics rather than "an equally constitutive component of sustainable development" (*ibid*: 4). In addition Littig and Griessler (2005) also note that the unequal treatment of the pillars is also a reflection of their treatment in the real world, that economic arguments often tend to be more convincing, and that the equal ranking of priorities is rarely an issue in the political context. Another reason can be seen in the central and local political structure and priorities and the power relations there in. In the context of UK, Hatter (2007) argues that while at the regional level major strides have now been taken to mainstream sustainable development due to the specific mandates of regional agencies, at the local level the picture is much less rosy. This, he notes, is due to lack of political priority thereby sidelining and subsuming Local Agenda 21 (LA 21) concerns to other policy drivers with more financial and political clout, often reducing it to recycling. This is in spite of new and unprecedented powers granted to local authorities in 2000 for the economic, social and environmental well being of their areas. This, he adds, is largely due to the centralised nature of state in the UK reducing local government to essentially a delivery arm of the central government.

Colantonio (2007) goes on to provide a good summary of different conceptual approaches to social sustainability and finds that there is not a set of agreed characteristics. For example some commentators such as Littig and Griessler (2005) focus on the role of work satisfying human needs while others, e.g., Stren and Polese (2000), highlight the tension between economic efficiency and social disintegration while also noting the importance of the physical environment including housing, urban design and public spaces. Yet we have other scholars such as Baines and Morgan (2004 cited in Colantonio, 2007) that have identified thematic areas of social sustainability as being basic needs and social well being, social capital, equity and social and cultural dynamism. Other variations include Bramley *et al.*, 2006 (cited in Colantonio, 2007) with a focus on social justice/equity and sustainability of communities' core issues, in particular noting the importance of social networks, community participation, pride/sense of place, community stability and security (crime). Some others such as Biart (2002 cited in Colantonio, 2007), however, have specifically focused on the importance of minimal social requirements for long term development or functioning of social systems while essentially ignoring the physical dimension (see Colantonio, 2007 for a more detailed review).

Considering the disparity of views on what actually constitutes social sustainability it is even more difficult to specify objectives and indicators for it. Here we agree with Littig and Griessler (2005) in that such indicators have not been grounded on "theory but rather on a practical understanding of plausibility and current political agendas" (*ibid*: 68). Social sustainability, therefore, is particularly context driven. This is the main reason that the international community has not adopted a single universal definition nor ascribed to one conceptual framework (World Bank, 2004a). We can however provide one broad definition that may include others in that social sustainability is about enhancing people centred development.[1]

As indicated in Figure 3.2, in spite of the lack of clarity on the precise definition and components of social sustainability the increasing number of studies dealing with the subject and its inclusion in the policy arena shows that in the first decade of the new century social sustainability may finally find its deserved place as an equal pillar of sustainability alongside that of environmental and economic spheres.

---

[1] The reader is also referred to Chapter 6 for a detailed discussion of social development that is directly related to our discussion of social sustainability.

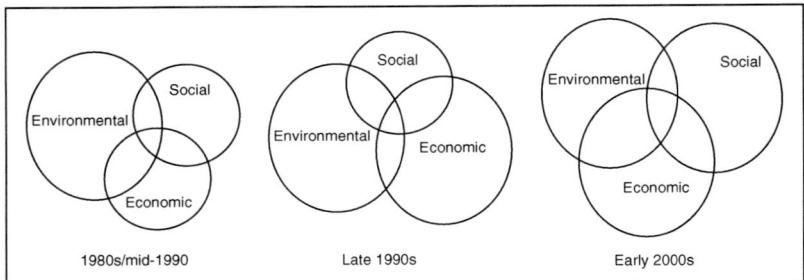

Figure 3.2 Relative importance of main pillars of sustainable development through time
Source: Colantonio, 2007.

Focusing more specifically on the urban scene we can also see the same trend is evident in the cities. Here the conceptual debate on sustainable development has now moved to fully incorporate the social dimension in a broader sense. Specifically we must highlight the concept of "just sustainability" with its emphasis on social justice in the implementation of environmental policies that was specifically developed in respect of place building in the UK and the US (Agyeman and Warner, 2002). The main argument is that the lives and communities of the poor and minority people should receive equal attention in all aspects of environmental policy, and that past injustices redressed. The point being that in their attempt to address the bigger picture traditional approaches can "lose sight of the social and equity dimensions that are critical in meeting the needs of the present and future generations" (Agyeman and Warner, 2002: 14). In effect just sustainability propels the social pillar of sustainable development to the fore, measuring the success or failure of initiatives in the other two pillars in terms of their impact on social and equity principles. The issue addressed here, therefore, is not only sustainability but also sustainability for whom?

In terms of urban policy, however, we can argue that in the main the economic pillar has tended to be more dominant in the initial stages. Nevertheless a similar shift for the inclusion of social dimension is also evident. During the 1980s and 1990s, for example, urban development policy in developed countries largely focused on economic/physical regeneration often relying on property-led development which scarcely mention of environmental, let alone social concerns (see for example Healey *et al.*, 1992). This is a policy which, we might add has been copied widely around the world including developing countries. In UK the collapse of property markets in the late 1980s/early 1990s and the failure to solve some of the more pressing urban problems through property development have led to a move to more diversified and comprehensive urban regeneration policies. In particular, social concerns have come to the fore with an emphasis on local neighbourhood level partnership development approach for bringing together local level actors in strategic partnerships both to define development priorities and implement policies (Wallace, 2001; Colantonio, 2007). In addition, there are signs that at the local level LA21 is gaining much greater significance in strategic policy development and local authorities are beginning to better assert and utilise their new powers for environmental protection and well being of their citizens (Hatter, 2007). Priority areas include issues such as jobs, crime, health, schooling, housing, pollution and physical environment. Importantly, however, economic development is no longer seen merely in terms of attracting investment in to cities and neighbourhoods but more crucially raising local skills, reducing unemployment, promoting self employment, making child care available to allow parents to seek work actively. In essence we have moved to focusing on neighbourhoods as communities rather than places. We, therefore, read:

> …, it is essential that neighbourhoods are not seen simply as places, but above all as communities. If neighbourhood renewal is simply 'done to' residents, the right solutions will not be found; new funding will simply flow through neighbourhoods rather than enriching the neighbourhoods; and residents will be seen as problems not as assets: these are the failures of many programmes in the past, and that is why community empowerment and involvement are at the heart of the strategy. (Wallace, 2001: 2165)

Later in 2003 broader concerns on sustainability were more explicitly included in UK urban policy to develop the Sustainable Communities Plan where a sustainable community is defined as:

> …places where people want to live and work, now and in the future. They meet the diverse needs of existing and future residents, are sensitive to their environment, and contribute to a high quality of life. They are safe and inclusive, well planned, built and run, and offer equality of opportunity and good services for all. (CLG, 2007)

In the 2005 Bristol Accord the European Union also adopted the UK approach by placing sustainable communities at the centre of its urban policy (ODPM, 2006; Colantonio, 2007). The eight key characteristics of sustainable communities adopted in the Bristol Accord are:

1. Active, inclusive and safe – fair, tolerant and cohesive with a strong local culture and other shared community activities
2. Well run – with effective and inclusive participation, representation and leadership
3. Environmentally sensitive – providing places for people to live that are considerate of the environment
4. Well designed and built – featuring quality built and natural environment
5. Well connected – with good transport services and communication linking people to jobs, schools, health and other services
6. Thriving – with a flourishing and diverse local economy
7. Well served – with public, private, community and voluntary services that are appropriate to people's needs and accessible to all
8. Fair for everyone – including those in other communities, now and in the future

In this context the essence of sustainable urban development, therefore, can be seen as enhancing the living environment of citizens encompassing environmental, social, economic and political spheres.

But what of developing countries? Can we assume that the same characteristics apply in the context of rapid urbanisation, scarcity of resources and extreme poverty?

Clearly at some levels the characteristics identified for the UK and EU sustainable urban communities are far fetched in the context of developing cities. As noted in this and other chapters of this book a significant minority or even majority of urbanites in most developing cities are struggling to have access to minimum shelter, utilities and social services, let alone living in 'well designed and built communities that are well served and well run'. Nevertheless, there are many similarities in basic requirements that can contribute to attaining sustainable urban development in cities of both the North and the South. Drakakis-Smith (1995) argues that developing urban sustainability at a macro level must meet the following requirements:

- equity, social justice and human rights;
- basic human needs;
- social and ethnic self-determination;

- environmental awareness and integrity; and
- awareness of inter-linkages across both space and time.

At the micro level these imply dealing with specific concerns that are mainly interrelated and must be addressed in an integrated manner. These are:

- Economic issues in terms of employment and poverty. This must integrate the external role of the city at regional and national levels with return on labour. It has a direct impact on environmental issues since the primary concern of poor people is to earn a living rather than look after the environment. This does not mean that poor people are not concerned with the environment rather that their priorities are firstly ensuring their own survival. Therefore without addressing the issue of employment and poverty it would be impossible to address environmental concerns. This takes us back to the debate on environmental justice and ensuring social sustainability as an integral approach to achieving sustainable urban development.
- Physical environment. Here the main concern deals with those elements that need to be provided at city level such as access to utilities, and those that can have a greater involvement of households such as waste collection. We must also emphasise the crucial role of public and commercial spaces that is provided by both the public and private sectors. These must be inclusive, facilitate reflexive and cross functional economic activities and engender a sense of pride and belonging in the citizens and users in general.
- Urban social environment. This concern deals with access to basic needs including shelter/housing, food, education, security and health.
- Finally we have human rights concerns. This issue is not only related to cultural, linguistic, religious and political freedoms but also some of the issues raised under social environment such as the right to shelter, education, food as well as the right to organisations of civil society, community and labour and professional associations and unions to be able to better participate in governance, win recognition for their rights and gain access to resources.

Similarly, in their discussion of social sustainability in cities, Stren and Polese (2000) identify employment and economic revitalisation as one of the six key policy themes that need attention by local authorities to ensure optimum employment generation both in terms of attracting investment and also ensuring that employment locations are not unduly segregated through ill thought planning, urban development and zoning policies that effectively exclude lower income and informal groups and traders from livelihood opportunities.

Addressing many of these concerns requires intervention at the city and neighbourhood levels usually by the public sector to provide for example utilities, service land for housing or investment in major infrastructure and social services such as hospitals or schools. Other chapters in this book examine both public and private interventions necessary for housing, utilities and social services. Here we shall focus on some aspects dealing with broader city regeneration, neighbourhood upgrading and community development.

3.2 City regeneration and physical upgrading: an evolutionary history

A defining feature of urban policy in both developed and developing countries in the past three decades has been major city-wide or neighbourhood level intervention for regenerating declining or blighted areas of cities. These have been aimed either at estate renewal primarily targeting physical upgrading of housing estates and/or wider area regeneration aimed at enhancing the broader urban economy as a whole. By definition, therefore, urban regeneration involves a variety of organisations with different qualities, motivations and resources to undertake projects at larger spatial-temporal scale (Jones and Evans, 2006). In both cases, however, physical redevelopment remained central to such efforts. In fact the emphasis on physical redevelopment as the catalyst for broader social and particularly economic area revival was such that in the 1980s these interventions came to be known as property-led urban development.

The origins of property-led urban development can be traced to the inception of a regional policy in the 1930s in the UK for building industrial estates in peripheral regions and similar initiatives by local authorities in early 1970s (Jones, 1996). From 1979 to early 1990s, however, property-led development became central pillars of urban policy, regeneration and city economic development in the UK and USA (see for example, Healey et al., 1992; Jones, 1996; Fainstein, 1995). The emphasis, though, shifted from direct subsidised public provision to subsidising direct private provision with the aim of engendering a more sustainable private market involvement without public subsidy in the long run. This did not mean that in the Thatcher period in the UK there was a complete lack of consideration of socially oriented programmes.

On the contrary, Ball and Maginn (2005) argue that in fact they generated a dualism of property redevelopment and socially-oriented programmes such as Garden Festivals, Safer Cities and Ethnic minorities Business Initiative. However, the property-led approach was the dominant form of urban intervention that was directly controlled by the central government. The underlying economic rationale for property-led urban policy was to resolve property market deficiencies/failures (in terms of lack of supply of appropriate infrastructure and property) to bolster private sector confidence for investing in inner city/peripheral projects (Jones, 1996). However, the reasons for its wide adoption can be seen in several macro-economic and political developments.

First, economic globalisation and the shift to a post-Fordist flexible service based economy led to major readjustment in the employment structure of urban economies and therefore urban development (Pugh, 1996; Sassen, 2001; Cullingworth and Nadin, 1994). It is sobering to note that between 1971 and 2003 the contribution of the manufacturing sector to London's economy reduced from 25% of total employment to about 6% (Harris, 2006). During the same time the share of business and financial services increased from 16% to 33%. As a result of such readjustment large areas of cities, particularly in previously industrial and water front port locations (that were feeding these industries) lay blighted and derelict and cities faced mass unemployment.

Second, the rise of neo-liberal governments in the UK and US from the late 1970s with pro-market ideologies had a significant impact on reorienting city planning towards a more flexible commercial development agenda (Atkinson and Moon, 1994; Tewdwr-Jones, 1994). This was reinforced through rationalisation of local public finances, particularly caps on local public spending and revenue raising capacity, which constrained the ability of local governments to use local public investment in housing or other infrastructure activities for redevelopment of blighted areas. Quangos or parastatal organisations, e.g., Urban Development Corporations and Enterprise Zones, were created to take charge of the development of specific neighbourhoods above that of the local authority (e.g., the London Docklands Corporation) or to act on a more national level as a facilitator for the private sector to regenerate land and buildings (e.g., English Partnerships) (Swyngedouw *et al.*, 2002; Jones, 1996; Wilks-Heeg, 1996; Ball and Maginn, 2005).

Third, liberalisation and deregulation of global financial markets and opening up of national economies during the 1980s further accelerated the economic globalisation process leading to highly mobile investment capital and intense competition between cities for attracting such investment. A condition that Sassen (2001) argued has led to a hierarchy of world cities with different but complementary functions in supporting the global economy.

Fourth the combination of these circumstances led to the emergence of entrepreneurial local governments whose main task was to increase the competitive position of their cities by creating favourable institutional and physical conditions for attracting national and international investment as the major resource for economic development. An important tool for this was private led physical redevelopment of rundown neighbourhoods or other major urban development projects including prestigious development projects and landmark buildings (Loftman and Nevin, 1996; Swyngedouw et al., 2002). The attraction of property-led development to local authorities is that this is the arena where they have most power in terms of land use control and acquisitions. Therefore, Jones (1996) argues "these powers used in a proactive way in combination with land banks and subsidies provide a local authority with its greatest potential for influencing local economic development. They also have the attraction of creating (short term) local jobs in the construction industry which concentrated in less skilled occupations of the unemployed" (p. 798).

Focusing on the cases of London and New York, Faintsein (1995), for example, notes that by the beginning of 1980s the governing regimes of both cities were increasingly relying on real estate development as their primary strategy for stimulating commercial growth. This was based largely on "addressing the office and housing needs of the upper echelons of the financial and advanced service industries participating in world economic co-ordination."

By the beginning of 1990s, however, orthodox Thatcherite policies of 'over-reliance' on the private sector and property-led urban development in the UK was coming under attack from several quarters. On the economic development front there was indeed evidence of local job creation. However, it was argued that much of the economic growth was in fact benefiting the region rather than the city and where growth was occurring in cities it was largely benefiting elite groups rather than poorer local residents (Loftman and Nevin, 1996). On the housing and social front liberalisation of markets had merely served to increase inequalities in the distribution of wealth and increase the levels of social problems in poorer neighbourhoods with severely rundown and unsaleable housing estates that were left behind from the public housing privatisation programme (Davoudi and Healey, 1995; Wilks-Heeg, 2000; Ball and Maginn, 2005). On the property front excessive procedural flexibility in interpretation of the planning system had led to massive over-building in the late 1980s leading to a severe slump in the property market (Healey, 1992). On the environmental front there was a conflict between Thatcherite market oriented policies and the new emphasis of the environmental movement that had now gained additional importance within the government as a result of the Rio Earth Summit. This required sustainable development and absorption of ecological conceptions of constraints into planning criteria while having some consideration for global impact, capacities and limits (Healey and Shaw, 1993).

Such criticisms led to the amendment of the Town and Country Planning Act 1990 in the UK that effectively put greater weight on the significance of Development Plans in the determination of planning applications, i.e., it reflected the then government's view that the planning system should be plan-led. This, however, did not mean an end to property-led-urban development in the UK. Indeed it has remained an important aspect of policies on urban physical and economic renewal. The difference, particularly since the 1997 labour government election, has been in the promotion of a more comprehensive, integrated and inclusive approach where at least attempts have been made to include social aspects and community development as well as economic and physical renewal considerations. This is particularly evident in funding and promoting more inclusive partnership arrangements to include community and voluntary sectors for delivery of urban policy at neighbourhood and city levels (Brindley, 2000; Carley, 2000; Wilks-Heeg, 2000). However, bringing community sector on board as contractual partners has its own complexities in terms of functions, conflict of interests and integrity of purpose where the lobbying and advocacy role of the community sector effectively becomes compromised.

Importantly, we should also note that even during the 1980s, property-led urban development was not the preserve of the private sector. In addition to facilitating private development, local authorities were also directly leading on a range of major prestige projects primarily targeted at civic boosterism. Loftman and Nevin (1996) note that between 1986–1992 Birmingham city council spent some £331 million on prestige business tourism and sport complexes including the International Convention Centre. Looking at 13 major urban development projects across Europe, Swyngedouw *et al.* (2002) argue that in fact during the 1990s property-led development and its underlying neo-liberal urban development model for increasing urban competitiveness through major development projects was not only alive and kicking but had come to be adopted by local regional and national governments across Europe irrespective of their ideological stripes and colours.

3.2.1 Property-led development and regeneration in the cities of the South

Property-led development has in fact spread far beyond continental Europe or the US. It is now a major driving force for urban change in many cities of the South that are emerging as international business and industrial nodes for attracting much of the relocated lower value added industries due to their comparative advantage in lower labour costs and yet developed infrastructure and transport capacities for supporting decentralised production and access to the world markets. At the same time many of these cities are also rapidly developing their institutional, infrastructure and human resource capacities to maintain and improve their competitive position not only in respect of industrial FDI but to climb up the hierarchy and becoming international nodes of higher value added functions in their own right.

The prime examples are Singapore and Hong Kong respectively shifting their economic base in successive phases from the sweatshops of the 1960s to becoming international centres of the high tech and information economy and regional HQ and export service centres of Asia (Macleod and McGee, 1996; Ho and So, 1997; Sim *et al.*, 2003). To this we must add the small oil rich cities of the Persian Gulf, particularly Dubai in UAE and Manama in Bahrain, that are shrewdly utilising their immense wealth and strategic location as an effective development strategy to becoming regional centres of HQ functions, IT, tourism and corporate and financial services to the greater Middle East (Keivani *et al.*, 2003; Parsa and Keivani, 2002; Stanley, 2003). This is achieved largely through attracting expatriate technical and managerial expertise, traders and importing skilled and unskilled labourers as well as rapid infrastructure and property development.

A unifying characteristic of all these cities is their reliance on property-led development in office, commercial, industrial and housing both within central locations and well in to their periphery to raise their competitive position. Many of these developments are in fact led by central/federal governments that have also set up special quangos and parastatal organisations for facilitating the redevelopment work (see Keivani and Mattingly, 2007 for greater discussion of this process, particularly in the context of Bangalore).

A similar but more exaggerated process is evident in the context of Chinese cities where local governments have emerged as powerful entrepreneurial developmental states in their own rights (Zhu, 2004) and are yet protected from consequences of loss making behaviour due to soft budget constraints (Xu and Yeh, 2005). In an effort to increase the competitive position and economic performance of their cities Chinese local governments have increasingly adopted urban boosterism and pro-growth strategies while utilising their land resources and manipulating planning procedures for attracting developers to engender a frenzy of physical development and infrastructure projects (*ibid*; Wu, 2000, 1998; Cao and Keivani, 2007).

A related issue here is the impact of growth of population in large cities in both developed and developing countries that has tended to lead to a decline of population in central locations and dispersal to peripheral areas as households are displaced by changing economic functions and expansion of other activities in the centre. Ingram (1998) observes that this trend has been seen in "cities as diverse as Bangkok, Bogota, Mexico City, Shanghai and Tokyo." Reasons for this are lower land and housing prices, lower rents and lower development costs in the peripheral areas as well as wider availability of motorised transport providing better linkages between periphery and the main city core. In addition growth of household size particularly in developing countries means that they prefer larger dwelling units. Given that housing costs are generally lower in peripheral areas there is a shift to such areas. In Bogota in 1978 household size increased regularly with distance from the centre from about two persons in the centre to five persons in the periphery (Ingram, 1998).

Changing economic functions in many cities often means that central city locations are gradually emptied of lower value added residential and industrial activities and turned towards more profitable service, cultural and commercial activities. In such a scenario many city centre locations become highly desirable space as concentrated Central Business Districts. These provide easy global communication and reflexive space for face to face contact and networking that are essential to the function of modern high value added activities in head quarter, financial and export services (Graham, 2000; Ingram, 1998). An additional functions of city centres, particularly older and more established locations is to act as a bridge, a meeting place that brings together different groups of people from different backgrounds and classes for other activities including cultural and leisure functions. As noted by Stren and Polese (2000), where people shop and work is also close to where they gather for other [cultural and leisure] purposes. "The social dynamics of public spaces (such as parks and squares)", they argue, "can not be separated from the workplaces nearby." (Stren and Polese, 2000: 32)

This pattern of changing economic functions and displacement is not only evident in major cities in the US, Europe and Japan that are functioning as power houses of the global economy but also in many emerging global cities of the South (Keivani and Mattingly, 2007). In many Asian countries, for example, the world is witnessing the rapid globally-induced transformation of a number of metropolises from Bangalore to Shanghai, including Jakarta, Kuala Lumpur, Manila, Mumbai and Taipei, into regional hubs of commerce, finance, IT and/or industry. This is leading to major changes in the socio-economy, demography and land use of these cities with rapid development of central locations with prestige projects particularly major showpiece office and retail developments (Benjamin, 2000; Wu, 2003; Douglas, 2000; Jones *et al.*, 2000; Firman, 1998; Morshidi, 2000; Shatkin, 2000; Grant and Nijman, 2002 and Aranya, 2003).

Glimmering skyscrapers in central business districts (CBDs) and vibrant commercial/cultural centres, however, are only one side of the story. Another side can be seen in very poor, dilapidated and socially excluded neighbourhoods that co-exist in close vicinity of major CBDs and modern skyscrapers in cities of both North and South. Perhaps the most striking example can be seen in London where the City of London beats as the financial heart of the global economy with high salaries, astronomical bonuses and state of art skyscrapers housing head quarters of banks and financial companies. Yet, cheek by jowl to it is Spitalfields, one of the poorest and most dilapidated wards in England. This pattern of uneven urban development is perhaps starkest in major metropolises in developing countries where many slum neighbourhoods continue to exist in central locations and/or in close proximity to major new modern developments. Yet residents have access to far less amenities and in some cases face continued threats of eviction and demolition rather than public intervention for regenerating their settlements. These settlements are what Shatkin (2004) describes in the context of Manila as forgotten places in the era of globalisation evidenced by the "increasing difficulty that low-income urban residents face in accessing legal shelter close to sources of livelihood and in the rising threat of displacement faced by many informal settlements". There are many examples which illustrate that many public interventions are normally aimed at extending utility or road networks through these settlements rather than for them, make over attempts at hiding the settlements from view or wholesale demolition to make way for new modern commercial, retail or high end residential developments. Benjamin (2000), for example, notes the redevelopment of traditional market areas in Central Bangalore with flyover and a new multi-storey retail and market complex displacing the original stall holders and traders of the old market. In Seoul and Bangkok during the 1980s it is estimated that three million and 100,000 people respectively were displaced in the redevelopment of the centre and adjoining parts of these cities (Douglas, 2000). Similarly Shatkin (2004) points to eviction of at least 150,000 in Manila only in the three year period between 1997 and 2000 due to various redevelopment and infrastructure projects in central areas of Manila. As a result he notes that there is an increasing shift of lower income groups to city peripheries where they can have easier and cheaper access to land. However, the fact is that this type of 'intervention' is not limited to the central slums and is also evident in more peripheral locations. The latest example of which is clearing a path for the Delhi metro through slum areas of the city that in one case resulted in over 200 shacks being demolished without any consultation with local slum residents (Ramesh, January 24th, 2007). There may of course be a reasonable argument that land needs to be put to its most economic use, create the necessary physical environment, and provide the necessary infrastructure to maintain and enhance the competitiveness of the urban economy as a whole. From the perspective of sustainable urban development, however, the important questions to ask are what are the social and environmental costs of such developments and how can we better intervene to ensure a more equitable development process?

In other cases rapid urbanisation and shifting economic activities have also led to displacement of higher income populations from original central city locations. However, instead of the formation of modern CBDs around high value service functions these locations have generally fallen in to a period of neglect, dilapidation and blight with little new investment, ageing fabric and little maintenance. The market process underlies such change of fortune. However, public intervention can also seriously undermine the economic basis of such neighbourhoods, not only leading to dilapidation of the old core but also spatial polarisation of employment and commercial activities that seriously disadvantage traditional traders and businesses. In San Salvador, for example, the municipality has not only neglected the old commercial centre but by promoting the development of new commercial zones and offices in other areas further to the west has effectively "created two San Slavadors: the old center, largely left to the poor, filed with street vendors and informal markets (and some informal industry); a new centre to the west, with modern shopping malls, offices, parking spaces, and a high proportion of white collar employment" (Stren and Polese, 2000: 32). Lungo (2000) explains that the situation in the old center of San Salvador has arisen as a result of Master planning objectives instituted in 1969 that designated new financial and commercial nodes due to perceived limitations in the centre for meeting increased demands for such services. However, the result, particularly following the 1986 earthquake has been flight of main banks and insurance companies and their replacement by largely informal activities, informal street vendors, etc.

Another case of such abandonment is the old central parts of Tehran around the main bazaar that was once home to wealthy merchants in grand houses at the turn of the 20th century. From the end of the second world war the original wealthy residents gradually moved to newer areas in the north of the city while the old centre became choked with increasing traffic and pollution and grand houses were turned into slum rental housing through many internal subdivisions for new comers and lower income groups in the city (Moatazed-Keivani, 1993). As such today the old central and much of the southern parts of Tehran comprise many dilapidated neighbourhoods, crumbling buildings and housing in serious state of disrepair and severely lacking green space. In the past two decades a major concern of successive Tehran municipalities have been regeneration of the central and southern parts of the city through large scale planning and physical interventions including undertaking major new road and transportation links between these areas and the rest of the city, creation of green space, and relocating and redeveloping sites of old industrial, warehousing and distribution activities. A prominent example of this is the relocation of the city's main fruit and vegetable market from a southern part of the city and turning the whole area in to a park as well as a current programme for renewing the original central parts of the city around the main bazaar as a historic/tourist core.

In different ways this scenario is repeated in many cities where old historic or commercial cores are abandoned or suffer from lack of investment in their upkeep and refurbishment due to socio-economic and demographic shifts in the city. In the case of Istanbul, Dokmeci *et al.* (2007) chart the decline and subsequent revitalisation of Beyoglu, the old CBD of Istanbul. They note:

> During the last quarter of the twentieth century, Istanbul like other large cities in the world experienced multi-centre development

causing the decline of its old CBDE. Decentralisation as housing, jobs and commercial activities (including shopping centres and hyper-markets) were set up in more peripheral areas of the city, and an increasing loss of accessibility due to the expansion of the city and traffic congestion and [loss of] attractiveness in the traditional shopping area paved the way [for the decline]. ... From 1960 to 1990, the percentage of Istanbul's firms located in Beyoglu dropped from 30.4% to 15.5% and in the service sector, from 20.9% to 17% between 1970 and 1985. (Dokmeci *et al.*, 2007: 156)

They add:

Until 1990, like many old central districts of Istanbul, and indeed like many inner cities in developing countries Beyoglu was losing middle and upper income people and receiving rural migrants instead. This decline led to substantial decrease in real estate prices, high vacancy rates and wide-scale abandonment. This trend was related to changing fashions in town planning, architectural style, housing and shopping preferences and the 'modern life style' to be found in newly developing parts of the city. Owners who could afford to buy properties in these districts moved out over time as Beyoglu lost its appeal as a prestigious housing alternative. (*ibid*: 167)

The historic character of Beyoglu as a tourist attraction nevertheless remained in spite of its overall decline. As a result with growth of tourism in the Turkish economy the municipality finally intervened in 1990 to kick start the revitalisation of Beyoglu as it was seen not only crucial for improving the quality of life in the neighbourhood but also to boost economic development in the city as a whole. These interventions were based both on planning measures such as pedestrianising the main street but also investment in infrastructure and large scale beautification such as reintroducing the tram to enhance the old character, repaving the street with specially designed slabs, new custom designed street lighting and street furniture. Importantly, there was also stakeholder participation from local businesses, citizens and conservation groups through formation of a voluntary organisation for preservation and revitalisation of Beyoglu as a historic commercial and cultural centre. Needless to say that these efforts have led to large scale private investment in Beyoglu turning it in to a bustling commercial centre with over a million visitors per week. At the same time there has been a functional shift with figures for the period 1986–2005 showing increases in office space from 11% to 43% on upper floors, movie theatres from 3% to 7% and banking from 4% to 16% on the ground floor (*ibid*). This trend now seems to be spreading to other adjacent street with new private investment in shops, cafes and work shops for artist and young professionals.

Inevitably this type of economic revitalisation has led to large increases in real estate and land values in Beyoglu, turning it again into one of the most expensive and desired locations in the city. The counter argument would be that this will restrict access of new migrants and low income people in general to housing in this part of the city. This may very well be true. Indeed, the same argument applies to most regenerations involving old neighbourhoods where there is a clear risk of gentrification. In other cases as already noted globally led private or public developments often also entail not only direct destruction of low income informal settlements but rapid increases in prices that would drive out lower income groups. Such processes have been noted in Manila and Bangalore (Shatkin, 2004; Benjamin, 2000). Nevertheless, we must also bear in mind that the economic benefits of the revitalisation in terms of creation of jobs in retail, service and tourist sector, particularly in old historic quarters, would generally benefit the lower income groups in the city as a whole in terms of greater job opportunities. At the same time increasing real estate values would also benefit the many lower income residents that had already moved to such locations prior to the start of their regeneration should they choose to realise capital value or rental opportunities from their properties due to the higher demand for the location. However, a major concern remains that the big losers in such cases are the low income renters who are always invariably driven out due to the higher status and value of land and property in the regenerated areas (Durand-Lasserve, 2002). Having said this, though, we must note that the actual impact of increased commercialisation of land is highly place-specific. A study on tenure forms in urban Egypt, for example, suggests that the majority of tenants – those renting before 1996 – are likely to benefit from increased commercialisation due to strict tenancy rights afforded to them by the law (Sims, 2002). For the owners of such properties to be able to sell and enjoy the full market price, they need to pay a negotiated amount to the tenant to leave. Thus both parties gain from the increase in land value. In other words it is the institutional context governing access to land and housing that ultimately governs the winners and losers from regeneration projects and their impact on gentrification and commercialisation of land.

On a different note Hoyle (2002) focuses on urban waterfront revitalisation in developing countries with the specific case of the Stone Town in Zanzibar. He charts the decline of Zanzibar since its glory days as the regional trading hub of East Africa in the 19th century. This was partly an effect of the changing global economic scene particularly the collapse of the clove market and partly due to political instabilities that have dogged Zanzibar since the 1964 revolution and the union with Tanganyika. However, the important point here is the opportunity that redevelopment of its historic waterfront area can afford Zanzibar in terms of economic development potential, particularly in cultural tourism. Nevertheless despite the opportunity afforded in the more positive and stable political climate and increasing interest of international investors in cultural tourism Hoyle identifies institutional weaknesses in leading and coordinating redevelopment activities as a major stumbling block. He writes:

> In administrative terms, waterfront redevelopment can not proceed to best advantage unless there exists, between various organisations and authorities involved, a common set of objectives and an agreed framework of methods. In Zanzibar, and elsewhere in East Africa, an appropriate degree of integration and coordination is frequently lacking. (Hoyle, 2002: 151)

Nevertheless, efforts are being made to renovate and conserve some of the 34 historic buildings on the water front. Two prominent successful examples both involve international donors in the form of the Aga Khan Trust for restoring an historic dispensary as the Zanzibar Cultural Centre and the EU for renovating and restoring an 18th century Omani fort and its grounds which is now used as a large open air auditorium for a variety of cultural activities. Another example involved the redevelopment of an old telegraph house in to an up market hotel involving a range of actors from the Aga Khan Trust, the Cable and Wireless company, UNESCO, EU and the Zanzibar government showing the possibility of cooperation among diverse organisations and local and international actors for effective intervention for historic conservation and economic development.

On a related theme we can consider the case of urban redevelopment in Old Accra. Here Razzu (2005) rightly points out that in the old district of Accra as in many other developing countries, concentration of poor communities in old historic areas have generally tended to exacerbate problems of conservation and maintenance due to the low priority of conservation for lower income groups in comparison to satisfying their basic needs. Again here, as in Tehran, Istanbul and Zanzibar, a combination of factors, including departure of wealthier residents to newer parts of the city and transfer of the main port functions to another location in 1962, have led to a strategic loss of economic resource and continuous decline of the local economy. As such the old centre of Accra is home largely to new poor migrants and remaining lower income groups. It suffers from extreme material poverty in terms of housing conditions and access to amenities, utilities and sanitation. It has nevertheless a rich heritage of tangible and intangible historic assets in the shape of forts, customs, chiefs' palaces, shrines, priests' houses as well as intangible culturally significant places for the endogenous Ga people.

A relevant observation by Razzu with respect to interventions in old declining and dilapidated historic neighbourhoods is that as this requires buying and/or renovating old historic buildings it usually entails relatively high levels of initial investment that is outside the scope of small credit availability to local households. As such it would normally require investment by an outside party. These can be local or central government, national or international NGOs, international donors or even the private sector in partnership with public sector or on their own. In respect of the tension between welfare of local people and historic conservation in conditions of extreme poverty he notes that according to guidelines of the International Council on Monuments and Sites, improvement of housing and local participation must remain part of the objectives of conservation. In other words all efforts must be made to bring the people on board that also include tangible benefits in their living environment. If carried out according to social sustainability principles not only is there no contradiction between cultural preservation and poverty reduction but that there are definite affinities between them. He writes:

> Cultural tourism, for example, can enormously benefit the local community but, at the same time, it can be enhanced by community participation. It is the community that possesses the cultural elements, such as religion, music, stories on the area and the people, etc. More tourists can be attracted to visit Old Accra if, for instance, guided trips are organized to the numerous shrines located in many houses or if they can eat local food, or if they can be introduced to

local customs... This can not be done without community participation. (Razzu, 2005: 416–417)

The point raised by Razzu on the inability of local residents to financially support interventions for the conservation of old historic neighbourhoods in low income countries is very important. As he notes neither the scale of required funding nor the nature of these types of investments lend themselves to micro credit systems or the saving capacities of the poor households. Particularly in a context of extreme poverty where conservation would inevitably have low priority compared to satisfying basic needs. In fact we would go further and argue that neighbourhood level interventions requiring large scale financial investments in general are out of the scope of local communities. However, as noted in the case of Old Accra, local communities play a critical role in providing non-monetary support and ensuring long term success. This can involve other inputs such as input in design of project, labour, organisation support, campaigning and advocacy, maintenance and after care, etc. This type of community intervention can be seen in Yeumbeul in Dakar, Senegal, an irregular settlement with some 800,000 inhabitants where 40% of the area does not have any proper urban infrastructure such as surfaced roads, sewerage and water main (Soumare, 2002). This translates into 60% of the local population not having access to electricity or main water. One consequence of this poverty is that people are coming together in grass roots movements and local associations to improve their living conditions and their physical environment. In this respect a small upgrading programme was initiated in 1995 primarily to improve access to clean water and sanitation, support income generating activities and promote community development and social activities. Notably the funding for the $80,000 project came from an outside international agency, i.e., UNESCO. However, while technical support was provided by the Regional Water and Sanitation Board and other agencies; local associations were involved in determining the objectives, supervising the work and setting up management committees to take charge of running and managing the new standpipes including collection of bills, maintenance and payment to the water company. In addition to extending water access to some 600 households, through fitting five new standpipes, the project succeeded in installing 65 sanitation units, providing three animal drawn carts for refuse collection and training for women and masons and labourers.

Another area of neighbourhood level intervention is in housing. Housing provision in general is discussed at length in another chapter. However, here we focus on slum redevelopment. Mukhija (2002) notes that conventional slum upgrading focuses on tenure legalisation and is predicated on a positive causal relationship between secure private property rights for squatters and their increased investment in housing improvement. Such programmes would normally also include targeted improvements in urban infrastructures and physical environments. Indeed as noted in the case of Yeumbeul many slum upgrading projects are primarily targeted at infrastructure improvement. This can also be seen in the context of Dhaka where Chowdhury and Amin (2006) show that a wide range of international aid agencies and local public actors are involved in many upgrading projects specifically targeted at improving the physical environment and infrastructure in informal settlements. These include "construction of drains and sewerage lines, footpaths, latrines or community latrines, garbage disposal bins, drinking water supply, improved housing, flood protection, and street lighting (*ibid*: 352).

Slum redevelopment on the other hand involves demolition of existing buildings and their replacement with new, often higher density, apartments. This can involve cross-subsidies to allow housing for original and lower income slum dwellers. Such interventions are particularly suited to slums where they are characterised by small lots, densely populated and irregular layouts with high land values due to relative central location of the slums that often occurs as a result of rapid growth of cities in developing countries turning originally peripheral sites into more valuable centrally located settlements. It is this higher land value that would allow the scope for cross subsidisation for the original slum dwellers since part of the redevelopment can be sold to relatively higher income new customers. One such scheme can be seen in Markandeya slum in Mumbai (Mukhija, 2002). Notably the main actors in this redevelopment were in fact the local settlement cooperative (Markandeya Cooperative Housing Society) and a local NGO, the Society for the Promotion of Area Resource Centres (SPARC) effectively putting the main public slum upgrading institution, i.e., Prime Minister's Grant Project (PMGP), on the periphery of this particular scheme. Here the slum settlement was replaced by a medium rise apartment block utilising a new state government programme called the Slum Redevelopment Scheme (SRD). This allowed private developers to be promoters of redevelopment schemes by cross subsidising the development through higher density development of the existing site. Mukhija (2002) notes:

> Unlike the PMGP's program, the SRD allowed private developers to be promoters in redeveloping the slums and the slum dwellers were expected to pay only Rs. 15,000 (23 percent of the estimated cost [in Markandeya]) for their new houses. To make this viable, the program changed the land development regulations for slum-encumbered land. The new property rights permitted a higher density and intensity (FAR) [floor area ratio] of development. This allowed extra units to be constructed and sold, at the market-price to outsiders, generating cross-subsidy for the slum dwellers and profits for the project promoters. The program also allowed for old PMGP projects, still under construction, to be developed as SRD projects.
> (*ibid*: 562)

In the final scheme a five floor block with a total of 180 housing units was constructed. Ninety two units were turned over to Markandeya's cooperative members while 86 units were given to the developer as their share to be sold on the market. In spite of the success in Markandeya, Mukhija (2002) notes that the overall success of such schemes was in fact rather limited with only 2242 housing units built in the ten year period up to 1998. Nevertheless, the new State government in 1995 in fact replaced SRD with a new but similar scheme based on complete cross-subsidy and absolutely no direct financial contribution from slum dwellers. This has led to a very high demand from slum dwellers for redevelopment schemes with 367 projects (producing over 75,000 housing units) approved in 1998.

Interventions for slum redevelopment are not of course unique to Mumbai. Such schemes have been pursued in many cities in the South as part of a broader range of housing policies. In Sao Paulo, for example, the municipality has an active programme for upgrading *favelas* or shanty towns whereby the old units are demolished and new medium-high buildings are constructed in the same location. The purpose is to provide better living conditions for the dwellers without moving them to distant sites. The municipality evaluates the priority areas and hires contractors to execute the works, and after conclusion of works, it grants permit of the area to the dwellers by means of signing a decree (Werna *et al.*, 2004).

3.2.2 Community development and urban governance

We noted earlier the evolution of regeneration policies from property led to community development and prioritisation of social development objectives in UK and Europe during the second half of 1990s. A critical factor in the design of these policies is the shift to partnership building with the aim of greater involvement of the private sector and community organisations in designing and implementing urban regeneration policies. In UK in fact the central government has set predefined statutory objectives for delivery of urban and social services. This inevitably limits the scope for design of urban policies at local levels that must work within the broader criteria of the central government. Nevertheless, there are concerted efforts for greater involvement of external actors in designing the form and implementation of regeneration policies. An example of this is the formation of Local Strategic Partnerships involving all main public, private and community actors at local level to provide strategic direction for local regeneration initiatives (Ball and Maginn, 2005).

Clearly, therefore, cooperation between the different tiers of government and external actors are central to the regeneration practice. This means the issue of urban governance becomes critical. In essence the shift in UK and European urban regeneration policy has been to expand the sphere of governance and include a greater number of external actors and groups as part of the regeneration practice. Indeed, Jones and Evans (2006) argue that understanding the governance mechanisms that create successful urban regeneration is essential to achieving the goals of sustainable development. In the context of UK and Europe this is an important observation as urban development is closely tied to urban regeneration and the partnership model of urban governance that underpins regeneration policy and practice. The basic principle of this however also applies in developing countries even though urban policy and regeneration itself as we have seen is less structured, and rather more chaotic and haphazard.

Here it would be useful to provide a short definition of governance. Jones and Evans (2006) argue that in its narrow definition governance is in fact the process of delivering government. Strictly speaking, therefore, we can have governance by government where the state is the primary actor of delivering services without any interaction with external parties or even other layers of government. In reality, however, the process of delivering government is much more complex and involves a variety of actors. One form of governance, for example, can be seen in governance by partnership as practiced in urban regeneration approach in UK whereby local partnerships are formed between government and business, but purely as mechanisms for delivering government policy (Jones and Evans, 2006). McCarney *et al.* (1994), however, provide a more precise definition where they state that governance, as distinct from government, refers to the relationship between civil society and the state, between rulers and the ruled, the government and the governed. Governance is, therefore, the process of interaction between the public sector and the various actors or group of actors in civil society. As such governance is broader than government and more inclusive of process issues (Sivaramakrishnan, 1996). Following World Bank (1994) definitions, this relationship and the above-mentioned processes are related to the manner in which power is exercised in the management of a country's economic and social resources for development. Urban governance, therefore, relates to the manner power is exercised in the management of such resources for development in towns and cities which is itself dependent on the interaction of the social actors that determine public decisions and activities (Werna, 1997). Indeed researchers on urban governance in both the North and South increasingly emphasise the centrality of power relations, associated networks and political processes in the effectiveness of the governance process towards stated objectives in be-it economic development or increased benefits to the poorer groups (Cars *et al.*, 2001; McGuirk, 2000; Devas, 2001; Rakodi, 2004). The crucial issue, therefore, is the ability to influence power relations within the urban governance structure to affect policy and service delivery.

This approach is followed by Warner and Negrete (2005) when they apply the growth coalition model to the context of Valparaiso in Chile to develop a more generic framework for consideration of sustainable place-building in developing countries. This framework relies on understanding the political economy of urban development particularly dynamics and conflicts that shape local place-building. In this respect they argue that we need to have both a set of institutional conditions and capacities to enable sustainable place-making. The former relates to a set of issues such as values, authority figures and regulations. The latter, on the other hand, are divided into community capacities, intermediary capacities and state/society synergy for sustainability. We are particularly concerned here with the community level capacities. These are described as:

- community/place integration,
- social capital,

- local knowledge,
- inclusivity,
- effective collective action.

Any intervention, therefore, that can lead to better community organisation, growth of social capital and empowerment of local communities to better engage in urban governance can be seen as contributing to the broader objectives of sustainable urban development.

There are of course many agents and partnership arrangements for enhancing local capacities in the areas noted including grass roots organisations/movements, political parties, local and central governments, national and international NGOs and aid organisations. We have noted in this book many examples that in some ways have contributed to community development and local governance capacities. However, one of the best examples involving most of these actors in a collaborative process for more sustainable urban development is perhaps the case of resettlement of the Payatas community in Manila following the collapse of the Payatas rubbish dump in July 2000. Here the slum residents of the rubbish dump capitalised on the international sympathy generated as a result of the collapse of the dump and resultant casualties to develop an international coalition including Global Campaign for Secure Tenure and Slum/Shack Dwellers International to support their resettlement campaign with the Housing Secretary, raise funds and bring legal action against the local government and private waste contractors for gross negligence and violation of environmental laws, zoning and health regulations leading to central and local government support for relocation of some 7,000 residents (van Vliet, 2002).

3.2.3 Protecting the urban environment

When discussing the protection of urban environment in developing countries we are faced with two different but related issues. First we have global concerns on release of greenhouse gases (GHG) and their impact on the world climate. Following years of inaction and half hearted commitments to enforcing environmental measures after the Rio and Kyoto agreements this issue has now gained political priority around the globe with the report of Intergovernmental Panel on Climate Change (IPCC) in 2007. This is seen in reaffirming international global targets for reducing GHG gasses in Europe, Japan and a number of other developed countries. The average global target in the Kyoto agreement was a reduction of 5.4% on the 1990 levels by 2012.

However, individual countries at the national level have increased this target due to the realisation of the greater severity of the problem. The UK for example is now committed to reducing GHG gasses by 60% from their 1990 levels by 2050.

The second issue is the environmental living conditions of the local populations themselves. We have already noted the consequences of rapid urbanisation on growth of informal and often ill constructed and ill serviced settlements in cities of developing countries. This can be largely attributed to unequal distribution of resources and income poverty in these cities. However, many commentators have also argued that in fact we have gone beyond the natural carrying capacity and energy sources of our cities to support the level of growth and activities that are currently undertaken in them. This is seen to be both a function of late capitalist growth and consumption models particularly the more recent consequences of economic globalisation and drive for expanded export-led production, transport and travel (Atkinson, 2007) and the historic antipathy of urban planners towards environmental concerns and ecological capacities of the location of cities. We therefore read:

> Given resources, a planner would happily plant a London in Calcutta, a Brasilia or Chandigarh or Islamabad any where in the world or a Moscow in Ulan Baator or a Los Angeles in the Middle East. Sustainability took a backseat as resources to support the system were considered (!) inexhaustible. (Deb, 1998: 34)

This point may be somewhat exaggerated but it does show an important underlying truth in respect of technocratic attitudes to urban planning and over-reliance on engineering solutions to address natural limitations. In many cases planners in fact prided themselves in beating the environment and creating mirages in the desert. Examples can be seen in the growth of Las Vegas in the US or some of the major concrete and glass cities in developing countries (e.g., the United Arab Emirates) where even drinking water has to be desalinated. As Deb notes, however, even major 'historic' cities such as New Delhi have now grown far beyond their natural capacities with serious shortages of basic resources such as water. This is perhaps the most pressing challenge not only facing Delhi but also many cities in the developing world from Lagos, to Tehran and Beijing. In the case of the latter, the latest controversy that has put such constraints in focus is surrounding the diversion of water from Western China to Beijing during the Olympic games of 2008. Thereby leading to complaints that the Western provinces will face major economic damage since many industries will have to shut down or reduce capacity during the Olympic period as a result of water shortages (Andrelini, 2008). (see Chapter 5 for more in depth discussion and other examples of shortages of utilities in developing countries).

Other concerns relate to general environmental pollution and loss of agricultural land arising from urbanisation and industrial activities. For example in China more than 1/3 of industrial wastewater and 2/3 of municipal wastewater are released into rivers without any treatment (Wen, 2005). This means that 60% of the country's main rivers are now regarded as being unsuitable for human contact. At the same time many Chinese cities face severe air pollution with some studies claiming that air pollution claims about 300,000 lives prematurely (*ibid*). At the same time rapid urban expansion and industrial activity has led to major loss of land, desertification and soil pollution. Figure 3.3 shows the trend in population growth and loss of agricultural land in China. One study between 1999 and 2002 in Guangdong province on 10,000 square kilometres of farm land found that only 10.61% can be classified as clean; 54.5% lightly polluted and 35.9% medium to heavily polluted (Wen,

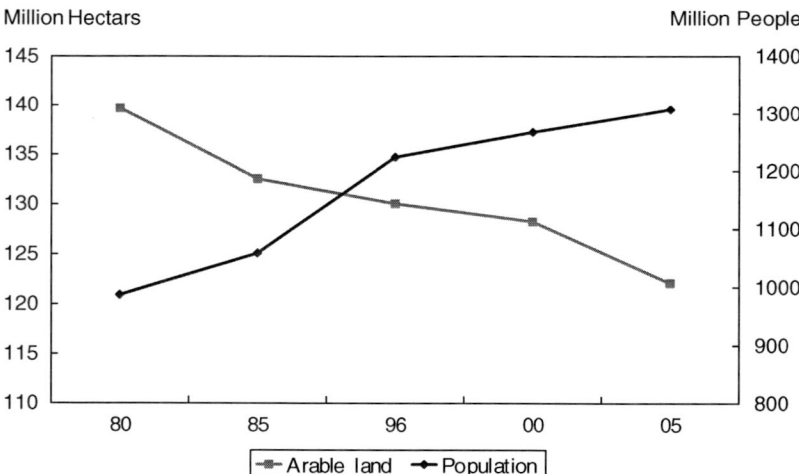

Figure 3.3 Trends of population growth and decline of agricultural land in China
Source: Cao and Keivani, 2007.

2005). Main pollutants were identified as cadmium and mercury largely used in industrial activity.

By and large we can say that to different degrees most developing cities are suffering from one or more of environmental side effects of urbanisation and industrial growth as that outlined for China. Examples can be seen in the loss of agricultural land around Egyptian cities estimated at a total of 1.4 million acres between 1952 and 2002 and severe air pollution in Tehran that is described as 'collective suicide' and estimated to kill about 3,600 people a month (El-Hefnawi, 2005; Terradaily, 2007). Having said this, though, other research also shows that while pollution initially increases at a certain point with rising incomes and economic development the actual rate of pollution actually reduces and is eventually reversed as has been noted in the reducing trends in production of particulate air pollution during the 1990s in Chinese cities, Mexico City and Cubatao in Brazil that was once known as the valley of death due to its severe industrial air pollution (Wheeler, 2000).

Overall, therefore, we would agree with Drakakis-Smith (1995) in that the scale of environmental pollution in different cities varies and is dependent on several factors relating to:

- the rate of population growth and urbanisation and derived demand on utilities,
- the nature of economic growth and industrialisation,
- institutional capacities for environmental protection and
- the ecological conditions and the natural environment itself particularly in terms of degree of vulnerability.

City-wide interventions for addressing urban environmental concerns can be divided into different categories that can relate to the outlined factors.

For example interventions relating to population growth and increased demand for utilities and general physical living conditions of poor households are generally around utility provision, social infrastructure and settlement upgrading that are designed to provide informal settlements and lower income groups with a better quality of life. These are discussed at length in other chapters of this book.

Interventions relating to the type of industrial growth are more in the area of macro-economic and industrial policy that determine the actual types of industries and their locations.

Interventions for strengthening institutional capacities also relate to policies on economic development but are largely concerned with laws, regulations and organisations dealing with environmental policy, pollution control and better urban planning and urban management to better coordinate urban expansion. By and large, however, in many developing countries we do not have a limitation of laws and regulations for environmental protection; rather, it is the implementation and enforcement of these policies that cause the main problem (Drakakis-Smith, 1995; Stren and Polese, 2000). In China and Egypt, for example, there are strict regulations aimed at controlling expansion of urban development onto agricultural land or green belt land around cities. In fact all city Master Plans usually have a protective boundary/or green belt around the city where all developments are prohibited unless with expressed permission and for specific and exceptional uses. In practice, however, it is lack of sufficient capability for enforcing these regulations and collusion of local authorities with developers that leads to continued expansion and loss of agricultural and protected land surrounding the cities (El-Hefnawi, 2005; Cao and Keivani, 2007).

Nevertheless we can also see major successes in terms of institutional interventions. For example the remarkable turn around of Cubatao in Brazil is largely due to the success in enforcing strict pollution control measures on industrial discharges that has led to more than halving particle discharge since the mid 1980s and for the city authorities to hold it up as a model not only of environmental recovery but also sustainable industrial development (Milliken, 2000). In terms of urban planning and city management we can also point to successful policies in multi-modal integrated transport policies including large scale bike routes (e.g., Curitiba, Brazil) that aim for a more efficient public transport system and reduce overall car journeys and related pollution (Globalideasbank, 2008). Finally, we can also point to various forms of congestion charging or limiting vehicular traffic into central locations that have been relatively successful in reducing traffic and pollution in at least the prohibited areas (examples include Singapore, Mexico City and also Tehran).

Interventions in respect of natural environments can take different forms including national and local campaigns for cleaning up rivers, lagoons, hillsides and forests. In addition we have interventions to relocate or protect settlements in dangerous locations. As noted by Drakakis-Smith (1995) many tragedies that have occurred as a result of land slides and/or collapse of rubbish dumps etc are not just as a result of natural phenomena, e.g., too much rain, but also a failure of the planning systems that have allowed settlements to develop and continue in such environments. As noted in the previous section a good example of such an intervention can be seen in the relocation of Payatas community after the collapse of the Payatas rubbish dump in 2000.

By and large, though, we should point out that direct non-public sector interventions are mainly possible in the first and last categories of interventions dealing with improving physical living environments, protection of the natural environment or reducing natural risks to informal settlement. As discussed in this and other chapters, this is carried out by various private actors, NGOs and community groups for direct provision of services or localised environmental protection measures. However, local and private actors can also play an important advocacy role in ensuring large public sector interventions in terms of more sustainable industrial policies and strengthened institutional capacities for more effective urban planning and urban management.

Finally, however, we would emphasise the point raised earlier by Drakakis-Smith (1995) in that environmental protection in developing countries is intrinsically tied to social and economic development in terms of addressing employment and poverty. This has come to be known as the Brown Agenda and is eloquently expressed by Stren and Polese (2000: 15) when they write:

> The connection between social factors and the environment is particularly clear in the development discourse. ... in poor countries, environmental considerations cannot be approached solely through such 'green' concerns as biodiversity, the protection of the ozone layer, and the creation of wildlife and forest preserves, but must first be channeled through far-reaching programs to reduce poverty – in particular, urban poverty.

3.2.4 Bringing the debate together

The discussion thus far has shown that achieving sustainable urban development requires a wide range of interventions covering all the main pillars of the sustainability paradigm.

By and large the public sector has borne the brunt of these activities. This is most evident in urban regeneration aimed at physical and economic revival of blighted areas in the cities. Often these have focused on property-led development initiatives but increasingly this focus has shifted to giving an equal weight or even prioritising social consideration particularly community development and inclusion of local actors in urban governance processes to offset criticisms of social polarisation and domination of private business agenda. In most cases interventions for urban regeneration are designed to act as a catalyst for greater civic pride/wellbeing and bringing in additional private investment particularly into blighted and run down areas.

At the same time it has also been shown that interventions for addressing environmental damage caused by rapid urbanisation and industrial development is a major priority issue in developing countries. Again the scale of intervention required at city level entails both local and central government action particularly in developing institutional capacities for better planning and regulation of industrial activity and urban development. At the same time, though, it has been shown that in developing countries environmental protection is closely tied to social development, particularly poverty reduction.

Nevertheless in all cases it has been argued that non-public actors, including the private sector, national and international NGOs/ organisations and community actors play a crucially important role either in partnership with public sector, for example large scale private investment in property-led regeneration, or direct involvement in, and indirect (advocacy) for, utility and social service provision, community development, urban governance and environmental protection.

3.3 CSR and citywide/neighbourhood intervention

The debate so far has shown that citywide or neighbourhood level interventions are mainly undertaken or financed directly by the public sector and/or international organisations and NGOs. Increasingly such interventions have taken a partnership/collaborative form involving a range of actors including private and community sectors in both developed and developing countries. In property-led regeneration projects, substantial commercial private sector investment can occur either as part of public private partnership arrangements or independent private development projects.

The issue at hand for us, however, is what role corporate social responsibility plays in this debate. The initial answer may be that given the high level of investment and organisational capacity required for such interventions they are in fact not suited to CSR type of activities and therefore not much can be expected. However, as the following case studies in this chapter and the rest of this book illustrate, this is an erroneous assumption. There are in fact many situations where corporate social responsibility plays an important role in all the main pillars necessary for sustainable urban development. What is often required is the right institutional environment that can recognise and develop the latent social potential of private firms as important members of civil society and the broader urban community.

3.4 Case studies

We shall examine three case studies dealing with different aspects of citywide interventions. Crucially, however, all three are based on partnership models involving a variety of private and public actors that together have created an effective framework for facilitating and applying corporate social responsibility of private firms in citywide interventions.

Case 1 concerns Societe Nationale D'Assurances (SNA) in Lebanon and its project for physical regeneration of Lebanese cities through rehabilitation of war torn and dilapidated buildings and infrastructure. This is based around a core partnership between SNA and a Lebanese NGO called Help Lebanon. There are, however, other partners and sponsors including several major banks. The activities undertaken aim at physical rehabilitation and beautification of public spaces in Lebanese cities.

Case 2 concerns another urban development partnership in Guarulhos, Brazil. Here the main business leaders of the city came together to develop a major NGO called Organizaçào da Sociedade Civil (OSC) Viva Guarulhos with the specific task of providing a partnership vehicle for bringing together different private, public and community sector actors to enable social, economic and physical development in the city. A major aim of OSC is their aim for facilitating community development and community leadership training that has a direct impact on empowering local communities for more effective engagement in urban governance and local leadership.

Case 3 describes an innovative partnership arrangement led by Schtroumpf, a small local restaurant chain for environmental awareness campaigns in Lebanon. This partnership formulated under the Go Green initiative involves not only local private and public sector actors but also major international private firms and international organisations such as UNDP in a direct collaborative arrangement. What is perhaps particularly important in this case is the illustration that commitment and synergetic collaboration are the key ingredients for high impact environmental interventions rather than high initial capital commitments. In other words firms do not have to be large conglomerates with high capital resources to make a major difference in terms of sustainable urban development.

Finally, we would refer readers to other cases examined in subsequent chapters of this book, particularly the utilities chapter. There again we will see highly effective partnership arrangements bringing together a private, public and community actors for multi-faceted citywide interventions that, while are focused on specific utility aspects (water and electricity), also have major contributions to environmental sustainability, community empowerment and economic development.

3.4.1 Societe nationale d'assurances (SNA)

After the 25-year-old Lebanese civil war, which destroyed the Lebanese economy, its infrastructure, people's morale and brought anarchy to the small republic, urgent action was needed in order for Lebanon to get back on its feet. As a result, community support has been pursued by many corporations, among them Societe Nationale D'Assurances (SNA), working to incorporate social responsibility into its vision and strategy. Such a vision and approach is not new in SNA's 'corporate family'. The corporate partners, Assurances Generales de France (AGF) and Allianz, also have immense community strategies adopted into every aspect of their operations.

SNA has actively supported the Lebanese community since 1963. Covering a wide range of areas, the company has worked on projects promoting art and culture, environmental awareness, renovating and beautifying Beirut, assisting the disabled and educating children.

Many of SNA's community initiatives that have been implemented for the past 39 years have been creative and have mainly addressed civic action or promoting Lebanon's image both locally and globally. This case will explore a unique project called 'Help Lebanon', which resulted from a partnership between SNA and Help Lebanon – a Lebanese NGO.

3.4.1.1 Current organisational profile

Founded in Lebanon in 1963, SNA Insurance is presently one of the world's leading insurers and providers of financial services.

By 1971, the company became not only active in Lebanon, but also abroad. Currently, SNA maintains presence in over 70 countries through its corporate partners – Allianz and AGF, and has partnerships with other insurance companies in Jordan, Egypt and Tunis. In Lebanon, SNA employs around 100 people permanently, and 200 agents. It has one head office, four branches and many sales offices all over the country. The company offers a wide range of services, which include: health, property (car, home), life, and corporate insurance (life, property & casualty). In 1998, SNA and AGF formed a partnership. AGF, is a subsidiary of the Allianz group, and presently has a 51% stake in SNA. This step was able to provide SNA with a new image of local expertise and international strength.

Throughout the years, and despite the Lebanese civil war during the 70s and 80s, SNA has managed to maintain an outstanding image of innovation and credibility. This has been done through the company's stability despite recession, as well as its active initiation and participation in community projects and events.

3.4.1.2 SNA's social program

Since 1973, SNA's management has engaged in community initiatives due to their firm belief that it is the moral role of every company to support its community and return a favour to its consumers. The company recognises that supporting the community is not only a matter of morality, but may also help enhance a company's respect, brand image, reputation, and allow the company to gain more publicity and exposure.

Since its establishment, the company has covered a vast area of themes through its community engagement. The majority of SNA's projects support arts and culture, education, and the rehabilitation of buildings and tunnels. They also encourage environmental conservation, and assisting disability. On the arts and cultural level, SNA has sponsored the International Sculpture Forum in Rachana and the Al-Bustan Festival since 1994.

In terms of education, it has offered children movie screenings and an educational activities club. While environmentally, SNA was actively raising awareness on environmental issues. This started with their first community project in 1973, distributing garbage bags to the public to encourage a cleaner Lebanon. Finally on the humanitarian level they advocated rights of people with disabilities.

They lent their hand and contributed to the LBC show 'Wakif Takkilak', further emphasising the rights of the disabled.

All the above-mentioned projects are framed within a yearly community strategy and budget, which is set by the communications office and studied by the CEO and communication committee. The budget is then allocated to projects requested by NGOs. Proposals submitted by

NGO's are normally screened by the Head of Communication, unless they are big enough to be discussed with the communication committee, composed of the Chairman, Head of Marketing and Head of Operations.

3.4.1.3 The 'Help Lebanon' project

As mentioned in the introduction, this case explores the 'Help Lebanon Project' that resulted from a partnership between SNA and Help Lebanon – a Lebanese NGO. This NGO was originally established as a humanitarian organisation in 1979 to help needy Lebanese children by providing them with food, shelter, medicine and education. The NGO has now shifted its focus from humanitarian aid to rehabilitation of buildings and surroundings in Beirut.

The fact that this new mission requires a substantive amount of time and money did not stop Ms. Lilianne Tyan, the NGO's president, from her belief in achieving her goals. She pursued her work through well studied and planned projects that were later discussed with other organisations for joint efforts. To keep costs down, Ms. Tyan executed facelifts rather than performing structural work. This was done with the help of many volunteers, freelancing architects, engineers and painters.

It is interesting to note how Help Lebanon and SNA came to work together. Just like most partnerships are usually formed, this one started by coincidence and very informally.

The idea to beautify Lebanon's streets came about in 1997, when Ms. Tyan was reading the newspaper and came across an article describing a government project by the then Prime Minister Rafik Hariri. The plan proposed to build a three floor metallic bridge for the trucks coming in from the port in Tabaris. Believing that the project would have destroyed many of Achrafieh's beautiful streets and a small garden in Tabaris, Tyan and other residents signed a petition and objected to the project. At the same time, SNA's headquarters were situated in the same area, and this project might have also had a negative impact on the company.

Disappointed with the idea as well, SNA's Chairman and General Manager, Mr. Antoine Wakim decided to take action. In an effort to stop the project, Ms. Tyan, Mr. Wakim, and several leading businessmen made arrangements to discuss the issue with the Prime Minister. Eventually, the government's proposal was dropped, and SNA and Help Lebanon continued the relationship they had built.

SNA and Help Lebanon came up with a proposal of their own, where a replacement project – initiated by Mr. Wakim – would protect the local environment, revive the historical setting of the buildings, and plant flowers in vacant spaces. Help Lebanon took the idea with enthusiasm and prepared a comprehensive study that took four months to complete. The first stages of implementation of what has become known as the 'Help Lebanon' project, began in the Bourj al-Ghazal area. The area has now been reformed with buildings, repaired, painted, and planted with flowers. To finance this project, SNA donated $USD50,000. This was topped off by an average of $USD10,000–$USD15,000 from the other private sector institutions.

SNA's work in improving Lebanon's buildings and image had started with the rehabilitation of the Sassine Tunnel in Achrafieh. By re-habilitating buildings, tunnels and other structures damaged by the war, SNA has also been able to promote this idea amongst other companies.

By 2000, Help Lebanon in collaboration with many other sponsors such as Banque Nationale de Paris Intercontinentale (BNPI), Banque Audi, Banque Saradar, Fattal, and ABN Amro Bank have spent hundreds of thousands of dollars to rehabilitate around 1200 buildings which were in a wide range of areas including Tabaris, Bustros Street, Avenue Charles Helou, Rue du Liban, Gemaize, Abdel Wahab El Inglise, Atshinak, and Karm El Zeitoun street. In 2003, the two organisations, Solidere and Landmark joined this monument.

SNA and Help Lebanon have a mutual agreement, but no contracts signed. Help Lebanon executes all joint initiatives, and at the end of the year they supply SNA with an annual report summarising the outcome of each initiative, including its expenses, duration, and progress to date. Furthermore, at the end of every year, they jointly map out a plan of upcoming projects in the following year.

As apparent, this project lies within a larger theme of bettering Lebanon, focusing on rebuilding Lebanon, which in turn would project a very positive image of the country both globally and locally. Together, Help Lebanon, SNA and their various partners have made a great contribution to Lebanon's development. Although the help Lebanon project was beneficial in many levels to the community, to some, it may have not been visibly beneficial to SNA. In Lebanon, community involvement has often been misperceived. To many, such actions are simply done on behalf of companies for advertising returns – a concept that SNA has always been very much against. But generally, is publicity of community involvement good or bad? The following section provides more information on SNA's and other perspectives on the issue.

3.4.1.4   Is firm publicity on corporate social responsibility good or bad?

The amount of publicity the SNA has generally received in the past on its community work has been marginal. This was largely due to the fact that management believed that a project should be implemented because of a desire and responsibility to do so, not as a marketing scheme. As a result, none of the projects were implemented with press conferences or other major publicity. In addition many cash and in-kind donations were given without (or with very little) mention in any literature or other venues. Exemplary of this is the Sassine tunnel that was rehabilitated by SNA, where in return for their contribution, SNA was very satisfied with a small discreet plaque that was stamped on the tunnel displaying the company's name.

Recently the communication unit realised the need to make additional effort to publicise its community activities. This was due to the fact that more awareness for the company was needed. For example when many sales persons would commute to clients, a big segment in the market had never heard of the company. As a result, SNA embarked on a communication campaign, which included publicising its community efforts more than they had done in the past. This began by briefly mentioning their projects in their annual report, and by developing a small brochure called "Parrainages et Actions Civiques SNA" that briefly outlines initiatives launched since 1971. This brochure has been distributed to the public in most of SNA's community initiatives. SNA also started sending out emails to their customers updating them with the company's latest community initiatives, especially with moving images of 'Before & After' from the Help Lebanon project. Finally, for the first time, in 2002, SNA invested in a social show developed by Lebanon's major TV Station, the Lebanese Broadcasting Corporation International (LBCI). The communication strategy adopted through the show was very effective for all the participating partners as it provided them with a lot of visibility. It was also very beneficial in advocating the many rights of disabled individuals, among them the right for employment. Due to its high number of viewers, the show helped introduce many NGOs and individuals to SNA. According to the Head of Corporate Communication, Ms. Gharzouzi, such efforts have been very beneficial not only for SNA, as it brought the company more awareness and networking with NGOs, but to the community as a whole. Such publicity has also allowed the company to mobilise many other organisations to join efforts towards implementing many other projects that have contributed to Lebanon's rehabilitation.

What is the opinion of those who work in the business-community field with regards to publicity? According to research that has been done on business-community relations in Lebanon, a few organisations mentioned that one of the major reasons for their involvement in the community was due to publicity. Furthermore, the public in general, as well as media agencies perceived the private sector's engagement in the community negatively, stating that such actions are simply done for publicity purposes. These findings could be attributed to the fact that the field is only emerging in Lebanon, and many organisations are still not fully aware of how to strategically incorporate the community in their vision, and how to communicate such activities.

Corporate Social Responsibility is a very broad topic, and incorporates many issues such as human resources and ethical practices, community involvement, etc. The return on investment through publicity is only a very small and minor aspect of the many other things that are usually brought about by effective community engagement. Companies and individuals who view that publicity through community engagement is the answer will be eventually disappointed as such efforts only yield short-term benefits that do not sustain.

However, others, who sincerely incorporate community involvement in their mission and every day practices, will be very pleased to enjoy all the other benefits that are brought about with strategic involvement including enhanced reputation, employee and customer loyalty.

To sum up, engaging in the community for publicity reasons is not so much of a good idea, because eventually the public will see right through the company, and all its effort will backfire. However, if complemented by a full communications plan, concrete action, and impact, publicity can do wonders for both the company and the community. After all, companies who sincerely try to do good for others by committing their human and financial resources deserve to receive good themselves.

In light of the above, SNA's efforts to publicise their community initiatives are appreciated and encouraged, as long as they are always done within the context of a strategic community involvement programme, which in turn will inspire other organisations to get involved, thus bring about more initiatives and will enhance the cycle of sustainability.

For more information on the impact of corporate community publicity, kindly refer to the 'Role of Media in Corporate Social Responsibility and Sustainable Development' case study of the 'Enhancing Business Community Relations' project.

3.4.1.5 Key lessons

Overall, SNA's community initiatives have been good, but scattered in different directions. It is recommended that SNA narrow down the fields of community initiatives it supports, and focus on one or two themes, such as the 'Help Lebanon' project. This will be more effective in terms of image and capacity building. Focusing on one area will also produce larger results, since the company will be more familiar with the logistics involved (i.e. NGOs working in that area, contacts, major needs in that field etc.) Finally, such a step will also enhance the sustainability of its initiatives, since SNA will be able to link one project to another, organise follow-ups, focus on recurrent themes, etc. For comparison purposes, when looking at SNA's partner, Allianz community program, it became evident that the corporation's priority is environmental. Everything from the building structure to the food served in the canteen has environmental friendliness in mind. When we think Allianz, we think environment! Such a link will make it easier for consumers and other companies to remember Allianz with. SNA is encouraged to consult Allianz about their programme's development, and possibly follow some of their steps in order to enhance their own programme.

Another recommendation for SNA is to put in place a measurement system for its projects, as none currently exist. This will help SNA evaluate its initiatives in such a way that it may continue to progress by effectively learning from past mistakes. This can be done via establishing a tracking system to assess the financial value of media awareness; measuring consumer perception and awareness of the company's social program through questionnaires, and doing employee satisfaction surveys focusing on Corporate Social Responsibility, etc. International measurement tools such as the London LGB model, or any other can be consulted in this case. Such measurement schemes may allow SNA to approach future developments with more efficiency and effectiveness. In the future, SNA plans to continue to participate in its annual events such as the Al-Bustan festival and Rashana forum. The company also plans to continue beautifying Lebanon through the 'Help Lebanon' project. Such efforts are applauded and encouraged, as they continue to promote a more positive image of Lebanon both locally and globally.

3.4.2 OSC[2] Viva Guarulhos

This case study explores the importance of alliances among state departments, private companies and the wider community in the search for improvements to an entire city. The OSC Viva Guarulhos is an NGO created by a broad coalition. Created in 2001, it aims to improve and sustain the quality of life and development in the city of Guarulhos, located in the metropolitan region of Sao Paulo, Brazil. OSC Viva Guarulhos acts together with two other entities, AGDC and the AGENDE, each of them responsible for different kinds of projects (see Table 3.1 below).

According to Ms. Viviane Alves Machado, communications assistant for OSC Viva Guarulhos, "our main goal is to make Guarulhos, between now (in 2003) and 2010, one of the ten cities in the country with the best level of quality of life."

3.4.2.1 Organisational history

In 1997 Guarulhos and its population experienced a chaotic situation in the city's administration. The mayor's impeachment for corruption affected Guarulhos' political image, not only within its boundaries but also all over the country and abroad. In particular, this negative image affected business credibility in the region and because of that, in 1998 and 1999 the idea of rethinking the city – searching for alternative initiatives to solve its problems – came up.

Table 3.1 Key organisations in OSC Viva Guarulhos

Entities	Participants	Projects
OSC VIVA GUARULHOS	Private companies	Social development
AGDC[3]	Individuals	Defence of ethics & citizenship
AGENDE[4]	Private companies, individuals & the state	Economic & technological development

---

[2]Organizaçào da Sociedade Civil (civil society organisation).
[3]AGDC: Associação Guarulhense para Defesa da Cidadania (Association of Guarulhos Citizens for the Defence of Citizenship).
[4]AGENDE: Agência de Desenvolvimento de Guarulhos (Agency for the Development of Guarulhos

The action started with three business leaders – Victor Siaulys (Chairman of Ache Laboratarios Farmaceuticos), Antonio Carlos Koch (then Chairman of Centro das Industrias do Estado de Sao Paulo) and Luis Roberto Mesquita (Alvaro Mesquita Companhia Ltda). In 2000 they proposed that business people and other community representatives invest in the programme 'Recover the Quality of Life in Guarulhos'. The proposal was accepted immediately by a larger group of 18 companies with links to the city, and they became sponsors and supporters of the programme. They also had the institutional support of commercial and community associations, social entities, churches and public departments.

Two consultancy companies with experience in urban renewal were hired to identify the city's main problems and its potential. In the first stage, the equivalent to US$55,000 was raised from the participating firms and allocated for consultancy work to enable the consultants to compile data, elaborate diagnostic material and plan to implement actions in the city. When the first stage was concluded, the consultancy companies suggested the creation of a civil society organisation. Thus, in the second half of 2000, the OSC Viva Guarulhos was born, and it was formally and finally established on November 7, 2001.

OSC Viva Guarulhos "was conceived with the aim of bringing together the state, private companies and the third sector to promote joint actions to foster social development for the benefit of quality of life in the city". The initiative also built upon the IDIS Programa Doar (Donor Programme), which has been developed in seven other cities in the State of Sao Paulo with the technical assistance of the Institute for the Development of Social Investment (IDIS).

3.4.2.2 Planning and creation of partnerships

The process of initial planning and creation of partnerships started with the Programa Doar, when Guarulhos city representatives from different sectors (private companies, social organisations and community representatives) were invited to participate in a seminar presented by IDIS to decide about their participation in the programme.

The four key strategies of the Donor Programme are as follows:

- Promotion of the concept and practice of philanthropic community organisations grounded in Brazilian culture and reality.
- Technical support for leadership development of a cadre of individuals and organisations from selected communities that promise

to become influential in the overall development of the sector in the coming years.
- Major effort to give technical support to implement local projects for creating or strengthening philanthropic community organisations, including the training and upgrading of staff members and volunteers to prepare them to meet the needs of such organisations in a more professional manner.
- Major effort to create a permanent forum for philanthropic community organisations, where key issues and directions can be addressed by such organisations and their representatives as partners in social development in Brazil.

The idea was to promote the IDIS Donor Programme to the employers, local government, community leaders and general public of Guarulhos and to discuss their participation in social initiative models. The Donor Programme was well accepted in the city, and business representatives started a movement to support an initiative to enhance the quality of life in Guarulhos, which led to the establishment of AGDC, AGENDE and OSC Viva Guarulhos.

According to Ms. Alves Machado, the number of people involved has grown steadily. This, she noted, shows their collective sense of identity with and commitment toward their city. OSC Viva Guarulhos forbids any member of the organisation to exercise political mandates or hold important positions in public administration. This prevents conflict of interest with their activities in the NGO. This stipulation, according to Viviane, grants members of the entity free access to the city council where they are respected and have the right to present their opinions freely and not as a member of any political party, even when on some occasions OSC Viva Guarulhos also works in partnership with public departments.

3.4.2.3 The sponsors' perspective

The sponsors of OSC Viva Guarulhos support the improvement of quality of life in the city. They feel the need to promote benefits for their own community, rather than seeking more feasible and promising marketing potential in other cities. In addition to financial contributions, some companies participate actively in projects of OSC Viva Guarulhos and assume direct responsibility for promoting changes in the city.

However, according to Ms. Alves Machado, the sponsors still have problems in involving their employees. Also, despite the initial momentum in terms of partnership, attracting new associates is a challenge for OSC Viva Guarulhos, because its product is not immediately tangible.

3.4.2.4 Focus on sustainability

OSC Viva Guarulhos is maintained exclusively by the monthly contributions from its member companies. These contributions are made through quotas, each company choosing a number of quotas regardless of its income.

In 2003, OSC Viva Guarulhos received the equivalent to US$2,143.00 monthly from membership contributions for administrative expenses. Its target was to reach the monthly sum of approximately US$3,000 by the end of 2003, which is not a large amount to run an office even in a developing country. To achieve this goal, OSC Viva Guarulhos advertised its actions through a quarterly newsletter, and its website was under development. At the same time, it had plans to advertise the trademark 'Viva Guarulhos' in mass media, especially on the city's business websites.

OSC Viva Guarulhos had two goals to achieve in its plan for eight years: to bring together the state, private companies and the third sector, and to promote joint actions to foster social development for the benefit of quality of life in the city.

One short-term objective was to transform OSC Viva Guarulhos into a new administrative structure, developed and officially recognised in the Brazilian Civil Code as a not-for-profit private legal entity (Law 9790/99), to attract and facilitate government and private-sector investments and partnerships for social projects. Other objectives include the development of activities that will strengthen OSC Viva Guarulhos' profile and visibility in the city and attract new members.

3.4.2.5 Key lessons

This case study offers an understanding of the value of establishing partnerships among public departments, private companies and various social agencies in an organised and responsible manner.

According to Ms. Alves Machado, partnership with the public sector is fundamental because ..."in Brazil most social entities depend on public money. This reality has to be considered. We can discuss if it is right or wrong but we cannot simply forget it." In this sense, it is easy to see how important it is to promote partnerships, because the relationship between a company and the community has yet a long way to go. Nevertheless, according to the OSC Viva Guarulhos spokesperson Antonio Carlos de Almeida, partnerships with the public sector are delicate, especially when they refer to political parties that can "contaminate the relationships" with "political protection" at election time. Such behaviour is not acceptable to private sector companies, which demand seriousness and commitment from social entities and expect to have reports that account for their investments. Private companies must be sensitised to make social investments, and entities should be prepared to receive them.

Another important aspect refers to the mobilisation of the region's business representatives in search of a common goal: the "recovery of the quality of life in Guarulhos". However, the involvement of some companies remains superficial, because they do not understand that active contribution means more than just investing money. It also implies voluntary action, dialogue and mobilisation work. This lack of involvement has been noticed in the community. Not as many people as there could be are actively involved in discussions. The voluntary work process is still tentative. A plan of action is poorly developed because of a lack of knowledge and commitment from senior managers of companies and the local community, especially when political issues are involved. Many people do not understand the constant necessity of learning how to work together to seek improvement for all.

It is clear that the initiative of OSC Viva Guarulhos and its partners represent an innovative model, which is maturing and constantly going through an educational process. With more experience and greater exchange of views and perceptions, there will be greater scope for improvement.

It is noticeable that while initiatives like the ones from OSC Viva Guarulhos tend to have a positive result for society, they do not necessarily exhibit concrete results in the preparatory phase. During this phase, community leaders from participant communities are identified and selected to take part in leadership training.

This training consists of two steps. The first step introduces the concept of servant leadership, explaining the main differences among common styles of leadership and explaining the reasons why servant leadership is the most suitable style to be followed when working on social development. The second step is designed to help leaders become aware of some relevant skills and the related knowledge and attitudes required for personal, organisational and community development. Indications of how to develop those capabilities are also provided. The structure of the seminars and the set of manuals that support the programme were developed by IDIS staff. It is a new and dynamic process, and there is a growing involvement from the wider community in these actions.

3.4.3 'Go Green' partnership

One of the pioneering multi-stakeholder initiatives in Lebanon is the 'Go Green' partnership that began in 2002, involving a variety of national and international actors. Its driving motor was 'Schtroumpf', a relatively small local restaurant chain but with a highly developed sense of social responsibility, particularly for protecting the environment. This includes activities related to the urban environment, which will be highlighted here.

Similar to the other two cases examined in this chapter, an important characteristic of this initiative is its formation as a partnership for bringing together expertise from public, private and NGO sectors to create synergies that are necessary for optimising the local impact of private initiatives. As noted elsewhere in this book, a decade ago community related partnerships around corporate social responsibility both locally and globally were limited, focusing primarily on philanthropic donations (cash and in-kind products) or corporate sponsorships. It remains to be seen what the effect of current political upheavals are on these sort of partnership work in Lebanon. However, in the early 2000s the country had already reached a point in which donations were not only relatively old fashioned, and less effective than partnerships, but also, in a sense, were considered as counter productive in terms of reinforcing the preponderant individualistic culture.

Such partnerships, which take time and skill to develop, typically involve both a benefit and a risk element to companies, but the benefits far outweigh the challenges. Although it can be challenging to maintain motivation and enthusiasm, especially if positive results do not happen quickly, they often result in a spirit of sharing and cooperation. In terms of the 'Go Green' partnership, however, we can note a win-win situation for both the key investor partners and the community alike.

Another important observation in this case is that CSR interventions do not have to have a necessarily high monetary value to be effective. In fact this is one case where a highly prominent role is played by a relatively small private entity that has facilitated high impact interventions in spite of its limited capacity for high monetary contribution.

3.4.3.1 The partnership

This partnership began very informally when some members from the United Nations Development Programme (UNDP) visited Schtroumpf's premises during the 2001 Environmental forum. The restaurant had already built up a reputation for environmental activism through a range of measures including education and clean up campaigns through its employees and waste management whereby it makes sure to use 100% Lebanese recycled paper in all their paper delivery packages, napkins, and hand towels, sorting large quantities of metal, plastic, and glass wastes as well as collection of card board boxes, papers and magazines for recycling. And the importance of a clean environment for cities and towns in general, and those in Lebanon in particular, cannot be overemphasised.

Impressed by the restaurant's environmental commitment, a dialogue started between the two offices. In order to strengthen his environmental program, Mr. Omar Sakr, Schtroumpf's environment program manager, decided to partner with other organisations working towards the same objective. As a result he informally approached UNDP/UNV to explore the potential for developing a partnership, as he had learned that the UNDP had a comprehensive environmental program, as well as a project promoting Corporate Social Responsibility called: 'Enhancing Business-community Relations' (EBCR).

For Mr. Omar Sakr, this was a natural step towards a better implementation of the company's community philosophy. As a result, in 2002 Schtroumpf and UNDP/UNV became the main organisers of this project, while the FTML, Coca-Cola and Tetra Pak East Med became the official partners.

3.4.3.2 Objectives

The 'Go Green' project had various objectives as jointly determined by Schtroumpf and UNDP/UNV, as follows:

- Promote the concept of corporate social responsibility (CSR) as a critical element in human development;
- Enhance awareness of environmental issues especially among youth by encouraging them to create a wide range of environmental projects;
- Promote and strengthen the concept of sustainable partnership building between different stakeholders (civil society, public institutions, private sector, international organisations etc) by actively

encouraging different sectors to work together through the 'Go Green' activities mentioned below;
- Exchange strategies, experiences, and identify common interests in relation to environmental protection and sustainability;
- Identify problems, constraints and priorities on one hand, and opportunities and possible areas of cooperation with various stakeholders on the other and;
- Build social capital by bringing various stakeholders together for networking and cooperation.

3.4.3.3 Activities

In 2002 the 'Go Green' project incorporated the following activities with an impact on the urban environment, implemented over a five-month period. With some changes these activities have been repeated annually.

- **'Go Green' Media Awareness Campaign**
  In April 2002 the project kicked with a press interview. During the rest of the year 25 articles were written in major newspapers and magazines. The initiatives also received a good amount of coverage on major TV stations as well, either through news segments, or live 15–30 minute interviews. Altogether, 12 live TV interviews were held either about the initiative or had mentioned it. It was also mentioned on websites of four international organisations. This activity has continued in subsequent years when various activities have been held under this initiative.

- **'Go Green' University Awareness Campaign**
  A university awareness campaign ran parallel with the media coverage. This campaign focused on promoting the 'Go Green' environmental contest and forum through flyers, placemats, posters, billboards, presentations, etc. Altogether around 80,000 copies of three distinct flyers were widely distributed. Altogether 18 university campuses were visited for leaflet distribution or poster exhibitions and talks.

  The latter is particularly important as it directly involved the 'Go Green' partners who personally visited most participating universities and held a PowerPoint presentation that provided more than 1000 students with an overview of their social programs. These visits were very beneficial as they allowed students and corporations to network together and become closer.

- **'Go Green' Environmental Contest**
  With the objective of sensitising youth to environmental issues, the 'Go Green' contest encouraged students to come up with environmental projects in the fields of engineering inventions and communicative artwork. It targeted close to 20,000 students in major universities across Lebanon. Altogether, around 200 projects were submitted and a total of $USD11,000 was distributed during the closing ceremony of the 'Go Green' environmental forum.
- **'Go Green' Environmental Workshop**
  The first 'Go Green' workshop was held on 12 June 2002. During the workshop, various stakeholders from private and public sector institutions, academic institutes, associations, NGO's, and UN agencies gathered at Schtroumpf's main branch in Jounieh to participate in the event, hoping to find solutions and come up with ideas that could contribute to environmental enhancement.

Attended by close to 100 individuals, the workshop caught the attention of many and received outstanding feedback from all those touched by the uniqueness of the 'Go Green' project. The important aspect of this activity is that it allowed people to meet and network with others in their field, and the working groups provided individuals from various sectors the opportunity to sample collaborative efforts on specific ideas.

3.4.3.4 *Important factors of success*

The process of developing the Go Green partnership has salutary lessons for all partnership work in developing countries. Some of the more important issues that can be outlined are:

- Selling the project internally to senior management of all partner organisations, starting with Schtroumpf and UNDP as the lead partners.
- Lead partners deciding on criteria for choosing other partners.
- Selecting partners and introducing partners to each other.
- Identifying and appointing a partnership broker that was accepted and trusted by all partners and a person who has sufficient weight and credibility for cajoling and getting the best out of the partners. In this case the UNDP/UNV area manager for Enhancing Business-community Relations was appointed to take charge of this task.
- Establishing good communication channels between partners.

- Establishing a set of protocols for partner involvement that is formally agreed in contractual form.
- Transferring the financial commitments from each partner to the partnership broker. Each part would then recover future costs of activities retrospectively through verifiable claims. These claims and receipts would then be sent to all partners for their scrutiny.
- Other important considerations include ensuring regular contacts and consultation between partners, creating a learning culture for partners, sharing on analysis of results and outcomes, getting regular feedback from the public, emphasising the long term benefits, encouraging all parts of member organisations to become involved, allowing space for mistakes and learning and finally documenting the experience and the success for further dissemination and publicity.
- Finally, we can note that the project had important and tangible benefits to all partners particularly in terms of increased publicity, enhanced reputation, networking and sharing of best practice.

3.4.3.5 Key lessons

What made the 'Go Green' initiative successful was the fact that there was a clear partnership building process being followed and that yielded a significant amount of benefits to the partners and the community. Such a process has built Schtroumpf's capacity to self manage and re-implement the programme in subsequent years on a much bigger scale with the objective of achieving sustainability in the long run. The uniqueness of 'Go Green' also lay on the fact that it reached a wide range of stakeholders from educational institutes, UN agencies, government institutions, NGOs, etc. Another important aspect of the initiative was that instead of taking the traditional sponsorship approach of making a donation in return for visibility, the companies signed on as partners by committing both their human and financial resources for the campaign. Financially, through pooling resources, 'Go Green' provided the community with a lot of benefits.

'Go Green' serves as an exemplary awareness campaign and a breakthrough in the business-community relations field in Lebanon, as it was able to touch many and bring together various sectors of society to work together on one cause. The 'Go Green' project has demonstrated that an initiative does not require a huge sum of money in order to be successful, and that a well-established strategy and process is key to a long-lasting impact. It also demonstrated that time is a precious commodity and because it is so precious, donating time to further a charitable cause can be a tremendously valuable contribution, one that is much more valuable than the one that could be made through traditional philanthropy.

3.5 Conclusion

This chapter has highlighted that many cities in developing countries are operating at the margins of sustainability. There are major strains on the living conditions of citizens and the city environment. On the one hand these are due to general demands of rapid urbanisation and industrialisation for land, utilities and services and associated waste products. On the other, they are exacerbated by lack of sufficient natural and economic resources and economic stagnation and restructuring in the cities. Many city neighbourhoods have been subject to long periods of economic, social and physical decline due to economic and demographic shifts, while many others are developed in informal and illegal conditions often lacking sufficient resources and in dangerous locations due to low incomes of the inhabitants.

At the same time concerns on global warming and lack of success in addressing social problems in the cities of the North through previously disjointed urban policy and lingering widespread urban poverty in the cities of the South has shifted the debate firmly towards the sustainability paradigm that provides an integrated framework based on the economic, social and environmental pillars of urban development. Decades of urban and industrial growth in both developed and developing countries has shown us that particularly in the former we can not address environmental and economic concerns without addressing social sustainability, particularly in terms of poverty reduction and employment generation.

Achieving sustainable urban development, however, requires interventions at city or neighbourhood levels that can either address immediate problems or develop long term capacities in economic, social and environmental spheres. The public sector and international organisations have been the main actors that have undertaken such interventions largely by financing direct projects, providing technical assistance or developing institutional capacities for better regulation and coordination of urban development and industrial activities. Increasingly, however, we note that the delivery mechanism for such interventions are based on a partnership model involving a range of NGOs, community and private actors. By and large, however, the latter have been involved as commercial providers of services, utilities, builders or investors that participate in commercial redevelopment projects.

Utilising three case studies, two from Lebanon and one from Brazil, this chapter has shown, however, that the private sector can in fact play a major role in supporting all the three main spheres of sustainable urban development through an alternative paradigm based on corporate social responsibility. Interestingly, all the three cases are firmly based around the partnership model bringing a range of actors together and an integrated approach to urban development.

In the case of Societe Nationale D'Assurances (SNA) and Help Lebanon Project we can see a large-scale physical redevelopment activities across Lebanese cities leading to rehabilitation of some 1,200 buildings by the year 2000 alone and concerted effort at beautification through planting flowers and shrubs etc. A major objective of this project is to raise the profile and image of Lebanese cities as better places to live, work and invest. They are in effect smaller scale property-led urban regeneration projects spread across a number of cities in Lebanon. The difference, however, is that the initial capital and organisational input is provided through the CSR mechanism and much of the work is largely carried out by volunteer architects, builders and painters and directly involves the local communities in planning and execution.

OSC Viva Guarulhos in Brazil, on the other hand, is essentially a partnership vehicle that has been created by the leading business groups in the city to bring together philanthropic and community activities of private firms towards a set of pre-defined and structured social, physical and economic development objectives. An important aspect of this intervention is training local cadres as future community leaders and training and upgrading of staff members and volunteers of community organisations to prepare them to meet the needs of such organisations. These are significant actions to better develop social capacities and empower local communities to engage in governance processes more effectively.

We returned to Lebanon in the third case study that focused on environmental protection. However, again here there is important emphasis on developing a sustainable partnership arrangement that would bring in other major private actors as well as the public sector, international organisations and local educational institutions and communities. What is perhaps most significant here is the ability of a relatively small private company with low capital commitment to initiate and lead on a high impact project with national significance.

From these cases we can distil three crucial elements of success.

First we can point to the presence of private entities with strong local identities and their perceived need to give back to their local communities. In other words they did not see themselves as merely commercial ventures operating in these cities/countries but also as an integral part of the civil society that had a stake in the wellbeing and development of the communities that they worked in. Second, we can identify the significant roles of established NGOs and international organisations in providing the necessary support to provide a structured framework based on the partnership model for more effective action, outputs and outcomes. Third is the partnership model itself that has been crucial in creating a synergetic vehicle for bringing on board many more private as well as public and community actors to achieve maximum effect through collaborative work. As we shall see in other chapters of this book what is repeatedly evident is that the most effective forms of CSR activity are in fact achieved through collaborative and partnership arrangements with NGOs and public sector actors rather than on their own.

Here we would like to point out that in all cases private firms involved have also benefited from the partnership model in a manner that traditional philanthropic donations or lone activity would not have allowed. This is because the partnership model allows for much wider publicity involving different actors that are involved in the partnership. It also provided a chance for learning and updating the organisational skills of the staff involved in terms of their interactions with and being exposed to best practice and experiences of other members of partnerships. In addition the partnerships provided a wide network of direct contacts with local communities and NGOs for the firms that would not have been possible through the more traditional routes.

4
Construction

Ramin Keivani

The building blocks for cities are numerous, and, as noted in Chapter 3, from a sustainability perspective these can be defined in terms of social, governance, economic, and physical dimensions. The physical aspect encompasses offices, roads, telecommunication networks, houses, rail lines and many other components that define the built environment. This built environment is important for the continued existence and functioning of towns and cities. The built environment is a product of the construction industry and yet rarely is the economic importance of the industry realised by the infrastructure users (Pheng, 1995). This chapter starts by addressing that omission, exploring the role that the construction industry plays in urban development. Different products of the construction industry will be noted, with particular attention to housing, given its crucial importance for developing countries. The analysis of construction concludes by noting the need for improvement, highlighting the possible added value of CSR. This paves the ground for the following part of the chapter, which presents case studies on CSR in the construction sector. The chapter concludes with an analysis of findings from the case studies, which later on in the book will be put together with the findings from the remaining case-studies chapters.

4.1 The importance of construction and the need for further support

There is a voluminous amount of literature acknowledging the important role the construction industry plays in national economies – in both developing and developed countries. For instance, Meikle and Dickson (2006), Pearce (2003, 2006a), Gorynski (1978), UN-Habitat (2005), Tipple (2000), Werna (1997) and Pheng (1995) all argue that the construction industry contributes hugely to the countries' national economic development. The assessment of the contribution of the construction industry to the national economy can better be achieved by first establishing some criteria with which the industry's share in the national economy can be measured and appreciated. This is done by estimating the share of the construction sector to the Gross National Development (GND) (O'Brien and Williams, 2004; Pearce, 2006b; Pheng, 1995; Turin, 1978). In a study conducted in the 1970s, for example, Duccio Turin discovered that the value added by construction industries of developing countries to the global economy amounted to about 10% (*ibid*). Even current studies confirm this figure. Another and perhaps even more informative criterion of measuring the performance of the construction sector, according to Turin (1978), is the value added in construction per capita. The share of construction in GNP and the added value in construction per capita increase with economic growth (Turin, 1978; Spence *et al.*, 1993).

The economic significance of the construction industries the world over cannot be overemphasised. Yet more often than not, the buildings that people live and work in, as well as the networks of other ubiquitous infrastructural facilities that criss-cross cities are usually taken for granted (Pheng, 1995). It is argued that the construction industry alone can be used to distinguish between rich and poor nations (Low, 1990 in Pheng, 1995). One of the earliest known works on the importance of construction was pioneered by Duccio Turin in the 1960s and 70s (Koenigsberger and Groak, 1978). From Turin's works, it was recognised that the construction industry could help cure the economic problems that were (are still) predominant in developing countries. This led to review, by international development agencies like the United Nations and the World Bank, of policies related to industrialisation in developing nations (Pheng, 1995). Since then, the subject of construction and its relationship with the economy has gained pace and today it is one of the key subjects that attract attention in economic development forums (Pearce, 2006b; Kohler, 2006; Crawford and Vogl, 2006; UN-Habitat, 2005; Tipple, 2000). Since the construction industry has a direct bearing on national economies, it can be used as an indicator of the economic development of a country. Research has also shown that there is a strong correlation between the per capita construction value added and the per capita gross domestic product (GDP). Construction also accounts for about 45–60% of fixed capital formation in many countries. The sector contributes 3–5% and 5–9% of GDP respectively in developing and developed nations. In terms of labour market, it is believed that construction accounts for 6–10% and 2–6% of total employment respectively in developed and developing countries (Pheng, 1995; Gnesan, 1978; Spence *et al.*, 1993). The industry is well known for absorbing unskilled labour by employing those in the lowest income brackets (Tipple, 1994).

Despite the economic significance of the construction industry, the sector is hampered, in developing countries, by lack of technological know-how, budgetary constraints, continued dependence on imported building materials and a lack of enabling policy frameworks (Pheng, 1995; Ganesan, 1978). Figure 4.1 presents a comprehensive view of the construction sector and its relationships with other sectors. The diagram was developed by David Pearce in 2003 and has become known as the Pearce Schema (Meikle and Dickson, 2006).

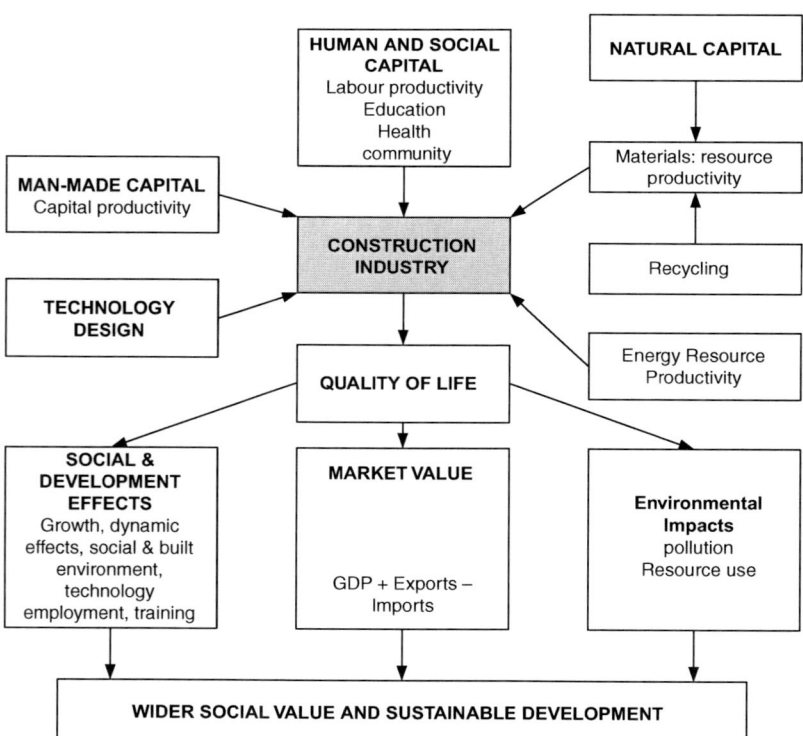

Figure 4.1 The Pearce schema: construction industry and its relationship with other sectors of the economy

Source: After Meikle and Dickson, 2006.

It can be deduced from Figure 4.1 that the Pearce Schema situates construction within the sustainability paradigm depicting the influences on the sector from different pillars of sustainable development. In his depiction he provides a specific perception of sustainability that defines the term as raising per capita endowments of man-made, human, natural and social capital[1] (Pearce, 2006b). What we are arguing for, however, is that, if the construction industry is to realise its full potential in engendering sustainability, it should be developed against the backdrop of the emerging concepts of Corporate Social Responsibility (CSR) and, particularly, business community relations.

The case studies to be presented later on in this chapter cover a number of sub-sectors within the construction industry. While the current section presented the importance of construction in general terms, it is beyond its scope to do it in detail for each sub-sector. Nevertheless, housing will be discussed in more detail next – on the one hand to exemplify the importance of a sub-sector of construction, and, on the other hand, due to the crucial role that such a sub-sector plays in development, which transcends economic contribution and assumes social benevolence.

4.1.1 Housing

Many writers acknowledge the importance of housing in the economies of the world (e.g. Angel, 2000; UNCHS/ILO, 1995; Tipple, 1994, 2000; Spence *et al.*, 1993; Werna, 1997; UN-Habitat, 2005). The development in 1988 of the *Global Strategy for Shelter to the year 2000* which was adopted by UNCHS, and the adoption by the same agency of the programme *adequate shelter for all and sustainable human settlements* in 1996 (Keivani and Werna, 2001a) is indicative of how crucial shelter is to society. Housing is not just brick and mortar. Other than being a commonplace, universally-recognised basic human need (UNCHS, 1996b; Buckley and Kalarickal, 2004), a house is also a crucial symbol of identity, progress, status and a source of prestige (Spence *et al.*, 1993). The sector constitutes one-third of the construction output (Spence *et al.*, 1993); it contributes 20–50% of fixed capital formation and about 5% to GDP (Angel, 2000). In terms of fixed capital formation, it is said that it is not uncommon for a country's housing stock to exceed its annual GDP. If housing constitutes one-third of construction

---

[1]The reader is also referred to Chapter 3 for a more detailed discussion of sustainable development.

output, and construction employs 10% of the employable population in developing countries as Spence *et al.* (1993) argue, then it follows that the housing sector accounts for approximately 3% direct labour market in third world countries. Others see housing as a productive (as opposed to consumption) capital asset, acting as a reservoir for human capital formation resulting from the rearing of children (Pugh, 1994). Indirectly, the sector also employs a huge number of people in linked sectors such as the building materials industry (UNHCS/ILO, 1995). Furthermore, housing is an income generating activity. Completed structures will generate direct income to landlords in form of rent and sale and indirect income in form of mortgage as people obtain loans for different types of businesses by using their houses as collateral. Thus housing plays a significant role in the financial markets. To government agencies like local authorities, housing is a reliable source of revenue through the various property taxes (UN-Habitat, 2005; UNCHS/ILO, 1995; Tipple, 2000, 1994). Housing does not employ only within the housing sector but also in other linked industries. Property management, estate agency, architecture, quantity surveying, notaries/conveyancers, builders, and a whole host of unskilled labour are but some of the well known business concerns that would benefit directly from housing activities as more jobs are created as a result of housing construction. Manpower will be employed before, during and after completion of housing construction projects. Each of the employees spends their salary on other sectors, thereby creating more wealth through multiplier effects (UNCHS/ILO, 1995; Spence *et al.*, 1993). In this way housing finds itself in a complex web of economic activities that may be too numerous to itemise and measure. Therefore, growth in the construction industry entails growth in linked industries through a mix of forward and backward linkages.

The other indirect role of housing can be seen in its (long term) effects on workers and/or children. It is generally argued that the economic productivity of a well-housed worker will be higher than that of a poorly-housed one (Werna, 1997). For example, workers with garaged dwellings are more likely to sleep without worrying about possibilities of their automobile being stolen, thereby enhancing their health and possibilities of higher productivity. Also, children who grow up in acceptable standards of housing are more likely to be motivated to go to and perform well at school and be potential future leaders and successful economic producers. In their book, *Home sweet home? The impact of poor housing on health,* Marsh *et al.* (1999) remind us of the commonplace impacts poor housing can have on health. More often than not we hear of outbreaks of diseases in unsanitary and overcrowded environments. These range from cholera (especially in sub Saharan Africa slums), reduced mental wellbeing, depression, impairment of social relations, and asthma (Marsh et al., 1999). Such diseases will have a dramatic effect on the individuals' economic productivity. In support of these views are writers such as Byrne and Keithley (1993) (including many fellow contributors of chapters to the book *Unhealthy housing: research, remedies and reform*) who rightly argue that practice has shown that dramatic improvements in housing are (always) accompanied by improvements in health standards. Therefore, good housing is always associated with good health and healthy people will be economically more productive.

There is a growing amount of literature recognising the role housing units play outside their traditional role of providing shelter. Spence et al. (1993), Tipple (2000) and Werna (1997) report that for many poor people in developing countries, a house is both a place in which to live and work. During the night a house provides space for sleeping; during the day, part of the space is converted into a 'factory' as occupants engage themselves in a variety of micro-level income generating activities.

4.1.1.1 Housing shortage

There is ample study evidence as well as common knowledge about the shortage or need for repair throughout the sub-sectors of construction in developing countries. For the reasons explained before, the example of the sub-sector housing will be presented in more detail.

Estimating housing shortage in developing countries is impeded by the unavailability of adequate data and lack of agreement on units of measurements. There is also inconsistency on what constitutes 'adequacy' (Tipple, 2000). Perhaps variations in the definition of a 'standard house' exacerbate the difficulty. Despite the difficulty in assessment, however, what is evident is that there is a housing crisis in developing countries. As the rate of urbanisation increases, population also increases. This raises the demand for shelter. Aldrich and Sandhu (1995) and UN-Habitat (2006a) (among many others) further report that in such cases the poor people are the hard hit because they fail to secure shelter with acceptable levels of amenities. The alternative for them is shelter in areas such as slums and squatters, let alone the problem of homelessness. The existence of slums and squatters has thus been seen to be the evidence of housing shortage (evidence provided in Chapter 2).

The trend in the nature of housing shortage seems to be escalating. According to 1996 data, for example, 100 million people in the world were without shelter (UNCHS, 1996a). These people slept/sleep in parks, under bridges, transport terminals, on pavements, in shop door ways, etc. A further 1 billion was estimated to be sheltered in insecure arrangements like refugee camps, public spaces or were squatting in someone else's shelter (UNCHS, 1996b). About ten years on, the situation seems to have worsened. The latest United Nations global report on human settlements still echoes the soaring housing shortages (UN-Habitat, 2006a). As noted in Chapter 2, the current number of slum dwellers in the world is approximately 925 million. If we adopt the availability of slums as a criterion for assessing adequacy, there was a housing shortage of 61.3% in 2001 in Africa alone (UN-Habitat, 2006a). Based on the report's estimates, about 2.8 billion people will require urban housing by the year 2030. In order to meet this figure, about 35.1 million dwellings per year (or 4000 units per hour) should be constructed. On the basis of the current rate of housing construction, is this a feasible target? Tipple (2000) provides us with more suitable data to developing countries. According to the author, the number of dwelling units constructed in such countries stands at about three houses per 1,000 people per year. However, about ten dwelling units are required per 1,000 people per year. This translates into an acute shortage of seven dwelling units per 1,000 people per year.

It is clear from the foregoing that housing shortage is indeed an issue that deserves a mammoth place in policy dialogue. How have developing countries kept themselves in tune with the challenges of the housing question? Which housing provision policies or strategies have they tried to adopt in order to alleviate the problem?

4.1.1.2   *Meeting the challenge: policy trends in house provision*

With such alarming levels of housing shortages in developing countries finding and implementing working policies to alleviate the crisis have been, and continue to be, a daunting task for the governments of developing countries. As a result there is an urgent need for scaling up housing production in developing countries through all possible means. This is now accepted and acknowledged by all policy makers and commentators in this field. However, the means of achieving this aim is subject to debate.

In Chapter 2, we explained in detail the debate over private (commercial) versus public provision in urban development in general. This chapter also included an analysis of the volunteer sector in such a context. The debate on the role of different actors in housing specifically (or the construction industry as a whole) echoes what has been said about urban development in general – and indeed many examples given in Chapter 2 are about construction/housing, seeing them as part of urban development. Therefore, a detailed analysis of the debate about the different actors in housing will not be presented here (for reference, see for instance Keivani and Werna, 2001a, 2001b). For the purpose of information, Table 4.1 presents a summary of the review of literature of actors on housing, structured in terms of formal and informal provision (for being such categories of paramount importance for housing in developing countries), but still related to the analysis of Chapter 2. The important point of the book is to highlight that Table 4.1 does not include CSR (again echoing what has been noted in Chapter 2).

Table 4.1 Summary of the main modes of housing provision in developing countries

Mode of Provision	Main Characteristics	Appropriate Setting	Target Group
Formal Private			
Speculative	Domination by formal developers	Middle to high income countries	Largely middle and high income groups
	(large and small)	The existence of well functioning development and building industries	In certain positive economic conditions, i.e., high and rapid economic growth and rising incomes this mode can also target the higher sectors of the low income households
	Formal finance		
	Industrial building technology		
	Compliance with planning regulations and building standards	Sustained and rapid economic growth and rising incomes	
Developer-Landowner	Mainly small scale joint ventures between developers and landowners	Middle to high income countries	Largely middle income groups
		A strong middle class	
	Mixed formal-informal finance	Well established development and contracting industry	
	Industrial/semi industrial building technology		

Table 4.1 Summary of the main modes of housing provision in developing countries – *continued*

Mode of Provision	Main Characteristics	Appropriate Setting	Target Group
	Compliance with planning regulations and building standards	Buoyant housing market Ability to build to higher densities than the original buildings	
Individual owner-occupier	Land owner commissioning building for his own use Mixed Informal-formal finance Semi-industrial building technology Compliance with planning regulations and building standards	Middle to high income countries Well established contracting industry	Largely middle income groups In certain cases, i.e., public land allocation, can include low income groups
Public Provision			
Direct	Large scale projects financed and initiated by governments Largely built by private contractors Formal finance Industrial building technology Compliance with planning regulations and building standards	Largely inappropriate in developing countries as a form of low income housing	Better suited as tied/service housing for essential public employees
Sites and services	Project based serviced land allocation Large degree of self build	Particularly suited to countries with large public land resource	Low to middle income groups

Table 4.1 Summary of the main modes of housing provision in developing countries – *continued*

Mode of Provision	Main Characteristics	Appropriate Setting	Target Group
	Initiated by national governments as well as international agencies	More limited but still applicable in other countries	
	Complicated organisation and bureaucracy		
	Problems with replication and cost recovery		
	Mixture of formal and informal finance		
	Traditional/semi-industrial building technology		
	Overall compliance with planning regulations and building standards		
Settlement upgrading	Extending services and regularising existing low income settlements	All developing countries	Low income groups
	Initiated by national governments or international agencies		
	Complicated organisation and bureaucracy		
	Problems with replication and cost recovery		
Co-operative	Formal organisation of workers, trades people and low income households for the purpose of housing provision	Largely undeveloped but appropriate in all developing countries	Low to middle income groups

Table 4.1 Summary of the main modes of housing provision in developing countries – *continued*

Mode of Provision	Main Characteristics	Appropriate Setting	Target Group
	Co-operation and negotiation with public authorities, banks and contractors	Requires government support for greater expansion	
	Initiated by governments, political parties or more organic		
	Mixture of formal and informal finance		
	Semi-industrial building technology		
	Overall compliance with planning regulations and building standards		
Public-Nonpublic Partnership	Exchanging cheap public land or other financial incentives for expansion of low cost housing	Applicable in all countries, particularly those with large public land resources and well established development and contracting industries	Low and middle income groups
	Can involve large scale private developers, private individuals or the co-operatives		
	Mixture of formal and informal finance	Requires government support for greater expansion	
	Industrial to semi-industrial building technology		
	Compliance with planning regulations and building standards		

Table 4.1 Summary of the main modes of housing provision in developing countries – *continued*

Mode of Provision	Main Characteristics	Appropriate Setting	Target Group
Informal Housing			
Squatter Housing	Land invasions	Countries with a large degree of communal and public land ownership	Established low income groups
	Largely self built particularly at the initial stages		
	Incremental construction over several years	Tolerant or weak governments	
	Lacking or inadequate services in most countries		
	Precarious locations		
	Manipulation by political parties and governments		
	Large degree of involvement of CBOs and NGOs		
	Informal finance		
	Largely traditional and some semi-industrial building technology		
	Low quality of housing in most countries		
	Largely lacking planned layout		
	Lack of compliance with planning regulations and building standards		
Informal Sub-division	Domination by private developers, particularly at initial stages	Most developing countries, particularly where squatter invasions are not tolerated	Established and higher sections of the low income groups

Table 4.1 Summary of the main modes of housing provision in developing countries – *continued*

Mode of Provision	Main Characteristics	Appropriate Setting	Target Group
	Defacto security of tenure		
	Illegal sub-division of land		
	Planned layout but not in compliance with official regulations		
	Illegal and sometimes precarious locations		
	Large degree of involvement of CBOs and NGOs		
	Informal finance		
	Largely traditional and some semi-industrial building technology		
	Incremental improvement in the quality of housing		
	Some self-build but a large degree of wage labour and contracting than squatter housing		
Informal rental housing	Largely small scale subsistence letting in low income settlements or dilapidated central city tenements	Appropriate for meeting the needs of the very low income and transitory groups in all countries	Very low income and transitory groups
	In some cases there are larger special rental areas developed by wealthy landlords or developers such as 'bustees' of Calcutta		
	Very low quality of housing		

Source: Keivani and Werna, 2001b.

The analysis of different modes of housing provision carried out by Keivani and Werna (2001a and 2001b) disregard the idea of one preponderant mode for developing countries as a whole. While markets can and should be supported as part of the wider spectrum of housing provision, they need not necessarily be the focus of policy initiative. Indeed, development of the housing sector in respect of expanded low income provision requires us to go beyond only enabling the private market. This means a more comprehensive and pluralistic approach. As shown in Table 4.1, the diversity of modes of housing provision in developing countries and the range of actors involved indicates that the process involves an intricate and complex network of relationships between various agents and the state. In designing policies for the expanded provision of low income housing provision in developing countries, therefore, it is important to take account of the social and political context and dimensions of land and housing supply (Jones, 1996; Baken and Van der Linden, 1993). For this reason it is important to identify and take into consideration the entire structures of provision and the interactions of the relevant interest groups and agents involved in the various sub-markets and forms of housing provision. This is as opposed to solely relying on adjustments to supply and demand which is the basis of the recommendations outlined by the World Bank and its allied writers. Such adjustments are unable to take account of the complex relationships between the different actors and interest groups, which are played out in cultural, social and political spheres which are country and even city specific and which directly influence the outcome of such policies.

The important question for us, however, is what role is there for CSR, and business-community relations in particular, in this debate. The fact of the matter is that there is absolutely no mention of these on either side of the debate on enabling private housing markets or housing and construction debate in developing countries in general. The closest that the debate has come to this issue is attention on a number of cases where private developers have been directly involved in low income housing provision/construction as part of their commercial business activities. In one such case in India, the developer, not only acted as developer and builder but also took on the role of NGOs and CBOs in organising the community to save regularly in order to be able to afford monthly payments into a construction fund for their housing units (Garg, 1990). In addition the developer also negotiated with the banks and acted as guarantor for extending credit to the low income people who would then repay the banks in stages. Finally, the developer also adopted a flexible approach to construction whereby the project was phased in stages in such a way as to account for the low income of the households. Similarly, Mukhija (2004) identifies how another major developer in Ahmadabad had specialised in commercial low income housing provision relying on a combination of formal-informal (and at times illegal) practices. We can also note the activities of private developers in illegal subdivisions that in fact form a major mode of informal housing provision in many countries including Pakistan in providing illegal land plots and main services or as in Bangkok the whole package of land, housing and services (Keivani and Werna, 2001a). These examples, however, are based on commercial activities of private developers/builders rather than any notion of corporate social responsibility or business-community relations. Nevertheless, leaving aside the informal and illegal aspects of their activities, they can be viewed as having similarities to bottom of pyramid approaches as conceptualised by C. K. Prahalad in as much as they provide a market based system for addressing housing challenges of the urban poor (Prahalad and Hart, 2002). The exception to these may be company housing that is provided by some, particularly large scale, employers for their employees often in lieu for payment of rent during their employment with the company. These were particularly prevalent in major company towns during the colonial period up to 1950s with firms involved in major extraction activities. A prime example of this was Abadan in Iran under the Anglo-Iranian Oil Company (Crinson, 1997). To different degrees the same system would be repeated in many other towns and cities built around major industries. To this day this model is being applied in different locations primarily for attracting and maintaining a stable workforce necessary for the activities of the companies concerned. This is still evident now in major mining towns in Africa or industrial hobs in Asia where clusters of major firms are to different degrees involved in direct or indirect housing provision for their employees as in Bangkok or Shenzen (Yap and Shrestha, 1998; Ding et al., 1997). As such, therefore, true forms of what we may now describe as CSR housing provision of any significance may only be seen in the activities of philanthropist industrialists towards the end of 19th century in the West, a prime example of which may be seen in George Cadbury's Bourneville experiment in the UK.

This book supports the idea of a pluralistic approach to housing – and construction in general – and within such a context, highlights the role that can be played by CSR. In the current context, CSR has not been on the radar of housing provision, or development of construction industry for that matter. Nevertheless, these concepts – and related modes of provision – can play a role at least at the local level in housing and other construction sub-sectors where specific firms are operating. If we are advocating a pluralist perspective, therefore, we would need to consider what possible roles such modes can play in promoting construction in developing countries with the aim of encouraging and up-scaling their effects both through identifying exemplars for activities of other private firms and exploring their inclusion in policy mechanisms as an additional source of contribution. We consider this by examining a number of examples in the next section.

4.2 Case-studies

Four cases are examined. The first case concerns the work of Água e Cidade. This is an NGO set-up by private companies that manufacture building appliances. It operates in Brazil with the primary aim of urban water conservation and improving urban water management. Most of its work is concentrated in educational campaigns and research efforts for more rational consumption of water resources, preservation of urban rivers and technical assistance to this effect. Institutional partners include universities, schools, research institutes, government agencies, public departments, sectional associations, class entities, technical associations, departments for consumer protection, professional entities, non-governmental organisations and laboratories, all of which are exempt from financial contributions. At the same time, however, it is the only one of our case studies that is involved in large scale housing provision both in terms of social and environmentally more sustainable housing on a large scale in partnership with private sector actors and international NGOs. This is an important issue as Água e Cidade has proved to be highly effective in setting up partnership arrangements with a range of actors but particularly private firms to progress both its water management and housing programmes. As such while housing provision is a side activity of the NGO it provides the best example for us to illustrate the potential in terms of low income housing policy in developing countries.

The second case concerns a leading company[2] in Ghana's cement industry. The sole producer of cement in Ghana until 2000, this company's monopoly power was broken by Diamond Cement Ghana Limited (DCGL). Prior to this development, the company's responsibility to society appeared to be *ad hoc*. The entry of DCGL changed its behaviour. The main CSR activities of this firm revolve around donation of cement to facilitate infrastructure development activities in

---

[2]The company did not want to be named directly in the original study.

health and education across Ghana. This firm has been included as an example of direct contribution to construction activities in deprived communities. At the same time, however, there are important lessons that can be learnt from both the effectiveness of the specific cement allocation programme in terms of targeted benefits to lower income groups and drivers for CSR activity in general.

The third case concerns a small road building activity by Ashfoam, which is a large foam manufacturing company in Ghana. This has been included due to the unusual consequences that have occurred since the completion of the road. While rather unique in terms of the set of circumstances that have led to a negative result for Ashfoam, it highlights the complexity of community-firm relations and the need for more careful study and targeted community engagement rather than *ad hoc* activity that can have unintended consequences.

The final case concerns Prima Woods in Ghana. This case is useful for our purpose for two reasons. First it involves construction related activities, albeit one-off small scale projects. Second, it shows that drivers for involvement in CSR activity can arise from the firm's immediate operational concerns that can also coincide with community priorities. This will undoubtedly have beneficial community effects for the duration of the operation of the firm in the locality. However, important questions are raised on the long term sustainability of such activities.

4.2.1 Água e Cidade

Água e Cidade is a non-profit association, created in 2000 supported by private companies and as a result of joint initiative between CEDIPLAC (Solutions for the Human Habitat) and PURA (Programme of Rational Use of Water). The former is an NGO primarily concerned with development of programmes of quality assurance, development programmes and programmes for professional qualification on rational use of water and the preservation of urban rivers. The latter is a programme of the water and sewage agency of the State of Sao Paulo.

Its goal is to involve society in the issue of water management in order to preserve life on the planet, but it has also been involved in housing provision, which will be presented below. To fulfill its mission of 'moving and making society aware of the need for the rational use of life in the cities as well as the preservation of urban rivers', Água e Cidade depends on the work of a team of professionals who are supported by partner institutions, individuals and water volunteers.

The supporting partners comprise not only industries; but also public service companies; state, private or semi-state companies; sectional associations; and other organisations that contribute fixed amounts according to criteria defined by Água e Cidade. Therefore, it is a good example of (support) partnership between private companies through CSR and other players.

Água e Cidade supports actions in four programme areas that are subdivided into various projects, all working toward the same overall objective:

- Our Water
- Water and Environment Management
- Healthy and Sustainable Cities
- Living Waters

All programmes are related to water and sanitation, which is the subject of the next chapter (utilities). The third and fourth programmes also include housing, and will be presented here.

4.2.1.1 Healthy and sustainable cities

Developed in partnership with Associação Brasileira de Cimento Portland and involves studies, projects and actions to develop technologies for the solution of social housing problems to guarantee the integration of the houses with their surroundings. The project is concerned with all urban services, especially clean water and sanitation, as well as the construction of houses with quality and productivity in all phases and their integration in a sustainable way.

Figure 4.2 Construction of healthy and sustainable districts and condominiums. The coloured pipes represent services as follows: Green – Electricity, Red – Telephone/TV, Blue – Water, Yellow – Natural Gas, Brown – Sewer

Figure 4.3 Team Living Waters – Brazil helping to build houses in Brazil

4.2.1.2 Living Waters programme

This programme works with the improvement of the quality of water and sanitation systems, infrastructure and public services that already exist or are to be built in Brazilian houses, making them healthy and sustainable. It also builds news houses, as presented above.

In August 2001, this programme, in partnership with Associação Habitat para a Humanidade Brasil, helped build 105 social housing units in Guapó, a small town in the state of Goiás.

The programme methodology for the execution of building systems and infrastructure systems focuses on the quality of execution and labour and material production that guarantee the quality of the material used.

4.2.1.3 Key lessons

NGO Água e Cidade, with the effective cooperation of its partners, has approached other companies and institutions to form new alliances to promote the rational use of water as well as housing construction. As a consequence, its programmes are being replicated in other Brazilian cities. Examples include the programmes Our Water, Water and Environment Management and Healthy and Sustainable Cities. This interest and participation from other companies occurs because of the credibility and the commitment of the partnering Brazilian companies already involved.

According to Juliana Castro Pastor, Água e Cidade's manager: "Our maintaining partners stimulate and enable the development of the entity as well as our purpose as a whole", and "without their support and commitment, the accomplishment of the objectives of Água e Cidade would not be possible." In conclusion, therefore, the key to Água e Cidade's success is its ability to network and involve a range of actors from different stakeholders to create synergetic partnerships for specified development objectives. In this case targeted around water management and housing provision.

4.2.2 Cement company – Ghana

This case study concerns a leading company in Ghana's cement industry. The sole producer of cement in Ghana until 2000, this company's monopoly power was broken by Diamond Cement Ghana Limited (DCGL). Prior to this development, the company's responsibility to society appeared to be *ad hoc*. The entry of DCGL changed its behaviour. The aim of this study is to demonstrate the vital role that competition plays in promoting business-community relations, with a focus on supporting decentralisation to local authorities.

The study begins with an overview of the case study company, followed by the company's cement foundation initiative. Next, the role competition played in activating this initiative is discussed, followed by the presentation of key issues relating to the company's community relations programmes. Subsequently, institutions that are supporting the smooth implementation of the Foundation are discussed. The case concludes by exploring the future actions that the company intends to pursue.

4.2.2.1 *Company profile*

The company is the largest manufacturing company in Ghana, with an annual turnover of 390.21 billion Cedis in 2002 (approximately $56,000,000). It is a joint venture between a Norwegian company and a Ghanaian private interest. It produces standard Portland cement, shortcrete products, and ready mixed cement. The company also provides marine transport services for loading of bauxite and manganese in addition to road transport for hauling bulk cement products.

Sales are conducted through a network of company depots spread throughout the country as well as independent agents and distributors. The company's mission is to remain the major reliable supplier of high quality cement products to the domestic market while at the same time securing a stable and safe workplace for its employees.

4.2.2.2 The Foundation initiative

In June 2002, the company launched a cement foundation to support infrastructural development. In the same year, the Executive Council of the Foundation donated approximately 15,000 bags of cement to needy institutions and deprived communities for developmental projects. This was expected to increase to 26,000 bags in 2003.

4.2.2.3 Foundation administration

According to the company's Communications Manager, the Foundation is administered by a three member Executive Council comprising of a board member of the company and two external appointees. The Executive Council has the sole discretion, power, and responsibility to evaluate applications submitted by potential beneficiaries. Other responsibilities involve deciding the time, quantities, and methods of distribution to beneficiaries. The Executive Council selects beneficiaries on a first come first serve basis.

In keeping with its policies and purposes, the company has set forth general prohibitions, which the Executive Council follows to ensure the proper and equitable use of the Foundation's infrastructural support scheme. The Executive Council is also expected to donate cement within the limits of the foundation's annual allocation.

The Foundation has also set up an inspection team that visits approved projects in the various communities to monitor progress. After each monitoring trip, the inspection team is expected to present its findings to the Executive Council. In some cases the inspection findings would be made available to the electronic media (e.g. Television).

In order to fulfill its philanthropic responsibilities within the limits of its resources, the Foundation's support scheme is guided by a series of strategic objectives and policies designed to enhance the operational efficiency of the scheme. In line with this, the Foundation operates in accordance with the following guidelines and policies:

- To donate cement freely to health clinics and educational institutions to improve their infrastructure

- Donations will cover both rural and urban areas with emphasis on deprived communities
- Small to medium size projects will be prioritised
- Significant element of community labour shall be included in the project
- Allocations will be made on non-partisan lines and will not be politically or religiously motivated

This statement of policy sets forth the current views of the Foundation with respect to the best use of its resources. It may be revoked or amended in any respect for any reason by the Executive Council of the Foundation. Accordingly, there is no guarantee that the above policy necessarily represents future policies or activities of the Foundation.

4.2.2.4 Application procedure

There is no formal application procedure. Proposals, preferably in concise letter form, are accepted and reviewed throughout the year. In order to permit evaluation of proposals, notification of final action may take as long as three to six months. Commitments for support are not made verbally, and personal visits and phone calls to the Foundation are not encouraged.

In evaluating requests for assistance, the Executive Council has developed criteria and guidelines to facilitate the process. Among the factors considered in evaluating proposals are the following:

- Projects shall be community initiated and should be viable and sustainable
- Applicants need to present drawings and/or descriptions of projects
- Applicants to state time frame for the completion of projects
- Location of projects must be stated as well as the financial source
- Institution or authority responsible for the project must be given
- Projects should be recommended by a recognised authority within the community (e.g. District Education or Health Directors, Chiefs or District Chief Executive)
- Cement meant for projects specified shall be used for such purposes only; breach of this leads to any donation being withdrawn
- Only screened and short listed applicants will be contacted

4.2.2.5 Drivers of the initiative

Prior to the entry of Diamond Cement Ghana Limited (DCGL) into the cement industry, this company controlled the entire market estimated at 44 million bags. With the absence of competition, the company became complacent and this has cost them dearly. The company has lost nearly 40% of its market share to DCGL. Currently the company, as market leader, controls about 64% of the market with sales volume of 28 million bags.

4.2.2.6 Diamond Cement Ghana Limited (DCGL)

As stated above, the company's main competitor is Diamond Cement Ghana Limited (DCGL). The new company was incorporated in 2000 and has experienced rapid growth. During the year of its incorporation, the company captured 20% of the total market share countrywide. This grew to 30% in 2001. At the time of conducting this research in July 2002, its market share was estimated at 35% and was expected to reach 40% by the close of 2002. The company is the market leader in the Greater Accra region with a 60% share. The company's presence and influence in the middle and Northern belts as well as Central and Western region is not very strong. However, it has had dramatic influence in three out of the ten regions of the country: Greater Accra, Eastern and Volta region where the company maintains its offices and manufacturing plant at Aflao. DCGL has marketing alliance with its sister company, West Africa Cement (WACEM) company based in the Republic of Togo bordering Ghana.

4.2.2.7 Threats to company operations

According to Mr Chitti Babu, Managing Director of DCGL, the company's present production is between 40,000 to 46,000 tones (i.e. only 2% of local requirements). At full capacity, DCGL's annual production level is estimated at 600,000 tonnes of cement. This constitutes only 25% of the total cement requirement of the country. The company's current low production volume of 2% is attributed to its lucrative marketing alliance with its sister company WACEM. This alliance allows DCGL to import finished cement product from WACEM which attracts only a 10% import duty. In addition to this low tariff rate, DCGL's proximity to sister company, WACEM in Togo, has enabled DCGL to enjoy other marketing advantages. These advantages are in the form of low transportation and insurance charges.

The focus company for this case study, on the other hand, produces all the cement it sells locally. As stated above, the company imports clinker, the main raw material for cement production from Norway. The raw materials attract a 5% import duty. Other expenses that have contributed to the company's unfavourable cost structure are high handling, insurance and freight charges of imported clinker. These factors have placed the company in a disadvantageous position. With the current state of affairs in the cement industry, it is currently far cheaper to import finished cement product from neighbouring Togo than to produce it locally.

4.2.2.8 DCGL seizes opportunity to gain market share

With its cost advantage as a result of low tariff rate, DCGL has employed price as its main competitive tool to achieve impressive growth. At the time of conducting this research (July 2002), the wholesale price of DCGL/WACEM cement was about 2,500 Cedis or 7% less than the wholesale price of the cement produced by the case study company. The pricing policy chosen by DCGL appeared to cover production costs and distribution expenses. The company introduced transportation and credit incentive schemes to entice distributors of the case study company. The DCGL transportation incentive involves absorbing 50% of transportation expenses incurred by distributors. Besides the transportation incentive, the company also gives two weeks credit facility to distributors. The implication is that, the pricing strategy of DCGL was aimed at gaining market share. With market share approaching the 40 percentage point within two years, this strategy is certainly yielding the desired result.

4.2.2.9 Internal weaknesses

Another significant feature of the case study company's operations prior to the emergence of DCGL was the non-existence of Human Resources and Communications departments. Issues related to human resource management were part of administration functions. "With the absence of a substantive personnel department, personnel functions were reduced to finding and training employees, arranging for them to be paid, explaining management's expectations and justifying management actions. Personnel functions concerning planning, monitoring and control as well as satisfying employee work related needs and problem were relegated to the fringes", according to the Human Resource Director.

> "With this snag in the company's human resource management", he recalled that "most of the employees became disenchanted; but there was no channel to vent their pent up feelings. The moment for expressing the pent up feeling came in 2000 with the establishment of DCGL as a credible option for employees. DCGL managed

to poach a sizeable number of... [our] workforce with little difficulty. This signalled a wake-up call for... [us]".

This sentiment was echoed by another employee at the Tema plant:

> During that period, there was no viable alternative and for that matter opportunity for occupational mobility was simply not readily available. This is because, the skills for undertaking cement production are specific and therefore we could not easily transfer our skills to other organisations.

The absence of a communications department at the company was an additional debilitating factor that worked in favour of DCGL. Communication is central to the conduct of organisational life. It involves both the giving out of messages from one person and the receiving and understanding of those messages by another or others. The communications department also links an organisation to its external environment.

A company's ability to respond to community relations issues is a function of what its information system can gather from its operating environment. Unfortunately, the cement company did not feel the need to be responsive to community issues with sufficient sharpness due to the absence of an information filtering system.

Thus, what they failed to see was invisible to them because there was no radar screen (Communication Department) to filter information pertaining to community issues from its operating environment. This situation weakened the company's responsiveness to the needs and concerns of society.

4.2.2.10 Reversing the trend

With a slump in market share and the loss of talented staff to DCGL, the company decided to take corrective actions to reverse this trend. To forestall the drifting of employees to its main competitor (DCGL), the company was restructured in 2001. The restructuring exercise led to the creation of a separate department for human resource management in 2001. The department has been very instrumental in controlling the high labour turnover at the company. This was confirmed by a shop floor staff member at Tema who declined to be identified; "Conditions of service have improved greatly and there is no incentive for us to leave for other companies".

To slow down the pace of DGCL's market share growth, the marketing department of the case study company recommended to management to partially adopt DCGL's distribution strategies (i.e. credit and transportation incentives). This option was considered unattractive to management. To steer the competing tide in favour of the company, management of the case study company realised that differentiating their market offering from DCGL would be the most effective approach. However, product differentiation was not deemed a viable option since competing offers for cement look the same in the eyes of the users or customers. This is because cement is a standardised product that allows little variation. Therefore the differentiation dimension that management settled on was image differentiation. The fulcrum around which this image differentiation strategy revolves is the company's Cement Foundation. The initiative is expected to enhance the company's reputation and brand image and by so doing provide the impetus needed to recover some of the lost grounds.

To achieve this objective, management created the Communications Department in January 2002, two years after the entry of DCGL. The Department links the company to its macro environment and it is supposed to be the ears and eyes of the company in the community. Three months after its creation, the Communication Department played a leading role in launching the Cement Foundation, for which it is administratively responsible.

4.2.2.11 Support institutions

The District Assemblies and Traditional Rulers have become a key support institution that is fostering the smooth implementation of the company's community outreach initiative.

District Assemblies were originally established in 1988 to facilitate the decentralisation of government to local authorities. They are assigned responsibility for bringing about the integration of political, administrative and development support needed to achieve a more equitable allocation of power, wealth, and geographically dispersed development in Ghana.

In the performance of these functions, the District Assemblies work through a number of sub-committees. One example is the Social Services Sub-Committee. In order to prevent fraudulent claims by potential beneficiaries, in each District Assembly this sub-committee has been assigned responsibility for recommending projects for consideration by the Executive Council of the company's Cement Foundation.

Another recognised authority that has been empowered by the Foundation's Executive Council to recommend projects is the chief or traditional ruler of a beneficiary community. Traditional rulers are the leaders of the communities whose responsibility extends over securing the welfare of their people. They are initiators of community development projects and have complete control of social and cultural issues in the community.

In 2002, 150 applicants had submitted their application to the company for consideration. Nearly 70% of the beneficiaries obtained their endorsement from the District Assemblies. The remaining 30% were endorsed by traditional rulers.

4.2.2.12 Key issues

There are two main issues that need to be mentioned as far as the company's Foundation initiative is concerned. The first has to do with the endorsement or recommendation role of the District Assemblies (DAs). This role assigned to the District Assemblies is well below the potential contribution the DAs could make towards the smooth implementation of the initiative. An initiative that focuses solely on allocating resources and not ensuring that the resources are used for the purposes for which they were meant engender patterns of behaviour that may defeat the objectives of the initiative. Monitoring and control systems are supposed to be the critical elements in ensuring that the objectives of the Foundation are attained. Without effective control and monitoring systems, the likelihood that donated cement would be used for the purposes for which they were donated cannot be guaranteed. In its current form, the monitoring and control systems of the Foundation appear to be weak. The control mechanism of the Foundation only takes a feedback form where, during monitoring visits, the Foundation's inspection team detect a deviation that has already occurred.

To strengthen the monitoring and control mechanisms, the Foundation's Executive Council should consider making its control system a mixture of feedback and feed-forward. A feed-forward control mechanism will enable the Executive Council to take action on the basis of prediction with the aim of avoiding deviation from expectations. The Foundation should set standards or targets for performance, or expected outcomes of a sequence of actions. The institution (i.e. traditional ruler or D.A.) that supported the application of beneficiaries could complement the efforts of the Foundation's inspection team by ensuring that the donated cement is used in accordance with established standards. It is hoped that the Executive Council would incorporate this observation in the Foundation's criteria for application.

The second concern is that profit oriented businesses do not possess the skills and competencies required to manage development projects efficiently. The company's foundation, as a social development initiative, would benefit from NGO expertise. Presently, the company is expending a tremendous amount of human resources in the implementation of the foundation's initiative. The company could improve the efficiency of the foundation by initiating a partnership arrangement with an appropriate NGO. A partnership arrangement would offer the company the necessary respite that would enable its employees to concentrate their efforts, time and energy on core business matters. This, however, does not mean that the company should delegate all responsibility to its NGO partner. Delegating all responsibility to an NGO would do little to build the company's capacity to effectively engage with the community as a key stakeholder.

4.2.2.13 The future

The New Academy of Business-UNV (2004) research on business-community relations in Ghana has shown that Ghanaian consumers are gradually becoming concerned about the social responsibilities of companies. That is, non-market issues are now influencing the purchasing decisions of some Ghanaian consumers. To make an informed purchasing decision, they require clear information about how choosing one product over another will benefit society. Due to its distinct qualities, the company intends to use the foundation initiative as a tool for shaping the purchasing decisions of their current and potential customers. The Marketing Director believes that 'good news' stories and features are more authentic and credible to readers than advertisements. He explains the company's next line of action as follows:

> With the introduction of competing products, the challenge for us is to protect our name so that our products can command brand preferences and even brand loyalty. To do this would require a great deal of long-term investment spending to improve positive brand associations. [The foundation]... initiative marks the beginning of the company's branding transformation. With the launching of this initiative, the next step is to design a creative advertising campaign aimed at improving our image. From experience, we know that advertising becomes more effective if it is more memorable. In view

of this, we intend to imbue our advertisements with the achievements of our… [foundation] initiative. This approach would be effective because when competing offers look the same getting associated with a social issue can make a difference. The message will get to our target audience as news rather than as sales directed communication; and this is expected to attract people who can relate to social issues.

In a business environment characterised by standardised products, fighting for consumer recognition and loyalty is very crucial. Simply offering a quality product or service does not guarantee success in such business environment since this could easily be imitated by rivals. The company recognises this, and is therefore seeking innovative ways to distinguish itself in the marketplace. One strategy that the company is seriously considering is cause-related marketing (CRM).

The Communications Manager argues that the company's "approach to cause related marketing would be two-pronged strategy. The first would involve donating 1% of the purchase price of our cement to a charity for a specific project, most probably education and health oriented. The second approach would allow our customers, through our agents, to direct a small percentage of their purchases towards specific charities. Whether we are looking for improved public relations, product differentiation, enhanced brand loyalty or increase sales, we believe CRM can deliver all of these benefits while simultaneously addressing social issues and concerns."

The foundation study suggests the following state of play. The macro environment of the cement industry is changing faster than ever and it is therefore necessary for the environment to be continuously monitored and the position of the company within it continuously assessed.

Second, beneficiaries are not always willing to act in the best interest of their benefactors. There is, therefore, the need to put in place appropriate control mechanisms to enable the Executive Council to monitor the outcomes of the allocated cement and take corrective action if those outcomes are contrary to the objectives of the foundation.

Third, this study has highlighted the relative importance of competition as a catalyst for ensuring corporate responsibility. That is, the competitive market place provides one of the most direct means of exerting pressure on businesses. This pressure may be in the form of the loss of market share which has negative consequences for the company. This is particularly true if a firm operates in a business environment that is characterised by intense competition. Conversely, companies operating in a static business environment or enjoying monopoly power are less inclined to be responsive to the needs and aspirations of their host community since the demand for their products may be perfectly inelastic (i.e. there is no substitute for the company's product). Thus, this case has revealed that if variety is the spice of life, then competition is the salt of business-community relations.

4.2.3 Ashfoam – Ghana

Ashfoam Company Limited thought that one way of improving relations between itself and its neighbours is to behave in a socially responsible manner. Unfortunately, the company has become a victim of its social responsibility. The victimisation has caused the company financial and operational setbacks. This case examines the nature of this victimisation and its effects on Ashfoam's future engagement with its neighbours.

4.2.3.1 *Corporate background*

About 300km north-west of Greater Accra region is the city of Kumasi, the capital and commercial centre of the Ashanti Kingdom. Kumasi which is the second most densely populated in Ghana, hosts nearly 24% of industrial activities in the country. One of these industrial activities is the manufacture of foam and rubber products by Ashanti Foam Factory Limited (Ashfoam).

Ashfoam Company Limited is the second largest foam manufacturing company in Ghana with annual sales of about 1.2 billion Cedis in 2000. The privately owned company employs more than 140 people nationwide and has a comprehensive range of products. Notable among these are mattresses, pillows and padding for furniture and car seats among others. The largest operating line is mattress production, which contributes nearly 90% of total revenue. With the head office in Greater Accra region, the Ashfoam manufacturing plant is based in the Garden City of Ghana, Kumasi. It has 40 distribution depots spread throughout the country.

Almost half of Ashfoam sales come from its distribution centre in Greater Accra (46%), while the rest of the country accounts for the remaining 54%. Currently the company has no presence outside the country.

4.2.3.2 *Business-community relations*

The manufacturing site of Ashfoam in Kumasi is located at Tafo, a suburb of Kumasi. In February 1999, Ashanti Foam Company Limited responded to the call by its neighbours and customers to restore the rugged road that serves the company and its environs. The road which is classified as a feeder, branches off Tafo-Mampong trunk road with a length of about 150 metres. It is a cul-de-sac that ends at the premises of the company. The company estimates the restoration cost at 150 million Cedis which translates into about US$54,000 in 1999. The objective of the initiative was to improve relations between the company and residents of the neighbourhood.

4.2.3.3 Drivers of the business-community initiatives

The quality of roads in Kumasi Metropolis can be described in developing country terms as below average. Only about 40% of the roads are tarred with bitumen. These tarred roads are in the main the major and ceremonial roads of the city. The remaining 60% untarred roads are left at the mercy of the weather during the rainy season between March and November. Tafo (where Ashfoam is located) is one of the flood prone suburbs of Kumasi. At the bottom of a sloppy and untarred road is the manufacturing site of Ashanti Foam Company Limited. The road services about 25 houses on both sides. Due to its sloppy nature, the road was subjected to heavy battering during the rainy season. The result was that each time it rained part of the top soil of the road was eroded. The erosion continued for many years leaving behind grave size potholes and ravines which caused many vehicles to break down on the road. Vehicle break down casualties included neighbours, visitors, customers of the company and the company itself.

Initially, the road restoration was thought by both neighbours and Ashfoam to be the responsibility of the Kumasi Metropolitan Assembly. Unfortunately, all efforts (by both residents and company) to get the Assembly to repair the road proved futile. Discussion with the civil engineer of the Metropolitan Assembly revealed that the meagre resources of the Assembly made it impossible to undertake the road restoration project.

With the non-response attitude of the Assembly, the residents and customers turned to Ashfoam to assist in the restoration of the road. At first, the company was reluctant but later yielded to pressure from the neighbours and customers. It considered the restoration project as its social responsibility to the community.

4.2.3.4 Key issues

The road restoration initiated by Ashfoam has aroused negative sentiments among top officials of the company. One of such sentiments is the assertion that the company has become a victim of its social responsibility. This assertion is explained by the branch manager (Mr. Tony Elias) as follows. Not long after restoring the road, neighbours started renovation and extension projects. The renovation work of one neighbour (Madam Fati Alifa) included three office blocks very close to the restored road. The location of these new office blocks was barely 100 metres away from the manufacturing site and warehouse of Ashfoam. These office blocks (constructed in 1995) had never been occupied prior to the road restoration project undertaken by Ashfoam.

On one fine Tuesday (11 May 1999) afternoon, Ashfoam was stupefied to find that these office blocks were being painted in the colours of its main competitor, Latex Foam. The company confronted the landlady of the office blocks. They (management of the company) put forward arguments that they thought would convince the landlady to rescind her decision of giving the space to Latex Foam. Unfortunately, these arguments fell on deaf ears. What mattered to the landlady was financial consideration. According to Mr. Elias, the landlady indicated that she would only consider rescinding her decision on condition that Ashfoam leases all three of the office spaces.

Competitively unwise for a key industry player to be so close, Ashfoam was keen to dislodge Latex Foam from this vantage point. Left with limited options, management of Ashfoam was compelled by this unfortunate circumstance to lease the office spaces for 20 (twenty) years at a total cost of 30 million Cedis (equivalent to US$11,000 at 1999 exchange rate). That is, each office block was offered to the company at 10 million Cedis. The office blocks are now painted in the colours of Ashfoam; but beyond that, the office blocks have not been put into any use due to excess capacity at the warehouse of the company. Mr. Elias contended that the company could have invested that money into something that could have improved its economic performance. But instead "we've been socially blackmailed to put money into something that we consider a white-elephant", he stressed. "What hurts most is the fact that the landlady did not make any effort to make her intentions known to us before approaching our key competitor", he added.

Madam Alifa, however, maintains that she constructed the office blocks in 1995 for rental purposes; but due to the poor state of the road she couldn't get any organisation to occupy them. She continued, "my husband was unemployed and with four daughters and two boys to support, life became unbearable. So I deemed it God's sent opportunity when after the road restoration Latex Foam approached me.

They offered to occupy all the three blocks at a price that I considered very attractive. What am I suppose to do? Tell them to go away with their offer and continue to live in destitution"? she queried.

When asked about why she did not first contact Ashfoam about her intentions, she expressed surprise at this accusation and stated that "I had for past four years prior to Latex Foam's offer erected a sign board in front of the office block that read: OFFICE BLOCK FOR RENT. She continued that "the location of the sign post was so conspicuous that there was no way the management of Ashfoam could claim that they did not see it". As to why she gave the place specifically to Latex Foam, Madam Alifa indicated that she did not approach Latex Foam but rather *vice versa*.

On the issue of whether in her estimation she had treated Ashfoam fairly, this is what she had to say: "not until I was confronted by Ashfoam, I did not know there was anything wrong with my actions". She went on to point out the factors that influenced her actions. "First, I have three office blocks that I have tried unsuccessfully for nearly five years to lease or rent out. Second, renting out the office blocks to three different tenants creates cumbersome administrative work. With these in mind I was troubled by the likelihood that if I forgo the Latex Foam offer I might not get an offer comparable to the Latex offer".

Asked about what she would do if Ashfoam fails to renew the lease when it expires in twenty years' time, the response was: "I will go back to Latex Foam and I am sure by so doing I may succeed in getting them (Ashfoam) to renew the contract on my terms". What one can deduce from this response is that, the landlady would use Latex Foam as the bargaining chip, to significantly raise the financial consideration of the office blocks after the expiry of the current agreement.

Asked whether such an action does not constitute overindulgence, Madam Alifa response gives an indication that her future actions would be motivated by vengeance. She remarked "the road restoration project that the company undertook has brought my residence right in the direction of the flood waters and this has caused substantial damage to my properties and possessions. All attempts to get management of the company to rectify this problem have been ignored. If one sees nothing wrong with that, then my future actions should not be considered excess".

4.2.3.5 Future engagement

The issues raised above clearly indicate that instead of improving business-community relations, the Ashfoam initiative has resulted in sour relations. The management of Ashfoam is bitter and has even regretted undertaking the road restoration project. At the time of conducting this case study research in 2002, some fault lines and fractures were very noticeable on the restored road. Unfortunately, the management of the company have expressed unwillingness to undertake future road restoration projects.

The company was also not unaware of the flooding problem Madam Alifa brought up, but Mr. Elias remained adamant.

4.2.4 Prima Woods – Ghana

Prima Woods specialises in the manufacturing and distribution of timber products. These products include sawn timber, lumber & moulding. Established in 1964 with only 30 staff, the company has grown to be one of the major players in the timber industry with staff strength of 252. The company maintains its headquarters and manufacturing site in Kumasi (Ashanti region).

The business-community activities of Prima Woods are concentrated in Mehami, a small human settlement, where it is undertaking its logging activities, rather than its headquarters in Kumasi. The construction activities have included renovating the Chief's Palace and building a police station, plus activities related to utilities and social development. The case has been chosen for inclusion in this chapter because construction in urban development is not only about large undertakings and/or large settlements. It is also about small settlements, where small construction activities make a difference. Indeed, better equipped small settlements may help to decompress large cities. It is important to note, this book does not argue for large cities dwellers to go back to rural areas (see Chapter 2). However, this does not preclude attempts for improving conditions in smaller settlements. Of course the sole contribution of Prima Woods to Mehami is not enough to provide all the necessary urban amenities to such a settlement – but CSR cannot address the problemetique of development alone, it can complement.

4.2.4.1 Key lessons

The overriding context for Prima Woods CSR activities is its security concerns for continuation of its activities. The company has over $744,000 worth of equipment in its area of operation. A major issue of concern for the company is preventing theft and damage to its equipment and safety of its operatives in a remote region. In this context it may be argued that renovating the chief's palace as a symbol of traditional authority and building the police station are in fact sensible business decisions that are as much to the benefit of the company as the local community. Nevertheless the local community claim, prior to the coming of Prima into Mehami, peace and order in the community was undermined by the absence of a Police station. Prima has been in Mehami community for nearly 12 years. During this period the community has enjoyed stable social conditions. Furthermore, the relationship between Prima Woods and Mehami has led to a drastic improvement in education and health conditions of the community. One would therefore not be far from the truth in saying that the community relations programme initiated by Prima is meeting desired objective.

However, one worrying aspect of Prima community relations programme is that there is no sustainability mechanism built into the initiatives. From all indications Prima's support to the Mehami community would come to a close with the exhaustion of the forest resources of the community by 2010. The net effect is that when Prima support is withdrawn or is terminated, all the positive gains attained by the Prima's community related initiatives would be eroded.

One particular issue that one finds very intriguing about the business-community relations programmes of Prima Woods is that the company has failed to be socially responsible to the community that is hosting its manufacturing or processing site. This is located at Kumasi, a distance of about 200km from Mehami, the source of the raw material which it sees as its host community. The company argues that the provision of employment for hundreds of inhabitants in Kumasi is its social contribution to the social stability in Kumasi Metropolis. Another social contribution is the payment of $50,000 towards the Metropolitan Assembly's road development fund. After lengthy discussions however, the company conceded that its business-community relations initiatives need to be revamped.

4.3 Conclusion

This chapter has shown that the construction industry and housing provide a central role in national and urban economies. As such they are central to urban development. Housing does not only satisfy a basic need but in the absence of financial resources it gains particular significance as assets that can be used for income generation. Small scale and often informal home based enterprises, for example contribute around 40% of household incomes in developing countries. At the same time we are faced with chronic shortages of urban housing where up to nearly a billion urban dwellers are estimated to live in insecure and inadequate shelter with a further 100 million estimated at having no shelter at all.

In response to this situation various policy measures have been proposed with the most recent emphasis placed on enhancing private market capacity as a means of raising housing sector capacity within the national economy as a whole. While private markets should be supported, this chapter has argued that the overemphasis on private housing markets, however, ignores capacities through other modes involving a variety of formal and informal private and public actors. As such it calls for a pluralist approach taking account of specific local institutional and resource conditions. In this context we have argued that CSR activities of private firms can provide an additional, albeit limited, mechanism for housing provision and enhancement of construction activities. In the main this resource has been ignored in all debate on housing policy in developing countries.

The examined cases illustrate that CSR, and business-community relations in particular, can indeed have beneficial local effects both in terms of local construction and housing needs. However, they also show that when such activities are undertaken on *ad hoc* basis their impact can be very limited and unsustainable and at times lead to unexpected complexities. Indeed as the case of Água e Cidade in Brazil highlights the most effective form of CSR activity in housing occurs in a context of a national programme capable of mobilising a large number of public, private and civil society actors for achieving a set of long term objectives. Crucially perhaps this case also shows the important role of a well organised NGO and the public sector as lead agents for initiating partnership arrangements that channel and direct private sector CSR activities to best effect and ensure its future sustainability.

On the other hand the other three cases in Ghana in different ways illustrate that while CSR activities of private firms have local beneficial effects their impact would tend to be highly localised, unsustainable and/or haphazard.

The case of the cement factory in Ghana, for example highlights that CSR can be an important tool for consolidating market activity of even large established firms that can help in countering competitive pressures of rival firms. In addition this case also highlights the potential of the CSR activity for effective engagement with important public sector and civil society actors, in this case District Authorities and local chiefs, that can be instrumental in consolidating and gaining market position. However, while undoubtedly allocation of free cement can indeed be beneficial in facilitating construction activity in the desired sectors, lack of sufficient institutional capacity for effective administration and monitoring of the CSR activity means that there is not clear indication of the final use of the allocated cement in line with the initial intended use as set out in the original applications.

The CSR activities of Ashfoam and Prima Woods, on the other hand, illustrate that even local *ad hoc* activities have local beneficial effects in providing necessary local infrastructure. However, these also highlight that such unplanned and *ad hoc* activities can have major unintended consequences leading to additional conflicts with local actors as in the case of Ashfoam and limited and unsustainable projects that are primarily designed to serve the firms' operational requirements as in the case of Prima Woods.

The key lesson from these cases is that while private firms may have different reasons for involvement in construction or housing related CSR activity in developing countries their activities have local beneficial effects. However, partnership arrangement with NGO and public sector actors provide the most effective mechanism for better channeling these activities in terms of targeted and sustainable developmental objectives. This is particularly relevant to larger firms such as the cement factory in Ghana where their CSR activities can be better targeted and administered at national or regional level. It is clear, though, that in many cases the institutional capacity for such partnership may be lacking. In terms of housing and construction policy, therefore, a priority activity for national and local public governments, major local and international NGOs and development organisations is to raise awareness on, and support development of, such partnership arrangements. A first step towards such capacity building may be the development of a dedicated CSR information centre/bureau by national government or major NGOs that can undertake educational campaigns and provide an information resource for private firms as well as public and civil society actors. Such a resource can also assist in better targeting and execution of *ad hoc* activities in the absence of partnership arrangements.

5
Utilities
Ramin Keivani

Utilities are part of the broader urban infrastructure and are crucial to both economic development and social welfare and wellbeing of urban citizens. In respect of the former, Kessides (1993) states that infrastructure is often referred to as an unpaid factor of production since its availability leads to higher returns obtainable for other factors such as capital and labour. As such the relationship between infrastructure including utilities, productivity, economic development and urban competitiveness is self evident. Without sufficient access to basic resources such as power and water, the ability for real time long distance communication and control functions and rapid travel, freight and shipping facilities, modern manufacturing and business activity would be rendered impossible. Similarly access to amenities not only enhances quality of life of local residents but also contributes to higher productivity of the workforce and enhances urban competitiveness in terms of supporting both inward investment and talent as a place to work and live. In the words of Graham (2000) it is the synergetic effect of the different infrastructure networks that creates the necessary technical and social environment that provides the basis for modern living and production activities. In terms of global competition various studies have shown the role of infrastructure capacity in the success of both established and emerging global cities (Keivani *et al.*, 2003; Graham, 1999; Sennett *et al.*, 2002; Wong, 1999).

In many cities of poorer developing countries, however, lack of access to utilities is a major impediment to economic growth and also a major cause of urban inequity and ill health that threatens the very survival of urban citizens. We can, therefore, note the assertion of the World Bank (1991):

> Failure of public management and scarcity of financial and technical capacity have resulted in widespread deficiencies in water

supply, electricity, transportation, communications, and solid waste management. These deficiencies impose heavy burdens on the productive activity of urban households and enterprises (cited in Azizi, 2000: 1346).

In developing countries the main mechanisms for financing utilities and other urban infrastructure is through traditional public expenditure, private finance or direct user fees (Azizi, 1995). The central government, however, plays the decisive role in terms of public and total expenditure with 90% of all spending (Arimah, 2005). The local government also plays a role in this equation largely through local taxation and levies. This, however, is rather limited in comparison to required expenditure and needs to be augmented from inter-government transfers or capital market borrowings. In reality, however, capital markets in many developing countries, particularly Africa are severely underdeveloped to be of a major use. The over-reliance on central governments creates major constraints on the level of spending particularly as it becomes largely subject to fortune to overall economic performance. Azizi (2000), for example cites the example of Indonesia where the reduction in oil revenues had led to major reductions in public investment in infrastructure. Similarly we can note the reduction in public spending on urban infrastructure in the Philippines from 5% of GDP between 1979 and 1983 to 2% for the rest of the 1980s or the eight fold reduction in public spending on sewerage, drainage and refuse collection by the state governments in Nigeria between the 1980s and early 1990s (Arimah, 2005).

Utilising the data from UNCHS Urban Indicators Programme from 1994 we can observe that among developing countries Latin America and the Caribbean have the highest level of spending (both public and private utilities) at $113 per capita followed by the transition economies at $82, Middle East at $69, Africa at $32 and finally Asia at $23 (Arimah, 2005). However, it should be noted that the Middle East sample comprises only Amman and Sana'a and Africa includes major North African cities. Hence there is a distortion in the indicators that does not fully reflect the general position in terms of spending on urban infrastructure in the cities of the regions noted. This is particularly the case for sub-Saharan Africa. As Arimah notes if North African cities are taken out of the equation the position of Africa falls to about $22 per capita which would be $1 less than Asia. This is an expected result, as basic intuition would suggest that spending on infrastructure would rise with income and GDP growth. Hence lower income sub-

Saharan and Asian countries would be at the bottom of the league. In fact Arimah's work indicates that for every 1% increase in per capita GDP there is a corresponding 0.35% increase in spending on infrastructure. Similarly and expectedly Arimah finds positive correlations between urban infrastructure spending with population growth, controlling corruption and increases in local government revenues and negative correlation with external debt servicing. Importantly revenues from taxation are identified as being important for increasing infrastructure investment. This is particularly the case for property taxation, which is generally seen to be very low in developing countries with only 1.3% of total public sector tax revenues and less than 20% of municipal government revenue.

Focusing on the economic impact of deficient utilities Lee and Anas (1992) argue that in many African cities deficient infrastructure provision have caused major economic inefficiencies. This is largely due to two major and interrelated factors. First we often have non-performing public utility companies that in spite of relatively heavy initial capital investment are unable to provide steady and reliable services even to those locations where they have connection points. At the same time and as a consequence we often see that many users of public utilities in fact have to provide such services in part or in whole independently of the public utility companies. This is perhaps best illustrated by considering the case of Lagos. Here we have a city of about 10 million people that is estimated to reach 16 million by 2025 (WUP, 2007). However, in spite of the country's oil wealth the city is faced with a severe infrastructure and utility crisis and general decline that has in fact progressively worsened since independence (Gandy, 2006). We therefore read:

> The recent history of Lagos has been marked by a stark deterioration in quality of life. Over the past 20 years, the city has lost much of its street lighting, its dilapidated road system has become extremely congested, there are no longer regular refuse collections, violent crime has become a determining feature of everyday life and many symbols of civic culture such as libraries and cinemas have largely disappeared. The city's sewerage network is practically non-existent and at least two-thirds of childhood disease is attributable to inadequate access to safe drinking water. In heavy rains, over half of the city's dwellings suffer from routine

flooding and a third of households must contend with knee-deep water within their homes (Gandy, 2006: 372).

The next sections will discuss the provision of specific types of utilities in developing countries, namely: water supply, sanitation, electric power and streetlights. This will be followed by the presentation of case studies focusing on such types of utilities.

5.1 Water

Recent international data indicates that in 2004 in urban areas of developing countries as a whole some 95% of the population have been covered in terms of access to drinking water (WHO/UNICEF, 2006). However, such general figures hide the severity of the problem and regional variations across the developing world. Researchers have noted that overall in low-income cities of developing countries only 50% of households have water piped to their homes (Arimah, 2005). However, half or one-third of these only operate intermittently. Other figures point to some 171 million people lacking access to affordable clean water in cities of the South (Nickson and Franceys, 2003). With specific reference to three cities in Kenya (Nairobi, Mombasa and Kakamega) we can note that only about one-third of households with private connection have more than 16 hours supply and 36% have less than eight hours (Gulyani et al., 2005).

Another study of ten African capital cities shows that in seven cities only 18–36% of households have direct piped connections to their homes (Collignon and Vezina, 2000). An additional 14–59% have access to public standpipes for collecting water. We can add the percentage of households with access to stand pipes to get the overall percentage of access to piped supply. However, even then in six cities only 27–49% have access to piped supply. This leaves four cities (i.e., Nairobi, Abidjan, Dakar and Ouagadougou) that can cover over 50% (in fact 76–86%) through piped water. Leaving aside the fact that even in the best cases 14–24% of the households are deprived from a connected supply of any sort, the connected households still have to contend with unreliable supply with utility authorities struggling to maintain existing services, let alone extend them to lower income settlements.

The same story can be seen in India and Sri Lanka. In the former a study of 35 urban centres representing 15% of the urban population of the country found that water was supplied on average only 7 hours per day (Nickson and Franceys, 2003). The Indian context is further elaborated by noting that unaccounted-for water ratio was in the region of 40–60% and only 47% of connections were metered with half of them being out of order. In Sri Lanka only 30% of households connected to pipe network had continuous 24-hour supply. Worst still overall in Colombo only 63% of urban residents were connected to the pipe network with growing incidence of water borne diseases suggesting that bacteriological water quality was deteriorating.

Lack of sufficient and reliable water supply gains particular significance when we consider the rapid rate of urban growth across the developing world. With average growth rates of 3.7% between 1975 and 2000 the urban population in low and middle-income countries have been doubling in less than 20 years[1] (Nickson and Franceys, 2003). As expected the situation is not uniform across countries and cities. Indian cities for example had a peak average growth rate of 3.9% per annum in 1991 while Dhaka in Bangladesh achieved a growth rate of 6.9% per annum in the past two decades achieving a doubling time of 10 years. With an average growth rate of 4.4% between 1950 and 2000 Africa, however, can be seen as the most rapidly urbanising continent. This trend is now continuing where by 2025 the total urban population in Africa is expected to rise to 700 million, an increase of 400 million in comparison to 1990 that raises the urbanisation level from 30 to 52% of total population (Mukami Kariuki, 2002). This rate of urbanisation poses major challenges to an already difficult situation. As Mukami Kariuki argues:

> According to the World Health Organization, urban Africa will require an 80 per cent increase in the numbers served to meet the recently established millennium development goal of halving the unserved population by 2015. This objective would require, on average, about 4–5 million new connections every year; or about 6000 to 10 000 every day. Political commitment to these goals, backed by resources and action, will be essential if utilities are to prevent widening of the gap between the served and the underserved (*ibid*: 2).

Clearly, scaling up to the level indicated is a monumental task in many developing countries due to lack of both material, financial and

---

[1]The reader is also referred to Chapter 2 for more discussion of urbanisation in developing countries.

human resources. This becomes even more daunting when considering that a large portion of the population in developing cities live in informal and shanty settlements where local authorities may in fact be barred to provide utilities due to illegal status of the settlements or due to precarious locations and unplanned and organic layouts that make extension of services very difficult even if governments were willing to extend them (Nickson and Franceys, 2003). Poor households, therefore, often have to pay vendors several times the unit price paid by connected non-poor households to the utility (Gulyani et al., 2005). Critically perhaps water vending can no longer be seen as a fringe activity in many areas. Rather, it has become a major source of revenue generation often for organised gangs and accounts for a large portion of the total water revenues in the city. This is exemplified by the case of Ontisha in Nigeria where water vendors collect 24 times as much revenue as the public utility during the dry season (*ibid*).

At the same time public officials are under severe political pressure from vested interest groups that already have access to water to continue with existing policies of water provision that often entail major subsidies but in essence perpetuate and exacerbate access inequalities. In Zambia, for example, official figures indicate that 70% of the urban population have access to piped water. However in peri-urban areas and informal settlements at least 56% of the population do not have access to safe water supply (Robinson, 2002). In a bid to improve the situation the government reformed the sector in 1997 removing the responsibility for water utility service from local municipalities and established commercialised utilities under a professional regulatory body, the National Water and Sanitation Supply Council (NWASCO). However, Robinson notes that political influences and constraints on the new institutional structures have in effect led to maintaining the *status quo* in inequality in service provision. This is seen in political influence by central government to maintain low tariffs and yet inability to fill the resource gap but relying instead on the perverse logic of encouraging profligate use of water to raise revenues. The result has been that water usage in urban Zambia has been estimated to be 300–400 litres per capita per day (lcd) that is 3–4 times per capita levels in Europe (100–120 lcd) and 6 times those of West Africa (60 lcd) (Robinson, 2002). To meet this demand the Zambian government has gone ahead with costly capital investment projects to rehabilitate the supply infrastructure to meet expected supply to existing household connection without raising tariffs. As a result the commercialised utilities are anything but commercial with a large shortfall between revenues and operating costs, lacking working capital and saddled with inherited liabilities. The result is that they have been unable to do anything to improve the situation in peri-urban and slum areas with the Zambian poor paying prices for water at kiosks that are three times the unit price for a connected household.

While the Zambian case may be rather extreme in their pursuit of increasing per capita level of water consumption, Nickson and Franceys (2003) point out that the same basic approach has in fact been followed throughout the developing countries in general. They argue that engineers have tended to design systems according to what they

Table 5.1 Per capita water use in Asian and Latin American cities

| | Asia | | | Latin America | |
City	Water use (lcd)	Year	City	Water use (lcd)	Year
Kathmandu, Nepal	91	1995/96	Florianopolis, Brazil	143	1990
Dhaka, Bangladesh	95	1995/96	Minas, Brazil	154	1990
Beijing, China	96	1995	Bogota, Colombia	167	1992
Mandalay, Myanmar	110	1995/96	Santiago, Chile	204	1994
Hong Kong, China	112	1996	Costa Rica	208	1991
Suva, Fiji	135	1995	Brasilia, Brazil	211	1989
Shanghai, China	143	1995	Sao Paulo, Brazil	237	1988
Colombo, Sri Lanka	165	1995			
Singapore	183	1995			
Kuala Lumpur, Malaysia	200	1996			
Manila, Philippines	202	1995			
Seoul, S. Korea	209	1995			
Delhi, India	209	1995/96			

Source: Gulyani et al, 2005.

perceive to be international standards of per capita water consumption that is based on exaggerated contribution of clean water to overall economic development. It is pertinent to note that the UNCED global target is in fact only 40 lcd. This compares to the figures already noted for urban Zambia and those noted in Table 5.1, indicating much higher actual water consumption than the minimum recommended target. This in itself is not an issue as long as the network capacity can be maintained and expanded to cover as many households as possible. However, as the African cases here illustrate this is in fact the reverse.

This is strongly illustrated by Gulyani *et al.* (2005) in the context of Kenya who argue that in fact the poor and non-poor are both ill served by the mismanagement of water provision both in terms of quality and quantity. In Kenya responsibility for water supply is through three main institutions. These are the ministry of Water Resources Management and Development, self-help or community organisations and small size independent providers. In Nairobi, for example, while the official production capacity is theoretically large enough to meet demand, total water available through the system for actual sale and use is significantly lower. This is largely due to technical losses (leakages) and commercial losses (unbilled and uncollected revenue) that means unaccounted-for water in the system is estimated to be 50%. As a result Gulyani *et al.* (2005) note:

> Due to inadequate utility service and coverage, a large and mostly unregulated parallel water industry has emerged. There are an estimated 1500 individual boreholes in the city and water tankers are ubiquitous. Kiosks and vendors are prominent in informal settlements; for example in Kibera – Nairobi's (and Africa's) largest slum with about 0.5 million residents – there are about 650 kiosks (p. 1250).

Importantly and in severely contrast to Zambia, Gulyani *et al.* show that water consumption in urban Kenya has sharply declined from 105 lcd in 1967 to about 40 lcd in 2000. This is in spite of the increase in water usage by un-piped households from 11 lcd to 35 lcd in the same period. Clearly indicating that the decline is entirely due to the sharp reduction in water use by piped households that has reduced by almost 70% from 117 lcd to 44 lcd. At this level of consumption water use in urban Kenya is in fact marginally lower than Uganda and 60–70% lower than the average water use in Tanzania that stands at about 71 lcd. These figures for Kenya and the other African countries can be compared to average water use in several Asian and Latin American cities shown in Table 5.1 that indicate much lower water use levels than even the lowest city in Asia, thereby highlighting the severity of the problem in the African context. The current consumption rate in urban Kenya hits exactly the minimum target set by UNCED. However, this has not been a policy choice to enable them to extend the network more generally. Rather it is a reflection of the dire straits of the piped water system, inability to maintain regular supply and huge losses through the dilapidated network clearly demonstrating that the mere fact of connection does not in any way mean reliable access to water. Rather it can mean the opposite.

In terms of relative share of connected and unconnected households it is worthy to note that there is in fact much less disparity between the two groups in the main cities of Kenya in comparison to some other cities. In Jakarta and Port-au Prince, for example, the rich are said to use respectively two to 14 times that of the poor (Fass, 1988, cited in Gulyani *et al.*, 2005). Researchers looking at different African cities have pointed out that water utilities generally supply kiosks at highly discounted rates (Gulyani *et al.*, 2005; Robinson, 2002; Collignon and Vezina, 2000). In their study of ten African cities Collignon and Vezina (2000) estimate that standpipe operators (kiosks) are able to have a mark up of 50 to 900% depending on the city concerned. In the case of Nairobi this figure is seen to be an underestimate with Gulyani *et al.* (2005) estimating the mark up to be twice as much at about 1800%. The relatively higher charges by water kiosks in Nairobi are also supported by Collignon and Vezina (2000) who estimate that among the ten cities of their study, kiosks in Nairobi are able to obtain the highest profit margin that is at least 80% while in 6 other cities kiosks have a profit margin under 50% with Cote d'Ivoire being the lowest at about 20%. However, in spite of the high prices charged by water kiosks, i.e., US$2.4/cubic meter, Gulyani *et al.* (2005) find that the median cost for the non-poor connected households at US$2.0/cubic meter is only marginally lower than the poor. This is an important observation as it demonstrates that the relative high cost to the non-poor connected households is not due to the high cost of utility charges that are highly subsidised but that due to the unreliable and poor utility service most non-poor households have to obtain the bulk of their water from other more expensive sources.

Nevertheless one should note that as Nickson and Franceys (2003) correctly point out there is a range of quality and price among private water providers. Here we can note the example of private providers in

Guatemala and Paraguay where competition among private water vendors has held down prices to a maximum of 2.5 times and 1.4 times the official utility price respectively. At the same time we can note that they rely on a private pipe distribution network drawn from private boreholes with investment costs estimated to be 20–60% lower than the government direct providers, operating costs 75% lower and administrative costs 94% lower.

In addition to independent small-scale private providers there are also many non-governmental organisations that are involved in water provision for the poor in developing countries. Here we can note the example of Kampala where local NGOs involved in health care support responded to the water needs of low-income suburb of 390,000 people to organise the local community to protect springs. This was achieved through setting up Local Water Source Management Committees. In many cases Nickson and Franceys (2003) argue NGOs play the role of intermediary between the government utility and the urban poor. Here they cite the example of an NGO (Dusthya Shashtya Kendra – DSK) in Dhaka where:

> ... in partnership with the government utility and the municipality, (the NGO) has been enabling communities to form water committees to take responsibility for a shared connection. The eight members of these committees are all women with a five-member male advisory board to limit social intimidation. The NGO finances the initial construction of a water point that comprises a round tank with a hand pump fitted for abstraction. (Nickson and Franceys, 2003: 112)

Overall therefore four main groups of actors can be identified in water provision in the cities of developing countries. These are the main utilities that are often public sector but in some countries this can also be privatised utility services, independent small-scale providers, self-help provision by individual households and communities that often also involves NGOs or community based organisations. In terms of scale of activity, however, while the utilities have traditionally played a major role their function is largely limited to the piped connection system and formal city neighbourhoods. Their dominance is increasingly challenged by small private providers due to general inability of utilities to maintain quality of existing services and/or expand coverage to largely lower income groups that are often in informal settlements. The important point to note, however, is that with a few exceptions where private boreholes have been dug, the utilities are still the main source of supply of water to the independent providers, NGOs and communities who then distribute the water in the city. It is therefore crucially important to consider ways of improving the effectiveness and efficiency of the main utility concerned.

Table 5.2 Percentage coverage of water and sanitation in selected regions and countries in 2000

Country	Water coverage %	Sanitation coverage %
Africa	85	84
Benin	74	46
Democratic Republic of Congo	89	53
Egypt	96	98
Ethiopia	77	58
Guinea-Bissau	29	88
Mauritania	34	44
Nigeria	81	85
South Africa	92	99
Tanzania	80	98
Asia	93	78
Afghanistan	19	25
Cambodia	53	58
China	94	68
India	92	58
Indonesia	91	87
Iran	99	86
Philippines	92	92
Republic of Korea	97	76
Yemen	85	87
Latin America and the Caribbean	93	87
Argentina	85	89
Belize	83	59
Bolivia	93	82
Brazil	95	85
Ecuador	81	70
Haiti	49	50
Jamaica	81	98
Mexico	94	87
Peru	87	90
Venezuela	88	75

Source: WHO/UNICEF, 2000.

5.2 Sanitation

Access to sanitation is generally more severe than that of water in the developing countries. The World Health Organisation estimates that in 2002 some 2.6 billion people lacked access to improved sanitation (WHO, 2004). This is almost twice those lacking adequate water. Over half of those lacking sanitation or about 1.5 billion people live in China and India. Table 5.2 provides figures on access to both water and sanitation in urban areas of selected countries for 2000 in all three main developing continents. It is important to note here that the countries' own classification of adequate water and sanitation levels have been used in compiling this table. Some of the more advanced developing countries such as Brazil or Republic of Korea give access levels that are lower than some of the less developed countries such as Tanzania. This is due to differences in standards of what provides an adequate sanitation facility. In many of the other less developed countries, particularly in Africa, generally a pit latrine is counted as adequate facility. Note for example that in their 1996 report on the state of water and sanitation in developing countries WHO/UNICEF point out that in Uganda some sources suggested an 80% overall coverage. However, if the pit latrines were to be excluded coverage would fall to only 3%. On the other hand, in more developed countries such as Brazil only flushed toilets are counted as adequate sanitation.

The situation can perhaps be more accurately gauged if we consider percentage of access to improved sanitation. This is shown in Figure 5.1 where improved sanitation is defined as:

- Connection to a public sewer
- Connection to septic system
- Pour-flush latrine
- Simple pit latrine
- Ventilated improved pit latrine

Other sanitation facilities such as bucket latrines, public latrines or open latrines are classed as 'not improved'. Nevertheless, given that the information has been derived from the countries' own definitions WHO/UNICEF (2000) provide the caveat that in many African countries lack of access to improved facilities does actually mean lack of any sanitary facilities whatsoever. In Latin America and the Caribbean, however, lack of access is more likely to mean that the local population or public authorities are unsatisfied with existing facilities rather than

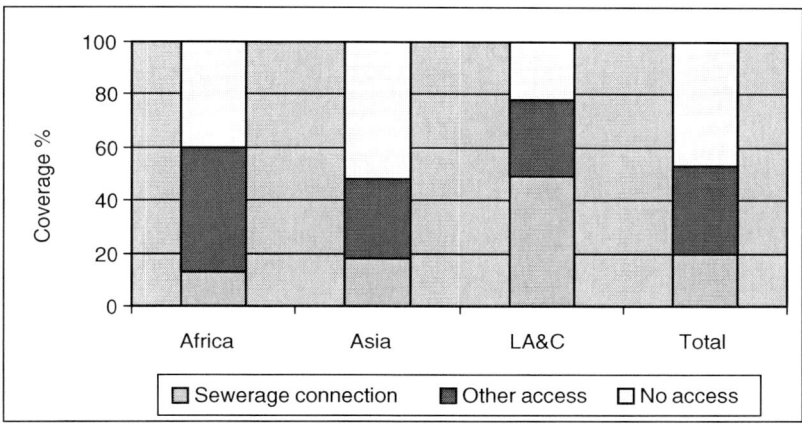

Figure 5.1 Overall access to improved sanitation by category of service in 2000
Source: WHO/UNICEF, 2000.

its actual absence. The data does not allow separation between urban and rural areas and are thus affected by the rural lack of access. Nevertheless, we can gain a more accurate picture of actual state of sanitation between the different types of areas.

Updated WHO figures in fact suggest that in sub-Saharan Africa 64% of the urban population lack access to improved sanitation facilities (WHO, 2004). In fact other researchers have noted that in developing countries in general less than one-third of households have access to good quality sanitation and between one-third and two-thirds of solid waste remains uncollected (Gulyani *et al.*, 2005).

The situation in many sub-Sahara African cities is particularly severe. In peri-urban areas of Zambia, for example, it is estimated that as much as 90% of households do not have access to satisfactory sanitation (Robinson, 2002). In Ibadan, Nigeria, on the other hand less than 1% of households are connected to the sewerage system. Collignon and Vezina (2000) in fact argue that in urban Africa the main utilities are practically absent from provision of sanitation with 70 to 90% overall, and virtually all poor households having to deal with their own waste by building their own latrines or septic tanks or hiring others to do it for them. They note:

> Since the public sector is generally not involved in this area, [small] private providers dominate the market and offer services tailored to

customers' needs and incomes, for the tasks that households choose not carry out themselves: masons who build latrines, manual latrine pit cleaners, suction truck operators for septic tanks, and manual or mechanized drain and latrine ditch cleaning services (*ibid*, p. 24).

In their ten-city study in Africa Collignon and Vezina (2000) show that in four cities (Abidjan, Nairobi Dakar and Conarky) the public sewerage system covers 20 to 45% of the households. In the remaining cities (Cotonou, Ouagadougou, Bamako, Nouakchott, Kampala and Dar es Salaam) this figure falls below 10%. They note that with the exception of the better off residential areas where the holding pits are cement lined and water tight with sludge removal carried out by suction trucks the remaining areas have unlined latrine pits and ditches where liquid waste is absorbed through the earth walls with removals either carried out manually by hired labour or as in some peri-urban locations simply a new latrine excavated when the old one becomes full.

The situation in sub-Saharan Africa may be somewhat extreme in comparison to many other developing countries. However, as noted in Figure 5.1, in many other cities of Asian and Latin America between 22 to 52% of the population lack access to improved or at least unsatisfactory sanitation. The situation is also particularly severe in Asia. In New Delhi, for example, less than 40% of households are connected to the main sewerage system (Khan, 1997).

As with water provision, however, the NGOs and local communities can also take an important lead in provision of sanitation to the poor. In India an NGO provider of sanitary services (Sulbah) in partnership with municipalities who often pay capital costs as well as power and water tariffs, provides sanitary blocks in poor neighbourhoods of Indian cities (Nickson and Franceys, 2003). While they charge for the use of these blocks (with children and destitutes having free access) to enable maintenance and provision of auxiliary sanitary products such as soap the customers seemed to be content at the 1 Rupee user charge. Using this approach the non-for profit NGO has been able to establish 4,000 such units in Indian cities. Similarly we can note the example of the Dharavi slum of Bombay. Here, local and international NGOs collaborated with female construction workers living in the slum to teach them to build latrines (Khan, 1997). As a result the local community now have access to modern latrines that each pay 2 to 5 Rupees per month for maintaining the facility. Importantly the project only cost 40% of those charged by private contractors and the Bombay Municipal Corporation recently pledged to support construction of 2,000 latrine blocks, each with five latrines. Finally Khan notes the example of the Orangi Pilot Project in one of the large squatter communities of Karachi with a population of one million. Here the project assisted the local residents to develop their own extensive sewerage system by providing technical advice and plans for simplified design, which reduced the costs by a factor of ten. Every family contributed about a month's wages to buy material and hire labour. After 17 years from the time when the project was first started in 1980, Khan argues, every family had a flush toilet connected to an underground sewerage line.

5.3 Power

In their analysis of the state of urban utilities in Nigeria, Lee and Anas (1992) focus on electricity provision to argue that inefficient and intermittent power provision has imposed major costs on Nigerian manufacturing firms since the vast majority of firms must resort to providing their own private generation capacity. In their analysis they show that only 14 out of the 179 firms that they surveyed do not have their own power generation capabilities. These were by and large small firms of less than 50 employees. This is an important point as the heavy incidence of power failures among small firms has a major implication for the growth of industries and the generation of employment in cities of the south that are overwhelmingly dependent on smaller firms for employment generation and local economic effects. In this respect Lee and Anas (1992) write:

> According to the 'incubator hypothesis' that was tested in earlier World Bank research on industrial location in Bogota (Lee, 1989) and in Seoul (Lee, 1985), it was observed that small new firms spend their early years near the city centre or in an old industrial area with easy access to good utilities and other essential services. They do so because it is prohibitively expensive for small firms to operate in outlying areas where infrastructure services are poor. As they grow and become more independent, they tend to move out of the central area for more space. In Nigeria and perhaps in most African countries, large cities with poor infrastructure cannot offer the incubator function for small new firms. Since small firms cannot afford their own generators, boreholes and other facilities, the burdens of inadequate public infrastructure services are especially severe for the small firms that start and grow in those

cities. This has a serious negative implication for the birth and growth of small firms and for the generation of employment and income. The studies mentioned above (Lee, 1985, 1989) showed that small new firms generate 60–80 per cent of the new jobs created in large cities in Asia and Latin America (*ibid*, pp. 1074–1075).

This research shows that the cost of private power generation in Lagos is 29% of the total value of machinery and equipment for small firms with less than 50 employees and 12% for larger firms. The Lagos experience provides a similar story on the impact of lack of provision of water, transport and waste collection on manufacturing firms. Again many firms have to resort to independent provision. In respect of water while the costs of provision, e.g., own boreholes, are relatively low in Lagos with 2.8% of total capital costs for small and 2% for large firms, in some states such as Anambara this can be far higher with 21% of capital costs for all firms (Lee and Anas, 1992). They therefore conclude that while due to lack of data one cannot provide definitive proof there is no doubt that many small firms in Nigeria have either shut down or failed to grow to a critical size due to infrastructure deficiencies. Similarly birth of new firms is reduced if many firms must shut down soon after birth. This is supported by Gandy (2006) who argues that on a more general level Lagos is the exemplar of failed industrialisation primarily due to failures in provision of urban infrastructure and states:

> From the mid 1970s onwards, however, the city suffered from acute and accelerating industrial decline marked by declining real incomes and huge increases in poverty and unemployment. ... Companies such as Lever Brothers and Guinness, for example, were having to pump water from half a mile below the surface to continue production and many of the city's 14 'industrial estates' – established in the 1960s and 1970s to attract inward investment – were in a state of total disarray (*ibid*: 381).

As Gandy notes, however, lack of utilities in Lagos is not only a barrier to economic activity of firms but also a major concern for the ordinary life of urban residents. Hence the apt observation that as night falls "the drone of traffic is gradually displaced by the roar of thousands of generators that enable the city to function after dark" (p. 383).

5.4 Street lighting

Street lighting has not received as much attention in the literature as other utilities. It is directly linked to electric power provision. Even with good basic physical infrastructure in terms of erection and maintenance of lighting posts the service is only as reliable as the overall power provision for the city. Notwithstanding problems of power supply alluded to in the previous section the fact remains that many urban areas of the developing world lack the basic street lighting hardware and/or its maintenance to provide adequate street lighting. As with water and sanitation this lack of coverage is particularly severe in the low-income neighbourhoods, slums and shantytowns.

One of the main concerns in terms of lack of street lighting is its impact on crime. The most recent report on the state of the world's cities notes that while overall recorded crime rates across the world is stabilising, 70% of urban dwellers in Latin America and Africa have been victims of crime over the past five years (UN-Habitat, 2006a). The same report also notes that the risk of being a victim of violent crime is in fact increasing with more than 1.6 million people dying as a result of violence every year. On average they note violence makes up 25 to 30% of urban crime and women are twice as likely to be victims of violent crime as men. Importantly it is the lower income groups and neighbourhoods that are disproportionately subject to crime in comparison to higher income groups with major negative developmental impacts. We therefore read:

> Urban insecurity presents a major challenge to the social and economic development of cities as it compounds other factors such as poverty and social exclusion. Violence and crime are no longer viewed exclusively as criminal problems but also as problems affecting the development of societies. Insecurity contributes to the isolation of groups and to the stigmatization of neighbourhoods, particularly those in which the poor and more vulnerable live. (UN-Habitat, 2006a: 143)

Clearly there are many causes for the increase in crime, particularly worsening economic situation, poverty, unemployment and failing states incapable of providing basic security for their citizens.

Noting the economic break down in Lagos Gandy (2006) writes in the nighttime:

> Many roads in both rich and poor neighbourhoods become closed or subject to a plethora of ad hoc check-points and local security arrangements to protect people and property until the morning. (*ibid*: 383)

Among these factors, however, lack of street lighting is also seen to have a major impact. Farrington and Welsh (2002) conducted a meta-study of research on the impact of street lighting in the United States and United Kingdom and concluded that while there is conflicting evidence on the separate impact of street lighting on crime in these countries there is clear evidence that increased lighting can be part of a package of measures that improve the environmental situation for residents and increase the risks and reduce rewards for criminal activity. They write:

> Depending on the analysis of the crime problem, improved street lighting could be implemented as a feasible, inexpensive and effective method of reducing crime. (*ibid*: 339)

The situation in developing countries is clearly different to that of the USA and UK. However the basic premise in terms of positive impact of street lighting on increasing community pride and also increasing the risks for criminal behaviour still applies. Consequently lack of street lighting can be seen to have similarly negative consequences in developing countries. It is, therefore, no surprise to see that improving street lighting is an important part of a range of measures to combat urban crime and create safer urban environments in countries such as South Africa (Sisulu, 2007). Similarly we can note the concern of the Nairobi urban sector profile that lack of streetlights and subsequently insecurity severely constrains mobility at night (UN-Habitat, 2006b). In another publication, Plessis-Fraissard (2007: 8) expresses a similar concern with respect to developing countries in general and writes:

> Municipal governments must take the lead in building safer communities. ... Examples include street lighting around bus stops that

reduce opportunities for aggression, allowing the poor to take better paying jobs outside their community.

As may be expected lack of street lighting is particularly severe in low-income slum areas. A measure of this can be seen in India where in Jabalpur and Gwailor respectively 70 and 60% of roads in low income slum settlements lack street lighting completely and in Indore 75% of roads had deficient lighting (UN-Habitat, 2007a, 2007b, 2007c). Lack of street lights in these areas has been identified to be particularly problematic for women and children at nights and aggravating hygiene and

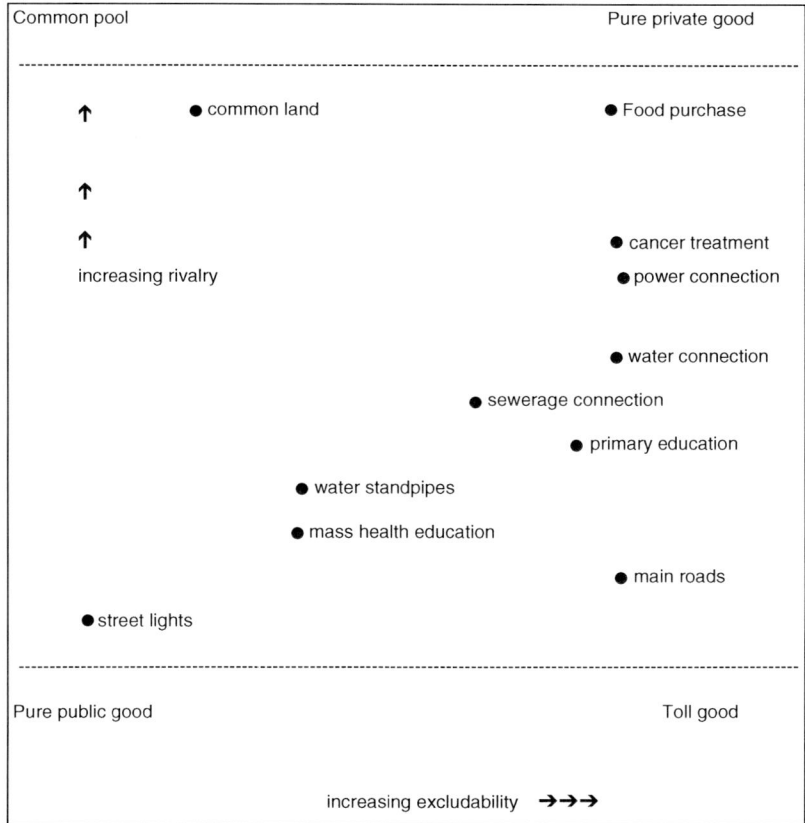

Figure 5.2 Continuum of utility/service provision
Source: Adapted from Batley, 1994.

health problems in rainy seasons when water remains logged for 4–5 days after only 30 minutes of rain.

5.5 What is to be done?

There is still a debate over how to best implement utilities, with a focus on public versus the private (commercial) sector. This relates to what has been explained in Chapter 2 regarding urban development in general, and to the following explanation about housing (as a sub-sector of construction) in Chapter 4.

Traditionally, utilities have been provided by the government, being defined as public goods (for the reasons explained in Chapter 2). Street lighting, for instance, is a classic example of non-exclusivity and non-rivalry. But the cases of other utilities are not so clear. For example, as shown in Figure 5.2, Batley (1994) puts different types of utilities – as well as other services/goods – in different places in a continuum between public and private goods, depending on the degree of excludability and rivalry.

The neo-liberal school of thought argues that major utilities are in fact private goods since we can exclude access through connection points, metering, etc., and limited production and coverage capacity inevitably means that usage by one group of people will lead to non-availability to others. In addition, the public sector is seen to be operationally inefficient, prone to political influence on policy setting, wasteful and generally inept in running effective or, for that matter, equitable utility services.

The experience of both developed and developing countries during the past two decades suggests that utilities can be completely or partially privatised. In both contexts the approach has been one of vertical unbundling to avoid creation of private monopolies. This implies breaking up the chain activities that were previously performed by a single entity and separating the monopolistic from the non-monopolistic activities of the sectors involved. Thereby allowing the basis for private market competition in the non-monopolistic activities. Various institutional arrangements have been developed to allow private participation in the different aspects of utility operations including the distribution networks (see for instance, Nickson and Franceys, 2003).

Other researchers have noted that private suppliers are already involved in aspects of utility provision due to intermittent and unreliable service of the main utility providers. Also, it has been argued that the government should play the role of promoting and enabling

Table 5.3 Performance indicators in water utilities in ten African cities

	Cotonou	Ouaga-dougou	Abidjan	Conakry	Nairobi	Bamako	Nouak-Chott	Kampala	Dakar	Dar es Salam
Population (M)	1.1	1.0	2.8	1.1	2.0	1.0	0.7	1.1	2.2	2.8
Concession	Parastatal	Public	Private	Private	Municipal	Public	Public	Parastatal	Private	Parastatal
% leakage	29	n.a	21	40	50	45	13	49	20	53
HH connection % served	31	28	76	31	75	18	19	36	71	31
Standpipes % served	0	59	2	3	1	20	30	5	14	0
Not served	69	14	22	66	24	63	51	59	15	69

Source: Collignon and Vezina (2000).

private sector provision. Public-private partnerships are encouraged, but with a clear limited role for the government in regulation; with supply being in the hands of the private sector. Following, authors such as Lee and Anas (1992) and Nickson and Franceys (2003), among others, put forward policy recommendations leading to institutional regulatory reforms to support private sector involvement in utilities. Moreover, it has been argued that failures of public-private partnerships in utility services in developing countries are due to lack of public regulatory capacity (e.g. Nickson and Franceys, 2003).

But there is also a set of counterarguments in relation to private provision. First, as noted in the beginning of this chapter, utilities are public goods/services because they meet collective needs of society, therefore should be provided by the government (e.g. Meirelles, 1996). Others accept that there are inefficiencies in public provision, but consider utilities as merit goods/services (explained in Chapter 2), and that the government has the responsibility to provide (e.g. Savenje, 2002, for the case of urban water services). As also explained in Chapter 2, sometimes the involvement of other actors such as NGOs in merit goods is also promoted to secure supply.

Furthermore, private involvement on its own, however, is no guarantee of more efficient and effective service provision. Table 5.3 indicates performance indicators of household connections and percentage of leakage and loss in a recent ten-city study in sub-Saharan Africa.

On the one hand, this information shows that two of the private utilities in Abidjan and Dakar with respectively 76 and 71% household connections and 21 and 20% leakage rates are the most efficient and effective utilities in comparison to their public counterparts. However, we still have the example of Conakry with only 31% connection, 66% of households not served by any form of public delivery and a massive 40% leakage rate that is in fact the second or third worst water utility provider among the ten countries of the study – thus showing that there is no assurance that the private sector is more efficient and effective.

In addition, it has been argued that, with some exceptions, divestiture (where the entire infrastructure and assets are sold to the private sector) has not occurred in developing countries. This is due to the reluctance of private firms to undertake the long term risk of full ownership in a context where the institutional framework is not yet sufficiently developed and there are complex regulatory environments and underdevelopment of local capital markets. As such the majority of private sector involvement is in service contracts and concessions that are in effect forms of private public partnerships involving major multi-national firms (Rodriguez, 2004; Nickson and Franceys, 2003).

There should also be a note of caution as to the social and political sensitivities and conflicts that may arise from private involvement of private sector in utility provision in developing countries. Here we can note the famous case of the failure of the Bolivian Cochabamba water utility concession after only five months due to popular discontent and riots (Tremolet, 2001; Nickson, 2001; Nickson and Vargas, 2002). In this case a combination of factors from higher tariffs to agitation by water vendors whose interests were threatened created the condition for the popular opposition even though Nickson argues that the poor would have been the most to benefit due to cross subsidisation involved in increased block tariff and reduced leakages.

Similarly, Gandy (2006) argues that in the context of Lagos it remains to be seen how the neo-liberal policy proposals towards greater privatisation can be applied in a complicated social and economic local reality involving a multitude of local interests that are benefiting from the current state of undersupply of public utilities. For example:

> When municipal authorities do attempt to extend water supply to poorer neighbourhoods, they are often met with violence and intimidation from water tanker lobbies, 'area boys' and other groups who benefit from the unequal distribution of water and the 'microcircuits' of exploitation which characterise slum life: the city's water corporation must consistently confront the 'water lords' who intentionally vandalise the network in order to continue charging exorbitant rates to the poor. (*ibid*: 383)

At the same time in its attempt to reform the administrative structure for water provision, the municipality has attempted to create 'community-based markets' utilising the traditional authority of chiefs as a revenue-raising strategy. Gandy (2006) notes the spectre of new forms of 'authoritarian governmentality' that combine neo-liberal concerns with 'full cost recovery' with a dependence on non-democratic sources of power in civil society.

The cases of local water suppliers in low-income settlements in Cochabamba and Lagos bring a complicating dimension to the private sector argument i.e. such water vendors are also part of the private sector – even though informal. Therefore, why should they be excluded? There is of course the explanation rationale of their possible monopoly/oligopoly, as well as a lack of appropriate supply. Yet, at the very least, the documented resistance in the two cities shows that the case in favour of the private sector is not devoid of problems within the sector itself.

In sum, there is still a debate over whether – or to what extent – the public and/or the private sector should provide utilities. This is further complicated by the possible roles of other actors such as NGOs and low-income communities, which have been noted in previous sections of this chapter. This leads us to the concept of a pluralist approach, already explained elsewhere in this book. Similarly to the case of housing provision, in each specific locality and time where a given type of utility is in need, it is important to identify and take into consideration the entire structure of provision and the interactions of the relevant interest groups and agents involved in the various sub-markets and forms of provision.

5.6   CSR and urban utilities

Having considered the situation of utilities in developing countries, the main question for us is what contribution corporate social responsibility of private firms can make. What is striking in the previous analysis is that, in spite of large-scale involvement of both small and large private firms in utility provision none of these were undertaken as part of CSR. Rather they were all carried out as formal or informal core business activity or as auxiliary provision to facilitate their core activities due to the unreliability of the main utilities.

In fact, the same debate on housing provision in developing countries also applies to utilities since in terms of human settlements the two are intrinsically linked together. In the same manner that informal sub-dividers provide housing on their plots for sale in the informal housing markets they also provide a basic level of utilities including access roads, local sewerage or lined individual sanitation wells and in some cases even negotiate connections to the main water and electricity lines through their contacts with local municipalities as in Pakistan and Thailand (Keivani and Werna, 2001a). Similarly we can also note that where major private firms have embarked on large scale housing provision for their employees they have inevitably had to provide extensive utilities as part of the broader package. Again we have already noted examples of company towns in a range of countries from Abadan in Iran during the 1950s to Bangkok and Shenzen today. To this we can also add major mining towns such as Ndola and Kitwe in the Zambian Copper belt where prior to the privatisation programme of the early 1990s the mines had in fact assumed a certain measure of quasi- municipal functions. Many of these functions particularly provision of housing and utilities are still being carried out by the international conglomerates that have bought the mines in respect of their employees. However, as in housing, none of these activities can be seen within the corporate social responsibility paradigm since they are all an essential part of either the direct or indirect business activities of the firms concerned. There are indeed cases of CSR in supply of utilities in urban areas. But sound analysis of such cases is still lacking.

Here we shall look at the role of private firms from a fresh perspective to consider the potential of their CSR activities in contributing to utility provision. This is in line with our overall approach in advocating pluralism to use all available resources for contributing to improving urban utility provision and at the same time providing a fresh angle to the topic of public-private partnerships that have been widely advocated.

5.7 Case studies

Two main cases are examined in this section. The first case concerns the work of Água e Cidade. This organisation was first noted in the Construction Chapter for its role in housing provision. However, as discussed in such a chapter, most of the activities of the organisation are related to water – and to some extent also to sewerage.

The second case examines the CSR activity of Davao Light and Power Company. This case provides an exemplary partnership arrangement between a local government and the only power utility company for the city of Davao to initiate a comprehensive street lighting programme that involved different levels of city government from local barangays to the metropolitan level as well as local community actors. This case also highlights the importance of street lighting for enhancing the city economy through increasing perceptions of security leading to increased tourism and local trade and business activities.

5.7.1 Água e Cidade, Brazil

We have already discussed the formation of Água e Cidade in the Construction Chapter. As also noted, Água e Cidade supports actions in four programme areas that are subdivided into various projects:

- Our Water
- Water and Environment Management

- Healthy and Sustainable Cities
- Living Waters

Here we will focus on the first three programmes. The fourth programme, in what concerns utilities, focuses on water and sanitation in housing units. However, all the information about utilities is intertwined with the information on housing, already presented in Chapter 4.

The first two programmes could in fact be considered as part of the broader urban sustainability agenda. However, they are focused on urban water management, particularly in terms of changing consumer behaviour towards more rational use of water and therefore demand management through educational and cultural initiatives. This is an important aspect that is in fact largely missing from the debate on urban water discussion in developing countries, perhaps since the main concern is dealing with such a huge shortage of supply and physical leakages from the system that consumer demand behaviour is pushed in to a secondary position. The third programme focuses on utility provision in general to make housing estates and neighbourhoods more habitable for their residents.

5.7.1.1 Our water programme

This programme teaches primary school students to use water rationally. It was developed primarily in Joinville in the state of Santa Catarina from 1997 to 2001 to improve methodology, check costs and overcome logistical difficulties so that the programme could be implemented in other Brazilian cities.

Throughout this experiment, the programme had the financial support of the Secretary of Education and two companies: TIGRE S/A and DOCOL Metais Sanitários Ltda respectively manufacturing plastic pipes and metal toilet works.

The companies DOCOL and TIGRE have their origins in the city of Joinville and have established a strong identity with the local community. Both companies are very much involved in community development programmes and are well recognised by the community as CSR – Corporate Social Responsible. DOCOL Sanitary Metals Ltd. was founded in 1956 and currently has over 800 employees. TIGRE S/A was founded in 1941 and currently has more than 1200 employees. This programme comprises four projects. These are:

Project for Teachers' Continuous Development

This project sponsors courses for elementary and high school teachers so that they can act as trained community agents and water volunteers working together with the school community.

Table 5.4 Community involvement

1998/2001
Water volunteers
450 school teachers and directors (enabled and mobilized)
165 schools involved
22.000 Students involved and benefited

Projects for the Production of Educational and Institutional Materials

These projects produce didactic and pedagogical materials to be used in the classroom by students and teachers.

Six sets of comic books (magazines) in a total of 30,000 copies of each issue were printed for 4th and 5th grade students from public and private schools.

Project for Visits and Excursions to Research Laboratories and Water Treatment Plants

- Offer the teachers some practical ideas and assistance for their teaching.
- Programme visits to research laboratories and classes in water treatment plants.
- Perform field activities so that high school students can apply their learning to practical situations.

Special Exhibitions (Fairs) about Water

This project helped to motivate schools to show the work developed during the school year in a big annual fair promoting the integration of actions developed and the sharing of experience.

5.7.1.2 *Water and environment management programme*

With the help of the water volunteers who coordinate the actions and assess the results, this programme mobilises and promotes awareness among businesses and industries, service companies, unions and other institutions (hospitals, schools, hotels, commercial buildings, public service agencies, shopping centres).

The Water and Environment Management Programme adopted a methodology that defined indicators to evaluate and quantify the commitment level of each organisation in the rational use of water and the preservation of the environment.

The organisations that participate in this programme become supporting partners of Água e Cidade.

In this programme, Água e Cidade had the assistance of supporting private partners DECA, DOCOL and TIGRE. The three companies' core business areas are related to water: Tigre S/A Tubos e Conexões was a pioneer in Brazil in implementing plastic pipes and accessories. DOCOL Metais Sanitários Ltda is well known in Brazil and abroad and manufac-

Table 5.5 Water volunteers

Water and environment managers – water volunteers		
2001		
393 water managers	São Paulo/SP (2000)	25
Mairiporã/SP		40
São Paulo – CTCC/USP		44
Cachoeira do Itapemirim/ES		41
São Paulo – CTCC/USP		21
Curitiba – PUCPR (two courses)		93
Campinas – Unicamp/SP		33
Joinville/SC – Centro DOCOL		50
Cachoeira do Itapemirim/ES		46
2002		
653 water managers	Joinville: SC – Centro DOCOL	49
Recife: PE – FECOMÉRCIO		42
Maceió : AL – TRIKEM		70
Curitiba: PR – PUC PR		86
Brasília: DF – CAIXA		25
Vitória: ES – CEPEMAR		20
Rio Claro: SP – TIGRE S/A		39
Brasília: DF – U. Católica Brasília		50
Jaraguá do Sul: SC – WEG		47
Fortaleza: CE		30
Goiânia: GO		53
Porto Alegre: RS		49
Rio de Janeiro: RJ – Firjan		37
Brasília: DF – Ministério da Defesa		56
Total of water managers trained and registered		**1,046**

tures exclusively toilet metalwork objects. DECA is the Brazilian leader in the toilet metalwork market. Their direct involvement with the theme of water gives them a natural interest in valuing and promoting the discussion of water quality.

Each organisation selects at least one person who will be a water volunteer to be qualified, certified and accredited by Água e Cidade as a 'business manager of the water and of the environment' (see Table 5.5).

Award Água e Cidade Project
This project is one of the ways that Água e Cidade provides recognition to organisations that seek to increase the level of awareness about the need for more rational use of water. Once a year, a nationwide evaluation of the organisations is performed and the best practices are selected.

In 2000 the following organisations were selected:

- Operational centre for TIGRE in Rio Claro,
- Industrial kitchen of SABESP headquarters in São Paulo,
- Galvan plastic section of DOCOL III in Joinville.

In 2001, the following organisation was selected:

- DECA-HYDRA metalwork factory in São Paulo.

Figure 5.3   1.5 million people on 1 May 2001

5.7.1.3 Healthy and sustainable cities programme

This programme aims to mobilise Brazilians and make them aware of the need for more rational use of water resources and the preservation of urban rivers, as well as the need to develop and improve systems for the collection and treatment of domestic sewage.

Água e Cidade develops and provides instruments for management, legal, technological, economical, international, educational and social actions that will make it possible to qualify people and organisations and support social demands.

The Healthy and Sustainable Cities Programme, in partnership with CEDIPLAC Solutions for Human Habitat in São Paulo, also has the support of TIGRE, Solvay, a chemical and pharmaceutical group and Braskem, the largest Latin American petroleum company. This programme is the most important activity for us in terms of its direct impact on utility provision. It comprises seven projects. These are:

Communication in Sanitation Project

This project, through a list of signatures from urban residents (some 800,000 signatures were gathered from 5,513 cities) has the objective of sensitising the media and society in relation to sanitation and about the need for universality of water and sewage systems.

Sanitation Dossier Project

This project documented the present situation of sanitation in Brazil as well as possible solutions to be implemented. In each local authority the mayor received a list of signatures collected in that town with demands and recommendations. This project encouraged local authorities to include sanitation in their plans, particularly the collection, transportation, treatment and disposal of sewage.

Website Project: www.esgotoevida.org.br

This project encourages the use of electronic resources to mobilise society and make people aware of the importance of sanitation.

Management Project: Indicators of Local Healthy Environment

This project was developed in partnership with FNU – Federação Nacional dos Urbanitários (National Urban Federation).

Studies were carried out to show how individual experiences were adapted and whether proposals were adequate to seek out indicators that may be obtained from 'the bottom to the top', in other words, with the direct participation of the whole society.

Institutional Project: Instruments for the Legislation and Regulation of Basic Sanitation – Hydrological Basins
Studies, projects and actions undertaken to understand and advertise legislation, regulations, technical procedures, codes for practices and prioritising systems for the management of hydrological basins. The goal was to contribute to the solution of problems, as well as to the development of social awareness, focusing on the use of water in sanitation.

Technological Project: Integrated and Innovative Solutions
Studies, projects and actions to develop technology for the problems of sewage, by implementing and maintaining the methodology of the 'System 100 per cent' that was specifically developed by CEDIPLAC, with technologies of operation and maintenance.

Social Project: Construction of Healthy and Sustainable Districts and Condominiums
This project has already been presented in Chapter 4, as it includes not only utilities but also housing.

5.7.1.4 Summing-up

As noted in the Construction chapter, the key lesson of Água e Cidade is in the effective role of a well-structured organisation in bringing together different stakeholders from the public, private and community sectors to implement a comprehensive programme for water conservation and utility provision (also including housing in some specific projects). This approach in partnership building is now being replicated in other Brazilian cities.

5.7.2 Davao Light and Power Corporation, Philippines

Davao Light and Power Company is a power distribution company exclusively serving Davao City and the municipalities of Carmen, Dujali, and Sto. Tomas as well as Panabo City in Davao del Norte. The company has a regular workforce of about 380 persons, and hires a sizeable number of non-regular staff. As of 2000, DLPC's State customers numbered 225. Residential customers were about 161,430, with a total consumption of about 26,285,376 kwH and approximately over 16% coming from outside Davao City.

Davao City, known as the largest city in the world in terms of land area (2,440sq./kms.), has a diverse topography ranging from urban cityscape to mountains and forest areas. Davao City has 180 barangays and eleven political districts, and the City Proper itself covers less than 10% of the whole city. The population is roughly 1.2 million people or a population density of 491 persons/sq. km., which is a far cry from Metro Manila's seven million population.

Despite the relatively low crime rate, 7.37 cases per 100,000 as of 2000, the reputation of this city has been marred by the general image of Southern Philippines as a dangerous place beset with insurgency, mistrust between Christian and Muslim population as well as those committed by purely lawless elements who took advantage of the decades old Moro-Christian conflict. As a seeming hotbed of violent upheavals during the insurgency years, economic activity in the city was sluggish. Poverty was rampant and there were very limited economic options for the people. For businesses that bravely chose to remain in the area, chances for expansion were poor and the cost of ensuring security of life and property directly affected the bottom line. Poor infrastructure in terms of roads, power and communications outside Davao City's more urban centre strongly contributed to the paralysis felt by both business and communities alike.

The perceived poor reputation of the city not only directly affected the Davao Light and Power Company in terms of narrowing its own investor pool, but also limited potential revenue growth due to risk-fearing investors. Essentially, DLPC's client base was largely residential, clearly showing the strong need for good community relations by the company.

The small municipal revenues obtained from a relatively meagre Davao City income was not enough to address all issues related to peace and order (e.g. infrastructure, police services upgrade, etc.). According to the Police Department, projecting a sense of security was needed as well which could very simply be answered by lighting up identified security-critical places. In 1993 the City Government started conceptualising this innovative crime prevention and tourist attraction plan, settling on the installation of bright sodium bulbs as these were more durable than traditional fluorescent lamps and could be seen even during foggy nights. This became the seed for a partnership between DLPC and Davao City aimed at igniting a massive lighting programme that would extend to the remotest areas of the city.

5.7.2.1 The first spark...

In response to the city's call, the senior management of Davao Light started brainstorming on how the company could assist the city through the procurement of sodium lamps. In 1993, the acquisition cost of one complete sodium lamp assembly was PhP19,000.00 (US$678.57). In 1996 when the street lighting programme was started, Davao Light, in partnership with Florida Electric, was able to obtain brand new surplus sodium lamps that only cost PhP8,000.00 (US$285.71) per set. This was further discounted to half the price. With the supply of bulbs assured, the City Government through then Mayor Rodrigo Duterte and DLPC through Executive Vice President and Chief Operating Officer (COO) Alfonso Y. Aboitiz entered into a Memorandum of Agreement (MOA) on 28 November 1995. The City Government was primarily responsible for identifying the communities most in need of light.

Under the MOA, the company donated sodium lamp bulbs, brackets and assembly and a utility vehicle with a hydraulic basket for the use of the city for maintenance purposes. The company also agreed to donate additional bulbs for replacement purposes until the end of 1998, as well as provide technical assistance to the city for maintenance of equipment and consumables. The city became solely responsible for the distribution, installation, maintenance and replacement of all streetlights. The city was also responsible for all applications by the communities for streetlights and also for payments of the electricity charges. Finally, the city pledged to provide a weekly status report of installed streetlights to the Company.

The city identified as priority areas those barangays the crime rate of which were risky to locals and foreigners, namely the Agdao to R. Castillo and Quezon Boulevard areas which were just within the periphery of the city. "Recipient communities were also given responsibilities in order for them to feel that they are not just beneficiaries but stakeholders of the project as well," according to Vic Sumalinog, the Community Relations Officer of DLPC. Communities have to monitor and report defective units to their local leaders who have to report this to the city's street lighting staff, as well as maintain the units by trimming tree growth that could impede the light coverage. The community officials also have to implement security measures to ensure that bulbs would not be stolen.

5.7.2.2 Lit up a corner

In 1996, Brgy. 22C Piapi in Quezon Boulevard had the reputation of being one of the worst barangays in Davao City in terms of criminality.

Prior to the streetlighting programme it had a crime rate of 20% or 2 to 3 incidences every month, statistics at the police office disclosed. In the first three months of the installation of mass lighting in the said barangay, the crime rate went down to a 10% monthly average. The police looked at the light installation as a major factor in their increased capability to respond to call for policy assistance from residents in previously unlit areas.

DLPC's Legal Department and its Transmission & Distribution Division provided volunteer technical assistance such as negotiation and drafting of the MOA, initial installation of the bulbs and the training of Davao City staff in installation, repair and maintenance of the units. The company's Community Relations Department developed information dissemination and public education programme for the people's project awareness including TV, print and radio, which allowed not only the company but also the city to present prompt information regarding the streetlighting to the general public.

In 1996 alone, the street lighting programme installed over 1,400 sodium lamps in three phases and almost simultaneously. While the good majority was very happy about the illumination of the city in agricultural areas, farmers were less exuberant. Plants and crops located near the streetlights grew slowly. Department of Agriculture technicians said sodium light hampers the maturation process. On the advantage side, the activity generated direct employment as the project created a streetlighting unit in the City Government's employ. The local government also hired sub-contractors for related services. These positive results were felt within the first six months of the streetlighting programme, thus bolstering the resolve of the city and DLPC to implement the programme city-wide.

5.7.2.3 And the light grew brighter...

Due to the success of the programme, DLPC after the term of the MOA in 1998 continued the project under a new lighting plan developed in consultation with the City Government. Under this programme, barangay authorities could go to DLPC directly and apply for streetlight installations. Streetlighting served as the stepping stone for the electrification of a whole community, with the installation of primary and secondary lines, transformers, posts, wires and cables largely shouldered by DLPC upon the request of the barangay. Starting 1998, the company sees the street lighting project as an expression of its corporate social responsibility.

5.7.2.4 Darkness diminished

All communities that were recipients of the streetlighting programme reported good results. Officials of Tugbok, a district near the City Proper supporting 18 barangays, said that there were increased investments, including the location of large companies such as Vitarich (poultry company) and Purefoods (food manufacturing) that paid about PhP145,000 (US$2,900) per month in local taxes. Community enterprises sprung up along the lighted areas, and public transport services were extended from 7 P.M. to 3 A.M. Community activities such as sports during the evenings became possible and incidences of civil misbehaviour were reduced. Records at the Local Civil Registration Office, in fact, indicated a reduction in the birth rates of areas served by the street lighting project in the Tugbok Centre.

On the whole, most community stakeholders (i.e., barangay leaders, trade officials, city planning officers, police officers) said that the project contributed significantly to the overall safety of the city. These stakeholders attributed about 20% to 80% of the economic progress enjoyed by the relevant communities to the streetlighting project. It had its greatest impact on the tourism industry, as several communities were able to open up commerce, transport and recreation facilities until late into the night. According to Engr. Froilan Rigor of the Office of City Planning, the streetlighting programme helped facilitate the image of Davao as an international city with a nightlife that could be compared to Manila or Singapore.

5.7.2.5 Effects on the bottom-line

The company obtained a return on its investment, as payments by the city to the utility reached a high Php12 million ($342,857.14) per month in 1998. The City Government recovered additional costs from increased taxes it collected from new businesses that sprung up in the lighted areas.

5.7.2.6 Key lessons

As a community relations programme within a business proposition, the communities did not see themselves as beneficiaries but as customers. The communities recognised that the earlier donation of bulbs and light stands as well as associated labour were a community relations' activity of the company. But in general, people felt that the long-term goals of the company were commercial and therefore they considered themselves to be consumers, or communities/stakeholders with a higher stake. That is, they want to play more significant roles in the identification of areas where sodium lamps should be installed.

This gave both community and the company an even position based on mutual need and gain, albeit limited, as DLPC was still the sole utility serving this franchise area. The company saw the street lighting programme as an opportunity to remain competitive in its franchise area because of the newly enacted Electric Power Industry Reform Act of 2001, which deregulated the power industry. The company believes that its willingness to provide services even to the farthest corners of its franchise area indicated its commitment to its community/customers. The recent electrification of Paquibato District, about 70 kms. from the City Proper at the cost of PhP6 million (approx. US$120,000) is indicative of this commitment. This area can very well be considered as Davao's 'last frontier'. It used to be the haven of the local communist rebels or the New People's Army (NPA).

Perhaps the most important lesson from this case, however, is re-emphasising the benefits of CSR and partnership working to the bottom line of both the private and public stakeholders when this is carried out in an enlightened and comprehensive manner. This case also highlights the importance of direct involvement of the community groups and stakeholders as equal partners both to ensure full support for the activity and to instil a sense of community pride and achievement.

5.8 Conclusion

This chapter has shown that lack of utilities in developing countries is a major impediment to both wellbeing of urban citizens and economic development. The lower income groups, therefore, face dire conditions in their living environments having to pay for example many times the official prices for access to water through private vendors and living in unsanitary conditions and insufficient or non existent power supplies or street lighting in their areas of residence. The small firms, on the other hand, may well go out of business due to their inability to maintain regular and sustained production due to erratic power and water supplies.

In many cities, particularly sub-Saharan Africa and Asia the situation has progressively worsened since independence largely due to rapid urbanisation and inability of public utilities to maintain the existing networks due to lack of financial resources, mismanagement and policies that are often focused on maintaining subsidies to those already connected rather than expanding provision to new areas and at more realistic tariffs to allow proper maintenance.

As a result much of the international emphasis for addressing utility shortages in developing countries is focused on facilitating public private partnerships through different institutional mechanisms for encouraging and enabling greater private sector participation in different contractual roles either to maintain different aspects of networks or direct providers. Importantly, however, while the literature has also noted a limited role for NGO and community actors, there is silence on a role of private contribution through corporate social responsibility. The two case studies in this chapter, however, have shown that in fact CSR can potentially have a major role both at local neighbourhood and overall metropolitan level.

As noted in Chapter 4 on construction, the first case from Brazil shows the crucial role of an NGO (Água e Cidade) for bringing together different actors particularly harnessing the CSR capacities of private firm in partnership with public and community actors to create such an effective synergy that their programmes are now being copied across Brazil. This perhaps highlights the importance of viewing CSR not merely as the responsibility of individual firms but the need for developing a supportive institutional structure that not only encourages private firms to engage in CSR activities but also channels such an activity in a structured and synergetic format to achieve highly effective results not only at local but national scales.

The second case from the Davao Light and Power Corporation in the Philippines, on the other hand, is an exemplary story for successful public private partnership in provision of street lighting with incredible wide results that have major impacts on the wellbeing of citizens and supporting the local economy. While provision of street lighting may be technically and financially relatively less demanding than other utilities, this example nevertheless serves as a lesson for the win-win paradigm of CSR for both private, public and community sectors when a relatively small investment by a major private firm can make a huge difference. What are needed are an enlightened and progressive attitude from both the public and private authorities and an entrepreneurial acumen from both sides. On the local government side it is the ability to identify an effective role for the private firm and creating the necessary institutional framework for their involvement. On the private utility side it is the recognition that investing in the community is in fact investing in the firm's future.

6
Social Development

Austine Ng'ombe and Edmundo Werna

The main dimensions of sustainable development were discussed in Chapter 3. It was noted that sustainable development was originally given major international prominence by the United Nations' World Commission on Environment and Development (WCED) report, *Our Common Future* (WCED, 1987) which states that for any form of development to be sustainable there is need to take into account not only economic and environmental issues, but also the social dimension. Subsequent to this, the 1992 Rio Earth Summit provided the main policy direction with inclusion of environmental considerations into broader areas of policy decision-making.

Current practice though suggests that the main focus among development agencies, writers and policy makers in the urban context has been on economic and environmental issues while the social dimension has by and large remained a Cinderella factor in urban sustainability and wider discourses (Castillo et al., 2007; Bhalla and Lapeyre, 1997). The stringent requirement in many countries to comply with Environmental Impact Assessments when conceiving development projects illustrates this assertion. It is perhaps partly for this omission that despite collective international effort to eradicate extreme poverty as reflected in the Millennium Development Goals (MDGs), poverty has persisted, especially in developing nations (Mutter, 2006).

This chapter first charts the social dimension of development; and second, it echoes the need to (re)consider it as a key agenda item for urban development. The guiding concept in this discourse is CSR, which is herein recommended as an instrument that adds value for development. Social development is discussed in terms of education, employment, culture and health. Afterwards, for reasons explained throughout the chapter, it focuses on urban children, and subsequently provides case studies on this theme.

6.1 The concept and importance of social development

There have been numerous attempts to operationalise 'social development', but, as agreed by the World Bank (2004a) and De Haan (1999) this has not been an easy zone. To date 'social development' remains without a universally-accepted definition. However, a major reason is due to the concept being particularly context-driven (*ibid*). Organisations and individuals define the concept in accordance with their area of expertise or operation. According to the World Bank (*ibid*), 'social development' is all about being people-centred in development efforts. It defines the concept in terms of what it attempts to achieve:

> Social development transforms societies by understanding the social context of the country as well as the needs and priorities of poor people. Poor people's own voices tell us that poverty is more than low income – it is also about vulnerability, exclusion and isolation, poor governance, and powerlessness. People's priorities and experiences are affected by such variables as gender, social exclusion, intra-household allocation of resources, incidence of crime and violence, geographical location, access to networks of support, and relations with those in power. By capturing different dimensions of poverty, a multidisciplinary approach can deepen our understanding of poverty and the lives of the poor.

Stren and Polese (2000) have defined social development as "development that is compatible with the harmonious evolution of civil society, fostering an environment conducive to the compatible cohabitation of culturally and socially diverse groups while at the same time encouraging social integration, with improvements in the quality of life for all segments of the population."

The above, and indeed other definitions embrace a common theme, which in the main is that social development is all about being people centred, taking into account political and cultural, but, according to Cheney *et al*. (2004), excluding the economic issues. Thus, the social dimension of development is about ensuring that basic conditions for human progress are met. At the most basic level, a social development model should promote equal access to services such as health, social protection schemes, education, employment, and justice, as well as the right to participation (*ibid*). This is in line with the World Bank's (2004a) proposed three crucial elements of social development: *inclusive societies, cohesive societies*, and *accountable institutions*. Inclusive implies a participatory approach while cohesiveness means people's ability to organise themselves for collective action in order to address common needs, overcome constraints, bridge social divides, and resolve differences amicably (*ibid*). Accountability, on the other hand, is about institutions that are transparent, responsive and which can serve the communities in an effective, efficient and fair manner. This is in agreement with Bhalla and Lapeyre's (1997) account of social development when they group its elements into three broad categories of 'citizenship rights', namely *civil* (freedom of expression, rule of law, or right to justice); *political* (right to participate in political processes like elections); and *socioeconomic* (personal security, equality of opportunity, right to minimum health care, education, employment and unemployment benefits). While the rights may be exercised especially in developed countries, they may not be enjoyed in totality in some countries.

Despite the focus on recent developments outlined above, the idea of social development is not new. In 1946, for instance, the United Nations Economic and Social Council (ECOSOC) established the 'Commission for Social Development' to spearhead social development discourses internationally. This was further supplemented by the establishment in 1963 of a specialist research entity within the United Nations system. The United Nations Research Institute for Social Development (UNRISD) was created specifically to study the social dimensions of problems affecting development (Wikipedia, 2008). However, it was not until the Copenhagen Summit in 1995 that the subject earned itself a meaningful global tag as a concept for public debate and increased research. At the Copenhagen Summit (commonly known as the World Summit for Social Development), the world leaders met to (re)emphasise the crucial role the concept plays in poverty alleviation. Arising from the summit, the world leaders adopted the Copenhagen Declaration, the Ten Commitments (listed below) and the Programme of Action (World Bank, 2004a, 2004b, 2004c). The Commitments are as outlined in Table 6.1.

Since the Copenhagen Summit, social development has gained prominence in research and policy circles, with some writers claiming that sustainable urban development is nothing else but essentially 'social' at its core (Devuyst *et al.*, 2001; Becker *et al.*, 1997, cited in Castillo *et al.*, 2007). Indeed the post-Copenhagen Summit has been characterised by many other efforts by organisations, institutions and governments to continue campaigning for people-centred development. The Millennium Development Declaration (2000) and, most

Table 6.1 The Copenhagen commitments

Commitment	Description
Enabling environment	To create an economic, political, social, cultural and legal environment that will enable people to achieve social development
Poverty eradication	To eradicate absolute poverty by a target date to be set by each country
Employment	To support full employment as a basic policy goal
Social integration	To promote social integration based on the enhancement and protection of all human rights
Gender equity	To achieve equality and equity between women and women
Basic services and promotion of culture	To attain universal and equitable access to education and primary health care
Development of Africa and the least developed nations	To accelerate the development of Africa and the least developed countries
Inclusion of social dimensions in structural adjustments	To ensure that SAPs include social development goals
Increasing resources for social development	To increase resources allocated to social development
Strengthening cooperation for social development	To strengthen cooperation for social development through the United Nations

Source: World Bank, 2004a.

recently, the Social Charter approved at the South Asian Association for Regional Cooperation meeting which was convened in January 2004 in Islamabad, Pakistan, illustrate the efforts. In parallel with this process, various international development agencies have the mandate to implement the Copenhagen Declaration. Although progress in this area has been limited (Mutter, 2006), some agencies (claim to) have actually tried to abide by the Declaration and have registered success stories (Sddirect, 2008). One such organisation is the World Bank, which we herein use as an exemplar to illustrate how social development practitioners can fulfill the Copenhagen Declaration.

In its effort to fulfill the Copenhagen commitments, the World Bank has identified specific priority areas which it pursues by using appropriate strategies. They include:

- increasing attention to social development in the institution's project lending, policy dialogue and development policy lending;
- listening to the poor and attacking poverty;
- social protection; community-driven development;
- participation and civic engagement;
- health; education; culture; and
- poverty reduction strategies.

The guiding principles that the World Bank has employed in order to realise these priority areas include:

- strengthening multistakeholder participation in development and monitoring of projects and macrostrategy documents like Poverty Reduction Strategy Papers (PRSPs);
- ensuring social development content in macro strategy documents;
- encouraging free standing country-level social analysis (of projects) to inform policy dialogue and strategies;
- promoting trade policies that foster transparency, innovation and entrepreneurship;
- facilitating poor people's empowerment by: promoting inclusive development and accountable institutions in which people have a voice; attacking corruption;
- supporting decentralisation, community-driven development, and gender equity; encouraging and supporting policies that tackle epidemics like HIV/AIDS;
- promoting policies that ensure efficient and financially viable pension systems to protect the aged; and
- supporting country-driven efforts to define and implement effective strategies to reduce poverty through PRSPs.

The World Bank further argues that economic growth is necessary but it is not sufficient to improve human wellbeing and reduce poverty in a sustainable manner (World Bank, 2004a). These assertions are based on research, which has shown that projects that incorporate social dimensions of development are more likely to have better outcomes, greater impact on institutional development, and are more likely to be sustainable than projects that do not address social dimensions (World

Bank, 2004a, 2004b, 2004c). In line with this realisation, and following Amartya Sen's comprehensive approach to poverty, the concept of poverty has been redefined to include not only economic but also social dimensions (Bhalla and Lapeyre, 1997). In this sense, social development is a key component of sustainable poverty reduction. Sen's approach to poverty calls for inclusion of social issues into poverty discourses, whilst realising the individuals' capabilities or opportunities to achieve valuable functions or states of being.

The World Bank has outlined four justifications for paying attention to social dimensions:

1. it improves project design through better understanding of 'the social';
2. it clarifies understanding of the potential impacts of the project;
3. it contributes to sustainability of the project; and
4. it improves relations with stakeholders/clients.

Joining the World Bank in illustrating the importance of social development is the Social Development Direct, a UK-based network of consultants on social development (Sddirect, 2008). On its website, the organisation provides an account of how the social dimension adds value to urban development. Assessing potential impacts of business is ethically important and makes business sense. This is because it can help avoid harmful social and economic impacts on local communities. Engaging local communities in early stages of the project also helps avoid expensive mistakes, leads to innovative and sustainable approaches and brings positive outcomes. Furthermore, culture needs understanding in order to determine programme or project impacts and possible interventions. This requires trained social development professionals who can offer insights into social contexts of projects, thereby enabling them to identify who can and cannot benefit from such development projects.

6.2 Social development in urban areas

As already noted, social development is a very broad concept. This section will present information on key issues in urban areas, namely education, health, employment and culture. Other issues often related to social development, such as housing and sanitation, overlap with key themes of urban development analysed in previous chapters, therefore they will not be repeated here.

First, regarding education, UNICEF (2007) reports that, despite overall growth in school enrolment, over 115 million children of primary age do not have access to basic education – encompassing both urban and rural areas. This is more so in developing countries where the case is even worse for girls. Girls normally drop out of school when they reach puberty so that they help out with household responsibilities or enhance (early) marriage prospects. Poor quality of education, high tuition fees and ubiquitous high levels of adult illiteracy are some of the noticeable indicators of problems that undermine achievement of the Education for All MDG (Millennium Development Goal) by 2015.

Although lack of proper education, and illiteracy in particular, are not specifically urban, they have specific and harmful effects in urban areas. To say the least, the access of the rural poor to basic needs is less dependent on one's ability to read and write – especially in subsistence societies. However, it is very difficult and sometimes even impossible for illiterate people to live in urban areas, because of the complexity of urban production and consumption patterns, noted in Chapter 2. Also, due to such complexity in urban life, it often is not enough just to know how to read and write. More robust education is needed, in order for instance to access proper jobs. There are still deep education deficits in urban areas, particularly in developing countries.

The second aspect analysed here is urban employment. Its importance derives from the fact that cities are the driving engine of national economies (Chapter 2). If urban residents are not properly employed, economic growth will come to a halt. Besides, it is common knowledge that lack of proper employment leads to poverty. Furthermore, literature states that such a problem leads to many other urban problems like street children, drug abuse, prostitution, etc.

The International Labour Office's (ILO, 2005) report *Global Employment Trends 2005* points out that there are 184 million people in the world who have no jobs. The number skyrockets to at least 1 billion if underemployed people are taken into account.

Over the next ten years, the ILO estimates that 500 million people will join the world's job markets, most of them young people in developing countries. They will join the 184 million unemployed and the 550 million working poor, all wanting to use their talents and abilities in a productive and gainful manner (International Labour Office (ILO) (2003) and International Labour Office (ILO) (2004)). Therefore, a large number of jobs have to be provided by 2014 simply to employ the new entrants.

In regard to the third aspect, urban health, as noted in Chapter 2, the urban poor face the 'worst of both worlds': while they still suffer health problems common to rural areas (such as infectious diseases and malnutrition), they also suffer problems which are particular to urban areas (chronic and psycho-social diseases). Unlike the rural setting where health services are (especially in developing countries) mainly provided at public health posts and clinics, urban health is distinguished by the prominence of for-profit private sector (Montgomery, 2008). Access to health services by the urban poor is thus limited by lack of resources. Whereas distance is the main barrier to health centres for many rural communities, the social, informational, and economic costs of access are the main barriers for their urban counterparts. The alternative health services for the urban poor are low quality services provided by less trained personnel at affordable fees. Others go to the extent of consulting traditional practitioners whose fee-paying systems are by-and-large negotiable. Even when they can initially afford a visit to the for-profit private provider, poor people abandon prescribed medication due to costs.

The final aspect to be mentioned here is urban culture. As UNV (2001) noted, the preservation of the cultural values of a society has a significant impact on development. Deterioration of tangible cultural assets (e.g., structures, sites, objects, books and archives) results in loss of heritage and identity, as does the disappearance of intangible cultural expression (e.g., music, language, folklore and crafts). A given community tends to have a greater stake in a development initiative when it relates to – or at least respects – the community's cultural foundations.

Cultural heritage also plays a very important role in reinforcing the pride of a community *vis-à-vis* the place where it lives. There is a social identification with a given city/town as a *place* (geographical entity): everybody within a local population *belongs* to the *same place*. Therefore, urban conservation enhances the social identification of the population with its city.

On the contrary, many development initiatives are wasted precisely because they overlook cultural foundations – exemplified by cases of vandalism in public infrastructure and buildings and the lack of use of public facilities. Therefore, it is imperative to preserve and reinstate the cultural dimension of urban settlements, and to reinforce the sense of pride that the citizens feel towards their built milieu.

However, cases of deterioration of cultural heritage still abound in cities and towns, particularly in developing countries. First, due to the impact of globalisation, many cities and towns have lost, or are losing, their specific cultural values. Second, this is also happening in developing countries due to the pressing need to focus on economic growth and livelihoods. Although cultural heritage would in the end reinforce both economic growth and livelihoods, more immediate problems often lead governments and people to ignore its added value for social development.

6.3 Urban children

The deficits in social development in urban areas noted before are particularly hard on children, whose fragility makes them more exposed than other sectors of society. Children bear the brunt of social problems that affect them in particular (such as lack of proper education, among others) together with those which affect their families and communities. Considering this, the case studies provided later in this chapter will focus on social development and children.

In their book *Children in the city: introducing new perspectives*, Christensen and O'Brien (2003) remind us that: "Children are now recognised not as passive players in the cities but active social and cultural actors and, as informants and participants in policy process." Furthermore, children have been a focus of urban development efforts, for instance by UNICEF and more recently since the conception of the MDGs and the United Nations Convention on the Rights of the Child (UNCRC) which documents critical issues or rights that are applicable only to children.

The remainder of this section will note specific problems faced by urban children, namely crime and violence, labour, drugs, housing and homelessness, and HIV/AIDS. Unless where age category is stated, 'child' in this chapter is intended to mean anybody under the age of 18 years as stated by UNICEF and the UNCRC.

First, as noted by UNV (2001), high rates of violence already constitute a crucial problem in many urban areas in developing countries, and these trends continue to spread to other cities and towns. The specific condition of urban violence is associated with urban features such as:

- **Intra-urban differentials:** cities and towns are relatively small geographical areas, which concentrate high disparities in income and standard of living. There is a growing body of research which shows how the day-to-day/constant cognitive perception of the poor as worse-off than other members of society generate behaviour patterns which lead to violence and crime (see, for instance, Werna, 2000 for a review).

- **Lack of social-cultural/family bonds:** this already noted problem also has an effect on violence and crime (e.g. adolescents and young adults who grow up without proper family and communitarian support).
- **Lack of social control:** the fact that everyone virtually knows everyone else in a given rural village constitutes a deterrent to violent and criminal behaviour, as the culprit is easily identifiable. This is not the case in urban settlements, due to their much larger populations.
- **Economic vulnerability:** as noted before, the urban poor are often extremely vulnerable to high prices and changes in income; and they do not have the option to fall back to an agrarian support system. Therefore, even when a given low-income individual (or group) is not affected by the above factors, she/he (they) may resort to crime and violence to make a living – although, it is important to say, crime and violence are not restricted to poor people.

The scale of urban crime and violence has led UN-Habitat to implement a specific programme to address such issues, named *Safer Cities*. There is ample evidence that young people have been drawn to urban crime and violence, including large numbers of teenagers. There is also evidence of significant numbers of pre-adolescents involved in crime. And those who are not involved are often affected, either directly and/or through what happens with their families and communities, particularly in poor areas. Furthermore, children and teenagers who become involved in crime and violence are definitely affected, as their involvement closes many or all doors to their integration into society as adults.

With regard to child labour, ILO (2006) notes that today, with rapid urbanisation, rising poverty, and growing number of children orphaned by the HIV/AIDS epidemic, young people are increasingly vulnerable to exploitation in illegal, underground and hazardous activities. In addition to these direct impacts, child labour undermines educational opportunities for children making it difficult for them to find decent and productive work later in life. The ILO estimates that in 2000 there were about 186 million child workers under the age of 15, with about 110 million under the age of 12 (ILO, 2006).

Children working in cities tend to come from poor families. They work mainly in manufacturing, trade and domestic service. In all three sectors, children work long hours for low wages, and when traditional social regulation (e.g. apprenticeship) is not operational, they are completely without protection. On the streets, or on waste dumps which are home and workplace for so many, they are visible sorting rubbish, carrying loads and surviving any way they can. Girls, who are mainly in domestic service, are exposed to physical, psychological or sexual abuse from their employers.

With regard to drug abuse, UNV (2001) also notes that cities and towns concentrate the largest portion of such problems in developing countries, and the connection with urbanisation derives from the following:

- **Behavioural pre-conditions** for drug-taking in sizeable shares of the urban population due to lack of socio-cultural/family bonds and livelihood pressures (noted before);
- **Large supply of drugs** induced by the existence of a large concentration of people and therefore of large potential markets – broader/easier access to drug supply;
- **Anonymity and lack of social control** – which makes things easier both for the drug dealers and takers.

There is ample evidence and there is now common knowledge that drug abuse is a widespread problem among teenagers. A large number of pre-adolescents are also caught up in such a problem. This affects their mental health, schooling and social behaviour, seriously hampering their future prospects.

Another critical problem relates to street children and homelessness. There are different types of street children, whose definitions by UNICEF and reviewed in Werna *et al.* (1999) are still used: (i) children on the streets, who maintain good family contact, often returning home at night; (ii) children who remain in contact with their families, but, because of poverty, overcrowding or sexual or physical abuse within the family, spend some nights or most days on the streets; (iii) children who are detached from their families and live in temporary shelters, such as abandoned houses and other buildings, hostels, refugees' shelters; and (iv) children who are in institutional care, who have come from a situation of homelessness and are at risk of returning to a homeless existence.

According to estimates from the 1990s, the number of street children worldwide is in the range of tens of millions, being the overwhelming majority in developing countries (Werna *et al.*, 1999). Since then, the situation has hardly improved (Holmgren *et al.*, 2004; Ennew and Swart-Kruger, 2003). A variety of facts have led children away from home, including for example family breakdown, poverty, manmade and natural disasters, abuse, exploitation by adults, among others.

In addition, many children who are not caught up in the above situations also end up in the streets because their families are homeless themselves. The consequences of living in the streets and being exposed to all sorts of natural and urban risks are well known and need not be repeated here.

The final problem noted here is HIV/AIDS. The widespread prevalence of the pandemic is currently a major problem in developing countries. According to the *2006 report on the global AIDS epidemic*, 33.2 million people in the world live with HIV/AIDS. As can be seen from Figure 6.1, developing countries in general and sub-Sahara Africa in particular are the most hit regions. Sub-Sahara Africa alone accounts for 30% of all the world HIV/AIDS deaths (UNAIDS, 2006, 2007).

Children are affected as many have become orphans and/or are born with the disease, which largely affect urban areas as they lack the stronger social norms of sexual behaviour prevalent in rural communities. It is also in urban areas where another cause of HIV/AIDS – intravenous drug abuse – prevails. UNICEF (2007) reports that about 11.5%

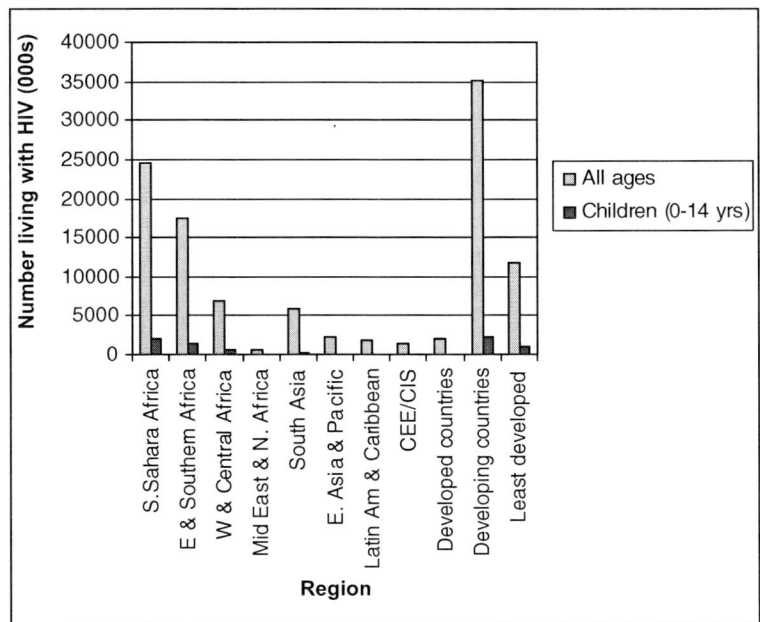

Figure 6.1 Number of people living with HIV by region
Source: UNICEF, 2007.

of the world orphans (0–17 year olds) were orphaned by AIDS in 2005, representing about 15 million children, out of which, 12 million were in sub-Sahara Africa.

6.4 CSR and social development

Combating the social problems that affect urban children requires alternative or scaling up of existing efforts. Existing global measures (e.g. MDGs, UNCRC, etc) are useful but not enough to respond to the challenges facing children in developing countries. International policy initiatives for children have produced limited success in terms of bringing down rates of urban children that are trapped by a host of social problems mentioned previously. In particular, private companies can play a crucial role in this cause. For example, business can use its purchasing power and influence to lobby for more ethically-made products to end child labour. The UK's Ethical Trading Initiative (ETI) is one such an alliance of companies that is committed to improve labour standards in supply chains, one of their objectives being to tackle child labour. Elsewhere, companies like the American Chocolate Manufacturers Association have pioneered causes that promote development of urban children. Companies can also campaign for ethical purchasing where only products with no potential harm to urban children are promoted. These are a few possibilities, among others. The next section provides further illustrations through a set of case studies.

6.5 Case studies

6.5.1 The African Oxygen (Pty) Ltd., South Africa

African Oxygen (Afrox) has been running initiatives that involve communities since 1995. The case study illustrates the different roles employees can play in fostering CSR by demonstrating commitment towards enhancing relationship between them and disadvantaged children in their 'adopted homes'. The adopted homes are basically institutions that take care of disadvantaged children e.g. childcare homes, orphanages, and centres for abused and abandoned children. This programme is executed in areas where Afrox has hospitals. The project encompasses the annual *Bumbanani Day*, a day when Afrox members of staff celebrate their ongoing relationship with their adopted homes by entertaining the underprivileged children. The day is characterised by fun, laughter and games. Because of total commitment from members of staff, the Afrox project has emerged as one of the best employee involvement exercises in the country, moving away from being a company-driven activity to one initiated by employees.

Afrox was established in 1927. The company employs a total of about 16,000 members of staff and it specialises in gases, welding products and healthcare. It has a market capitalisation of well over 4.5 billion Rands (about US$570 million), with 325 million shares in circulation. Of these, 55% are held by the British Oxygen Company Group plc (BOC). In 2001, the company's revenues were R5.2 billion (US$650,000) (i.e. up by 11%) and realised a net profit of R363.9 million (US$45,000), out of which 0.28% was spent on the community involvement programme.

6.5.1.1   Community involvement

The community involvement programme was initiated in 1995 by Royden Vice, the then chairman of Afrox. The chairman introduced the programme not only as a response to the government's call but also as a means to provide employees with an opportunity to do something in communities where Afrox was operating. One million Rands (about US$125,000) was allocated by management for this cause. Afrox offices were asked to identify homes, organisations or institutions dealing with underprivileged children that they would like to 'adopt' and support. Afrox employees then formed working committees which would spearhead the Community Involvement Process (CIP). Following preset criteria, new homes could be selected after which a business proposal could be designed and sent to the central CIP office for funding.

Although the programme was initially received with a mix of scepticism among employees, it gained support over time. The initial uptake of projects was only 15 in the first year of operation. The number grew to 113 projects seven years later and by 2003, the programme had supported over 200 projects countrywide. Genuine sense of satisfaction among employees is said to be the reason for the success of the programme. By 2003, the programme was supporting 54 orphanages, 25 schools or aftercare facilities, 16 centres for children living with HIV/AIDS, 15 centres for mentally-disabled children, eight shelters for street children and two hospital children wards.

6.5.1.2   Benefits to the company

The programme has helped build staff loyalty and improved relations among them. The CIP has helped to break down the traditional organisational hierarchies and barriers. Furthermore, in the field, all the employees are equal and are unified by the desire to achieve a common goal. From the company point of view, diversity management is one area that Afrox has enormously benefited from. The fact that the programme runs not only in South Africa, but also in other countries like Mozambique, Namibia, Malawi, Kenya, etc, has provided the company with an opportunity to manage employees who have been exposed to different cultures. The company also discovers some employees' abilities and skills out of their involvement in CIP. This could not be possible if the staff were not involved in the programme.

6.5.1.3 Key lessons

As already noted in this book, copious amount of literature has outlined a number of advantages of being CSR-compliant. In particular, employee involvement in CSR is upheld as a positive good. The general understanding is that employee involvement benefits the employees themselves, the company and the hosting communities. As discussed in Chapter 1, such benefits include enhanced employee skills and motivation, building personal networks, sustenance of the company's 'license to operate', increased employee teamwork, and promotion of loyalty and job satisfaction. Furthermore, good CSR policy would attract and retain employees (Monaghan, 2002; Hall, 1988; UNV, 2001). Similar lessons can be learnt from a different case study, which follows.

6.5.2 The Learner School City, Brazil

The Learner School City (LSC) is a demonstration of how a civil society organisation engages the business community to access resources in order to sustain itself. The in-depth research carried out about this case study (New Academy of Business-UNV, 2004) highlights that volunteerism within the community was also a major aspect of the initiative.

Established in 1997 and with a total of about 150 members of staff, Learner School City is an NGO that specialises in the development and implementation of educational projects. The aim is mainly to disseminate new knowledge and teaching methodologies in order to contribute to the educational system. The organisation invests not only in programmes that are related to education; it also invests in arts, citizenship and work. The organisation aims to continue influencing the country's education system and hopes to have its education model accepted in the official system. The LSC owes its success to a diverse group of participants which includes educators, professionals from different areas, trainees, as well as a number of sponsors and supporters. The organisation's operational base is in the west zone and central region of the city of São Paulo. Its annual revenue is in the range of US$2 million.

6.5.2.1 Institutional history

The LSC was introduced in the book *Aprendiz do Futuro* (The Future Learner) which was published in 1997 by the president, creator and founder of the organisation, Gilberto Dimenstein. Since its inception, the LSC has grown to be the national model and reference in terms of educational methodologies. This is done by providing a new tool for organised civil society, creating discussions and debates about education. The objectives of the LSC educational model include:

- Gathering resources that guarantee the organisation's sustainability,
- Disseminating methodologies using educational experimental models,
- Developing activities with children and teenagers who participate in the programme.

6.5.2.2 How does LSC construct partnership with civil society?

Many organisations seek to be associated with the LSC brand 'Aprendiz' (Learner). In addition, the organisations cherish being associated with the founder of the LSC, Gilberto Dimenstein. This is because Gilberto is a well known figure not only nationally but also internationally. Thus, the success of the LSC can partly be attributed to Gilberto's facilitator's role in the construction of partnerships with the organisation's sponsors and supporters. Many of the LSC's sponsors (e.g. the Bank Boston Foundation) offer support for alliance activities that are in line with the ideas, values and culture of a network of organisations that support it. The main motivation for organisations to establish partnerships with LSC include creation of better company image, tax benefits and the solidarity and humanitarian spirit that emerges from the partnerships. As already noted, New Academy of Business-UNV (2004) stressed that volunteerism in the community (mutual-self help) was also a major aspect of the initiative – although unfortunately this publication did not provide in-depth data on this.

6.5.2.3 The CSR initiatives

While initiatives such as the Café Aprendiz (the Learner Café), Agencia Aprendiz (Learner Agency) and the Learner Cyber Café were mainly established as income generating activities for LSC, they are also examples of how the NGO contributes towards its objective of educating children. The Learner Café, for instance, also facilitates access for students to computers and computer programmes and the creation of new learning spaces, thereby demonstrating that knowledge dissemination can be done even outside the classroom setting. But perhaps one of the most noticeable direct initiatives by LSC is the 100 Walls Project. The arts-related project involved transforming grey, lifeless and visually polluted areas that had an excessive amount of disorganisation and unfocused publicity. After the 100 Walls Project, these areas are now back to life. They are attractive, enjoyable and interesting not only to the residents of the neighbourhood (Vila Madalena) but also to all the visitors.

6.5.2.4 Key lessons

The success of the LSC programme is a result of commitment from the employees of the organisation, and, most importantly, the effective role of the leader with visibility. To this end, LSC is considered as an exemplar of an NGO (with private sector sponsorship) that has contributed enormously towards children's education in Brazil.

6.5.3 Aluminium company[1], Ghana

The Aluminium Company was established in 1971. The company was a product of Kwame Nkrumah's dream of driving Ghana's economic growth through industrial development driven by electricity. With its rated annual capacity of 200,000 tons, the Ghana aluminium company is part-owned by an American-based aluminium corporation. The company obtains electric power from a local dam while a Jamaican company and third parties supply alumina, the material for producing aluminium. Most (90%) of its production is shipped to Europe, while 10% is sold out locally. About 99% of the company's 1,200 workforce is Ghanaian.

The drivers of the company's CSR initiatives have direct links to the manner in which it was conceived. This dates back to 1957 when Ghana became independent. Kwame Nkrumah's immediate post-independence dream was to kick-start industrial development through electrification. Thus the hydroelectric Volta River Project (VRP) was initiated, with the first phase of damming of the river at Akosombo, getting completed in

---

[1]This company requested not to have its name disclosed.

1965. The total cost of the dam was US$196 million in 1960. Having obtained 50% funding from other sources, Ghana needed to fund the remaining 50% of the cost. Of this, US$47 million was provided by the World Bank as loan. In order to access the loan, Ghana was subjected to very stringent conditionalities, one of which was to find a customer who would guarantee sufficient use of electricity in order to repay the loan. The parent American aluminium company was thus negotiated into the investment. But the parent company subjected Ghana to more conditionalities. Despite the abundance of bauxite in the country, the parent company opted to import the material cheaply from the Caribbean. Furthermore, electricity was offered to the parent company at comparatively cheaper price in order to attract the company to put up the investment. Thus Ghana accepted an unfair bargain just to get the dam up fast and have a buyer for its electricity to justify the costs. Given that the company itself uses 60% of the generated power, it turned out that the price the company pays for power does not bear a direct relation to the cost of producing and transmitting the power to the country. The cost of the company's operation to the country far outweighs its social contributions by a cost/benefit ratio of 10:1.

6.5.3.1   CSR initiatives

It is argued that the company's CSR initiatives are a way of compensating Ghana for the economic costs of its operations in the country. However, the company itself argues that its CSR initiatives are guided by the philosophy of helping the community to help themselves. It is felt that this will help to earn its the license to operate because the company will be operating in a community where there is social stability and peace.

The CSR initiatives of the company include a host of activities. In line with the focus of this chapter, only the initiatives that are social in nature are discussed, with attention to children.

a) Company Trust Fund: Through its Trust Fund, the Aluminium Company makes the largest charitable donation in the country. These contributions have amounted to about US$600,000 per annum since the company's inception. This contribution is more than ten times that of the second largest trust fund in the country. Between 1971 and 2001, the fund had contributed some US$41 million to the social, cultural and economic development of Ghana, including purchasing of buses, scientific equipment and textbooks for educational institutions.

b) Miscellaneous CSR contributions: In addition to the Trust Fund stated above, the company makes miscellaneous contributions to the promotion of juvenile sports and the development of tertiary education in the city of Tema, which is the location of its plant. The social contributions include:

- a total of US$140,000 towards the promotion and development of soccer in secondary schools through kit donations and sponsorships;
- through the institution of the Annual University awards, the company has contributed over US$150,000 to three premier universities in Ghana since 1995. This is intended for research and facility upgrades;
- annual scholarships for deserving children of natives of Tema, as well as Newton and Kpone, the communities adjoining the plant. The scholarships are for education in government-approved high schools of the children/parents' choice.

As a way of promoting transparency and ensuring support and smooth running of these initiatives, various stakeholders participate in the CSR agenda. The key players are the Government of Ghana, the Tema Municipal Assembly and the Ghana Education Service.

6.5.3.2 Key lessons

The approach the company has adopted in implementing its CSR initiatives has been criticised in some quarters. For instance, the company is criticised for spreading some CSR activities throughout the country (beyond the specific ones to Tema and surroundings, noted before). This stance, it is argued, is not beneficial to the company's immediate neighbour, where the plant is located – a position which has a connection to the specific theme of this book. Businesses should focus on the communities within geographical areas of their operations (and spheres of influence). Consideration of the whole country as a beneficiary would make it difficult for the company to reach tangible results. Furthermore, the company's CSR efforts are diluted by its failure to conduct social responsibility audits. These are important in order for the company to establish whether or not it is meeting its predetermined objectives. Criticisms notwithstanding, the Aluminium Company deserves commendation in its efforts to embark in social CSR initiatives that support children and promote social cohesiveness within communities In parallel, it has earned the company its much-needed licence to operate. There is still room for improvement, however.

6.5.4 The Schlumberger case study, Nigeria

Schlumberger Oil Services is the world's largest oilfield service provider. It is also the leading supplier of technological services and solutions to the international petroleum industry, with operations spanning over 100 countries where it provides a range of services, including well services, drilling, among others. The company was established in 1927 by brothers Marcel and Conrad Schlumberger. It has been operating in Nigeria since 1948. The focus of its CSR activities are youth and children, mainly related to developing science and technology as a driver of growth and development.

6.5.4.1 *CSR initiatives*

While the company is involved in a wide range of CSR initiatives (e.g. the University of Ibadan-Schlumberger Learning Centre), we focus on the Schlumberger Excellence in Educational Development (SEED) initiative, in line with the major theme of this chapter.

6.5.4.2 *The SEED initiative*

SEED is generally an initiative that is implemented in partnership with NGOs, primary and secondary schools. The programme provides educational services to 8–18 year olds. In Nigeria, SEED has partnered with ANPEZ Centre for Environment and Development (ACFED) to initiate a project in the city of Port Harcourt. The project was commissioned in 2001. Its aim was to deliver computer literacy to children. In addition, the project seeks to connect the local children to the internet, thereby promoting the sharing of experiences with other more privileged children and users around the globe. In particular, Schlumberger provided two-year internet connectivity at the cost of US$8,000 per annum. Furthermore, the company provided the centre with 12 computers, two printers, a projector, furniture, air conditioners, a generator and two years office rent. According to the company the project costed about 20 million Naira (about US$170,000). SEED enables ACFED to provide free computer and internet access to schools, students and community youths who visit the centre. It also connects the children to Science World, a website that promotes study of science among school children.

6.5.4.3 *Key lessons: sustainability*

The sustainability of the SEED project with ACFED and other initiatives will be determined by issues such as ownership and independence as well as funding and business planning. The sustainability of the activities may be limited by heavy reliance on Schlumberger's financial goodwill. Continuity of the SEED initiative with ACFED will be threatened if the latter cannot generate income to sustain itself including payment of rent and internet connectivity charges after Schlumberger is gone. A solution may be for Schlumberger to assist ACFED to develop a commercial business plan.

6.6 Conclusion

Social development in urban settings remains a major challenge. As noted in Chapter 3, environmental and economic issues have taken precedence over 'the social' in urban contexts. Moreover, as the present chapter has explained, social development encompasses a broad range of issues, from education to health, employment and culture, which are not easily addressed within a single development activity. This chapter has highlighted what we feel are key social issues in urban areas, and key problems related to children specifically. But one could easily add other issues or specific problems (e.g. prostitution), or approach from another angle, such as for instance human rights. In a way, the issues analysed in previous chapters may be easier (or less difficult...) to target, because they are more specific – as well as tangible – as opposed to the wide spectrum of social issues. Even so, the previous chapters have highlighted the extent of the problems in such areas. Addressing the plethora of social issues presents greater challenges. Despite the efforts of many development agencies, urban social problems are still at levels high enough to question the achievement of the MDGs by 2015. Nevertheless, as already noted in the book, the social dimension is a fundamental part of sustainable (urban) development, therefore it is not a question on whether or not to address it, but how. The situation in developing countries requires scaling up existing efforts and innovating alternative development instruments, such as CSR, that can work in parallel with current efforts. The latter option is supported by empirical evidence from case studies.

The African Oxygen case study, for instance, demonstrates how even with a limited financial investment and without formal public private partnerships, strong support from management can contribute towards the success of an employee-involvement CSR strategy. It is partly for this reason that the Afrox's Community Involvement Programme (CIP) has been successful. Afrox employees gain self-satisfaction in their relationship with children in the 'adopted homes'. The employees have been motivated by management to the level that they start seeing the programme as their own. In return, benefits to management are in the form of diversity management, identification of employee skills, employee loyalty and enhanced corporate image. However, the case also shows how disaggregated administration of CSR strategies can limit success. In this case, while the CIP is managed by the Human Resources Department, the other Afrox social investments like donations and sponsorships are handled by the Managing Director's office. For any CSR strategy to be successful there is need to integrate all efforts.

While involvement of Afrox is very diverse in that the company participates in a wide range of areas including but not limited to HIV/AIDS, child skills development, educational programmes, abused children, street children, the other three cases discussed in the chapter are by and large involved in educational programmes. The Brazilian Learner School City (LSC) case study and the SEED project executed by Schlumberger in Nigeria, for instance, are reminders of how crucial partnerships are in the success of any CSR agenda. In the case of the LSC, these partnerships could not have been possible without the leadership and commitment from the president, founder and creator of the LSC, Mr. Gilberto Dimenstein. The success of the LSC programme, which is evident from projects like the 100 Walls in Vila Madalena, is as a result of the wide network of supportive and participative relationships with other organisations. The faith the partnering organisations have in the LSC founder has contributed to the success of the CSR initiatives. The other key lesson from the LSC case is sustainability-related. While the NGO receives support and sponsorships from such organisations as the *Fundaçao Bank Boston*, the NGO has taken some insurance measures whereby it has initiated projects like the *Café Aprendiz, Agencia Aprendiz* and the *Learner Cyber Cafe* specifically to guarantee sustainability of LSC's CSR initiatives. This ensures continuity of social causes in case sponsors pull out, and reduces financial demands on sponsors. Success notwithstanding, the LSC case echoes the need for partnering organisations to go beyond the mere provision of funds. While financial support is critical for any CSR initiative, and indeed appreciated, there is need for all stakeholders to collaborate and act together in a manner that leads to the achievement of a common goal rather than expecting to reap 'good image' arising from sponsoring implementing agencies. The SEED project in the Schlumberger case is an exemplar in this area. The partner organisation ANPEZ Centre for Environment and Development (ACFED) gets involved by going beyond the award of funds. The organisation participates by offering computer and internet access freely to schools, pupils and community youths who visit the centre on scheduled basis and connects them to Science World. Although, as noted before, sustainability is still an issue for SEED.

In turn, the activities of the Aluminium Company in Ghana, while bringing benefits, have been questioned. Are the CSR activities merely intended to compensate the citizens for the costs that the country incurred following an allegedly unfair deal that saw the birth of the company, and the eventual construction of the Akasombo hydro station on Volta River? Putting the debate on justifying the CSR drivers aside, this case study is another example of the important role that partnerships play in CSR strategies. The company's successful participation in CSR initiatives by way of contributing funds towards development of soccer and provision of scholarships to children of Tema communities, for instance, could not have been possible without the full support of public actors/agencies like the Tema Municipal Assembly, Ghana Education Services, and the Government of Ghana. However, while this case is generally a success in terms of bringing benefits, involvement in too many initiatives by way of cash donations without management fully considering how such activities would support its business objectives are limitations of the company's CSR policy.

All activities implemented by the companies studied in this chapter are important; from the care of children in especially difficult circumstances, to promotion of sports and education (the latter including support to traditional education, plus computer literacy and innovative approaches such as 'street education'). Such activities are likely to contribute for a better future for the children involved – all of them under the poverty line, and in a number of cases also orphans, abused or/and abandoned.

A big question perhaps is the extent or significance of CSR interventions to support urban children, given that each company has a limited scope, while the numbers of urban residents in general and children in particular affected by poverty (which entails social development deficits) are massive. As noted in Chapter 2, there are around one billion people living in slums, which is a condition associated with poverty. In addition, there are also many other poor people in urban areas, living outside slums or many times homeless. A second, related question would be how to prioritise specific interventions, given the broad scope of problems and needs. Furthermore, how to place each single specific intervention in a concerted way within the broad framework of urban social development, and, even broader, sustainable urban development.

The answer to the first question is that, as emphasised elsewhere in this book, we do not argue that CSR is a panacea, but rather a useful complement – still under-utilised – to the existing urban development cooperation process. CSR alone will not address the plight of billions of urban poor, but business can join hands with other actors to find innovative long-term solutions.

The second question, about priority setting, can be addressed by companies planning their CSR projects through ample consultation – and ideally joint decision-making – with local actors. This may seem an obvious suggestion, but one should take into account that there is a component of public relations for the companies in CSR, therefore sometimes activities are chosen on the basis of their visibility and perhaps other strategic advantages for the companies. While it would be naive to neglect that companies do also wish to benefit from CSR, it is important to advocate that they should always keep in mind the priority development needs of their intended beneficiaries.

The third question is the broadest and the more difficult to answer – how a myriad of isolated small-scale activities make up a concerted, sustainable social development process and ultimately an urban development one. Part of the answer is related to the one above – consultation, as well as partnership. But of course the solution to accomplish a sustainable social/urban development process is beyond the scope of this book. Nevertheless, we believe that an international concerted effort to establish some priorities and indicators – such as the MDGs process – is a good path to take. Following, it would be best if individual companies bear in mind such general principles when planning their local CSR activities – therefore bringing to the CSR arena the well-known motto of the environmental movement: 'Think global, act local!'

7
Conclusion

Edmundo Werna, Ramin Keivani and David Murphy

This book began with the account of United Nations Volunteers' (UNV) efforts to promote CSR in urban settings. The idea was to work with an international organisation representing low-income communities – the SDI (Slum/Shacks Dwellers International) – and associate it with private construction companies to upgrade low-income settlements. As explained in the Introduction, it did not succeed. However, as also noted in that chapter, there is room for optimism. UNV eventually succeeded in linking some companies and urban low-income communities on an individual basis. Following, this book has noted that urban CSR has picked up momentum in the past few years, and the case-study chapters offer detailed evidence. This is not to say that the process is devoid of challenges, as also noted throughout the book. The final chapter will first explore the advantages and challenges of CSR from the perspective of its different elements and practices, followed by final conclusions leading to general recommendations on how to further strengthen CSR in urban areas.

7.1   CSR practices

As noted in Chapter 1, CSR encompasses many different elements. Each element may also be defined as a specific CSR 'practice', if it is the focus of a given case. The final sections of the four previous chapters drew conclusions on the CSR cases in relation to various urban development themes. The present section will analyse the cases from the perspective of CSR practices. The understanding of such practices and what they entail may enable companies and their partners to improve their CSR initiatives.

Table 7.1 Types of CSR elements/practices per case study

Field of urban development	Case-study	Country	Main CSR practice
City-wide interventions	Societe National d´Assurances	Lebanon	Corporate social investment
	Go Green Partnership	Lebanon	Partnership
	Organização da Sociedade Civil VG	Brazil	Partnership
Construction	Cement Company	Ghana	Corporate philanthropy
	Ashfoam	Ghana	Corporate social investment
	Prima Woods	Ghana	Corporate social investment
	Água e Cidade	Brazil	Corporate social investment
Utilities	Davao Light and Power Corporation	Philippines	Corporate social investment
Social development	Africa Oxygen (Pty) Limited	South Africa	Corporate volunteering/ employee involvement
	Aluminium Company	Ghana	Corporate social investment
	Schlumberger	Nigeria	Corporate social investment
	Learner School City	Brazil	Volunteerism and development in the community

Often, there is a mix of different CSR elements in a given initiative. This indeed has taken place in all cases studied in this book. Nonetheless, it is worth analysing the different practices individually, for the purpose of understanding their respective advantages, potentials as well as limitations. For each case study, it was possible to identify one primary area of CSR practice, as noted in Table 7.1. They include:

- Corporate philanthropy and social investment
- Partnership
- Corporate volunteering/employee involvement
- Volunteerism and development in the community

Each practice area will be analysed in turn. This review will be supplemented by consideration of another practice area, corporate citizenship and responsibility, which was a secondary focus in some of the case studies. Given its more strategic and cross-cutting nature, corporate citizenship and responsibility will be analysed separately to identify recommendations for companies and their partners.

7.1.1 Corporate philanthropy and social investment

Corporate philanthropy is the oldest form of CSR, as noted in Chapter 1. Philanthropy remains a prevalent form of CSR, and some academics and practitioners have in recent years sought to redefine it as strategic philanthropy (Porter and Kramer, 2006).

Despite this new impetus, corporate philanthropy may still be classified as part of the conventional 'donor-recipient' paradigm, which the international donor community has generally tried to move away from, with different degrees of success.

Another way of looking at corporate philanthropy from the perspective of corporate social investment can be defined as the planned, monitored and voluntary use of private funds for projects of social interest (e.g. New Academy of Business-UNV, 2004). Despite efforts to transform corporate philanthropy and social investment, one of the limitations of both of these concepts is that they continue to be largely based on a business perspective of what is strategic. Strategic approaches to corporate philanthropy and social investment equally need to take into account broader development questions. How do corporate philanthropy and social investment encourage communities and companies to relate in relationships and contribute towards the achievement of the Millennium Development Goals? When do corporate philanthropy and social investment increase the likelihood that communities and companies relate in ways that promote sustainable development? Without due attention to these kinds of questions, there is a danger that corporate philanthropy or social investment could create energy sapping dependencies between 'uppers' – those with power and influence – and 'lowers', in conformity with the criticisms of the donor-recipient paradigm.

Although some of this new language represents genuine efforts to be more responsive to the needs of local communities, much corporate philanthropy and social investment remains paternalistic and imposed from the top down. If social investment is usually what designated government departments or community organisations do, then companies that invest in communities should approach this area of activity with due care. Key differences between *ad hoc* philanthropy and long-term developmental social investment emerge from the way in which the work is connected with community needs and the official development plans and activities of public institutions. *Ad hoc* philanthropy tends to be less concerned about the influence of the act of giving upon existing processes and relationships.

In making the transition from traditional forms of philanthropy towards more collaborative forms of social investment, businesses need to consider how their actions sit alongside community understanding and government planning. The role of government in enhancing business-community relations is also of central importance in developmental social investment by companies. At any rate, while social investment is a step forward in comparison to philanthropy, it also has limitations, as noted above.

The case studies that fall under such types of CSR have brought benefits for both the companies and target groups, as noted in previous chapters. Some are small-scale and deemed unsustainable, such as Cement Company (philanthropy), Ashfoam, Prima Woods and Aluminum Company (social investment). Others have achieved broader results, such as Água e Cidade, Davao Light and Power and Societe National d´Assurances (social investment). Even with the broader results of the latter cases, it is recommended that companies should strive to go beyond both types of CSR. As noted before, all of the company cases in this book illustrate different dimensions of CSR, in addition to their primary focus. Therefore, the companies that focus on philanthropy or social investment should strengthen their efforts in other areas to build a more comprehensive approach to CSR. For companies that are beginning to embrace CSR, it is suggested that they should start with a wider focus beyond philanthropy and social investment to encompass other practices, which are noted below.

7.1.2 Partnership

The definition of partnership in general is broad, and encompasses a wide variety and levels of relations between the actors in a given joint initiative. All of the case studies included in this book entail some kind of partnership, and indeed the word has been used somehow freely throughout previous chapters. However, this sub-section centers on a more robust kind of partnership where risks and benefits are shared (Tennyson, 2005). Partnership is classified here as one type of CSR practice. Two case studies have a primary focus on partnership, i.e. Go Green (Lebanon) and Organização da Sociedade Civil (Brazil). Many other cases include partnership as secondary focus.

Since the 1990s there has been a growing impetus for solutions-based relationships between businesses and other stakeholders with the emergence of numerous cross-sector partnerships to promote voluntary initiatives for sustainable development and socio-economic justice. In this period, in the world of business, the language of partnership grew from an emphasis upon partnership between companies to include partnerships with other non-business actors. In many respects, the notion of partnership is grounded in volunteerism. Partnerships are based upon the voluntary actions of parties to come together to design a joint project for mutual benefit. Partnerships are also often seen as being inherently good or positive.

The case of Organização da Sociedade Civil shows a partnership with broad objectives (social, physical and economic) and related results. Go Green, in turn, focused on green educational and awareness raising campaigns, which also achieved positive results. At any rate, rather than an open-ended acceptance of all partnerships (or a dismissal of the possibilities they open up), we suggest that it is important to ask questions about how to improve partnership arrangements. This will be beneficial to the two case studies, and to other companies that wish to strengthen the partnership dimensions of their CSR activities. Specific ideas for starting or strengthening partnerships are summarised below.

Process and content are important in different ways. These two aspects of partnership thrive off each other. Without something worthwhile or energising to address, the process of engagement does not matter. Similarly, without good processes, working towards the desired content of a partnership will be meaningless.

- How will a good process be facilitated?
- How is responsibility shared?
- What would happen if the process is running well?
- How would individuals talk to each other?
- What kind of energy will be created?
- How can you balance the time for paying attention to the process of engagement, when deadlines and resources are short?

Sometimes small is beautiful. It can be difficult to avoid the impetus to promote the partnership activity so that the relationship tries to grow up before it is ready. Pressures from various parts of the system (e.g., head office and other stakeholders) tend to call partners away from nurturing long-lasting relationships.

- How can you give the relationship enough space and time at the beginning to develop slowly?
- How can you avoid the pressure to become big?
- What signals might indicate that you are caught up in the needs of the system for fabricating quick results?

Things go wrong (and do so fairly regularly). Partnerships do not allow the partners to spend excessive amounts of time trying to prevent all possible mistakes. Instead, partners are prepared to talk and communicate about mistakes as they arise and seek creative ways to learn from them.

- How can you learn to embrace the problems that will arise?
- What techniques can you use to talk about the difficulties openly?

One cannot know everything and your 'ways of knowing' will never be sufficient. With multiple issues, perspectives and challenges emerging all the time, uncertainty and 'not knowing' are inherent parts of the process of engagement in partnership.

- How can you balance the need for clarity with the sense of not being able to know everything?

The relationship between a community and business is something that is recreated every day through numerous interactions. Partners seek to create conditions for engagement throughout the system and organisation since responsibility, impact and influence are dispersed. For example, the people in a community development office are not the only ones to create difficulty in relationships. Similarly, there are more people in a business than just the head of a company or its spokesperson who are responsible for creating a better relationship between a company and its community. Meaningful partnerships will only develop between businesses and communities when individuals expand their horizon beyond formal community development activities to relationships involving areas of core business operations.

- How can you find ways to work on the boundaries of the organisation?

7.1.3 Corporate volunteering/employee involvement

The case study of Africa Oxygen falls into this category as a primary focus. Other cases include an element of employee volunteering, such as the Go Green partnership, Davao Light and Power Company, and Lerner School City.

As a concept and practice, formal corporate volunteering and employee involvement programmes have largely emerged from the experience of Western-based companies. But they are finding their way into developing countries.

Many of the business benefits of corporate volunteering and employee involvement programmes are similar to those often articulated for business-community relations or CSR more generally. What distinguishes corporate volunteering from other forms of CSR is that it has the potential to strengthen interactions between employees in various departments and levels of the company and ultimately make important contributions to employees' personal and career growth through developing and enhancing their skills in areas such as employee leadership, teamwork, confidence and social and interpersonal skills. In 2002–03, employees of Africa Oxygen were involved in 128 child health and development projects. The approach of this company encourages team volunteering and staff ownership of the projects to build staff skills and commitment.

Although the field of corporate volunteering and employee involvement remains relatively new in many developing countries, this area of practice appears to offer considerable scope for enhancing business-community relations in a development context. Benefits for the employees include the following:

- Enables integration into local community
- Provides satisfaction from doing worthwhile work
- Develops and enhances skills & broadens employee experience
- Enhances community awareness
- Improves mental and spiritual wellbeing
- Builds personal networks

In addition to the concrete benefits provided, the communities gain from the direct engagement with the employees, a fact that has both humanitarian and technical aspects. And the companies also benefit from the fact that the employees gain a different type of capacity from engaging directly with communities, rather than working only on commercial projects and/or in company offices.

7.1.4 Volunteerism and development in the community

The mutual aid or self-help dimension of volunteerism has a long tradition in developing countries, as noted in Chapter 2. This involves individuals and groups undertaking voluntary activities in support of community development projects and other local causes. Much of this voluntary action is not necessarily captured as formal volunteering. This form of community volunteerism is also generally not provided with formal institutional backup (such as in the UK with Community Service Volunteers).

As mentioned in Chapter 2, it is true that community volunteerism has faced criticisms – the most important being the fact that low-income communities have a right to receive public benefits, therefore the government, not the communities themselves, should provide. However, when the governments do not provide, it is better for communities to be engaged in provision – otherwise, at least the present generation would just lack the benefits. At the same time, community involvement adds value by bringing to an initiative a deep knowledge of local characteristics and needs. Finally, it may strengthen community-based organisations, and eventually their relations with the government and the possibility of better public services. Therefore, there is value for CSR to include community volunteerism.

One case analysed falls into this category as a primary focus, which is Learner School City. A number of other cases include an element of volunteerism and development in the community, such as Água e Cidade, Organização da Sociedade Civil and Societe National d´Assurances. They offer examples of the importance of community-based models of volunteerism as a means of enhancing business-community relations.

7.1.5 Corporate citizenship and responsibility

The previous sections reviewed individual CSR practices that constituted a major focus in the case studies analysed. As already noted, while each case includes different elements, it is still worth analysing such elements separately for the purpose of better understanding their respective characteristics, leading to the recommendations made above. The CSR practices found in the case studies do not represent an exhaustive list. Indeed the theory and practice of CSR continues to evolve and be re-invented. Such a wider analysis is beyond the scope of this book. However, in addition to the CSR practices analysed earlier in this chapter, we will now examine a final area, namely corporate citizenship and responsibility. Although not a major focus of any of the case studies, citizenship and responsibility did appear in a few cases as a sub-theme, and this practice area has particular importance for future undertakings.

The idea of corporate citizenship or corporate responsibility has come to be recognised in recent years as both a framework to enhance understanding of the role of business in society and as an area of practice in its own right. As a business-in-society framework, corporate citizenship brings together questions about issues pertinent to this book, related to different aspects of urban development – e.g. the role of business in urban regeneration, the creation of healthy communities and ethical dilemmas, such as child protection. Current corporate responses nonetheless range from the minimalist to the discretionary to the strategic. Corporate citizenship embraces a "complex relationship of interlocking [business] rights and responsibilities" (McIntosh *et al.*, 1998: xxi), and is based upon three supporting pillars (Tichy *et al.*, 1997): the moral ('doing the right thing'), the social (community integration) and the economic (long-term survival). Of particular relevance to this book, current thinking about corporate citizenship has a strong emphasis upon sustainable development issues.

As a means of enhancing business community relations, citizenship and responsibility practices encompass a range of corporate accountability measures, such as social and environmental certification, triple bottom-line accounting and reporting, among others. Most of these initiatives have their origins in Northern industrialised countries and often have been responses to pressure from consumers, the media and civil society organisations (e.g., trade unions, NGOs and church groups). In some cases these activities have been developed by the private sector, while in others they have resulted from partnerships between business and other sectors similar to those outlined in the previous section.

Companies are increasingly being challenged by their stakeholders to address the issues outlined above (and many others). There is evidence of innovative corporate responses emerging in the form of improved citizenship and responsibility initiatives. An example of the latter is the growing importance of environmental and sustainable development issues for business, as noted in Chapter 3. While many of the business responses are linked to environmental legal compliance, there are also examples of companies adopting proactive approaches to environmental sustainability in both a commercial and community context. The case of the Lebanese restaurant Schtroumpf and its 'Go Green' campaign – which includes an element of corporate citizenship and responsibility – illustrates how small and medium enterprises can integrate sustainability principles into their business, achieve financial success and foster wider social change. Another case which also has an element of corporate citizenship and responsibility is that of Schlumberger in Nigeria.

7.2 Final remarks: what is possible, necessary

This book has shown that there is room for optimism regarding the role of CSR in urban settings in the developing world. It has also shown that the process is not without problems and challenges. CSR cannot be taken as a panacea, but it still can add value to urban development.

Although some of the criticisms and limitations of CSR were considered in Chapter 1, one cross-cutting issue is worth highlighting in this final section. The criticism is that private companies are profit-making organisations, and that CSR has tended to be about giving back part (and only part) of such profit to communities and disadvantaged groups. This means that the companies and their shareholders are the major beneficiaries of business profit – and, through the CSR process, companies may realise some additional, indirect commercial benefits.

The above is indeed the current reality of a global market-based economy (with very few exceptions), and that the notion of profit is at its core. A private company would not survive if it did not re-invest its profit in the business whilst ensuring that shareholders realise a financial return on their investments.

There have been indeed proposals for a different world, which would not be market-oriented. A critique of CSR would be more justifiable within such a framework. However, a big question would still remain. A radical shift from a market-based economy, even if it comes at some point in the future, is not currently on the horizon. Therefore, given the present context, and being pragmatic, what are the implications for the large numbers of poor people that inhabit the planet? It is important to also think about ways to improve their current living conditions. With such a pragmatic view in mind, it is indeed worth considering the positive attributes of CSR activities that can bring direct benefits to low-income communities and ideally improve the internal dynamics of private companies through ethical behaviour, environmental accountability and other issues discussed in this book.

While the book has focused on the specific CSR context of business-community relations, the internal dynamics of companies cannot be disregarded. It is not enough to help low-income communities if a given company does not pay attention to its internal workplace and supply chain conditions, continues to pollute the environment and/or does not compete fairly in the market. As noted earlier, business relationships with low-income communities can also trigger internal dynamics in companies. This is an added value, although enhanced business-community relations will not ultimately lead to radical change in business strategy and practice. An in-depth analysis of other aspects of CSR is beyond the scope of the book, and should be the object of further research, particularly in the context of developing countries.

Returning to the focus of the book, based on its analysis and conclusions it is recommended that (urban) development cooperation institutions should more actively promote business-community relations and CSR. As noted in Chapter 2, there have been CSR activities in urban areas led by multilateral agencies, such as UNV and UNDP. It is also important to remember the extensive Global Compact initiative, led by the UN, noted in Chapter 1 – although it does not have a focus on urban development and low-income communities, its broad CSR framework is also relevant for such initiatives. Activities led by bilateral agencies and NGOs have also sprung up. Chapter 2 also noted a broader urban initiative led by UN-Habitat. Although it also includes commercial activities of enterprises, it is a larger urban initiative that includes CSR – and business-community relations in particular – as a major topic. It is here suggested that the UN-Habitat initiative could develop a specific component to boost CSR alongside commercial activities. Perhaps such an initiative could also be broadened to include other international agencies as partners, such as UNV with its mandate and operations to promote volunteerism (including volunteerism in urban development). More importantly, UN-Habitat should consider the inclusion of associations representing businesses and low-income communities internationally. This will not only give more impetus to the process, but also would encourage institutionalisation of the initiative within such organisations. This would promote sustainability and help to ensure that the initiative does not become dependent on a UN entity for its survival.

In addition to the above, it is important to pay attention to the growing number of independent CSR-based initiatives between individual companies and urban communities. Development cooperation organisations should strive to promote such initiatives with awareness-raising campaigns, and designing CSR indicators, benchmarks and capacity-building tools that can be widely disseminated, plus setting up specific CSR bureaus at city/national levels or raising awareness of the role of CSR among urban development public professionals in order for them to actively identify and promote CSR opportunities. There is value in encouraging and facilitating a partnership approach for CSR activities to build different capacities towards more effective project outputs and larger outcomes.

Much more needs to be done to promote and enhance CSR, particularly in developing countries. While CSR may retain its focus on industrialised countries, this book has shown that CSR practices are on the increase in developing countries. However, a large number of developing country enterprises are still not engaged. One interesting area for research and practice is to consider ways of engaging the massive number of small and medium-sized enterprises, which abound in urban areas in the South.

The engagement of new companies in CSR initiatives will not take place in an empty, new field. CSR as a process or movement is already moving forward around the world. The seeds have already germinated. The challenge for both CSR researchers and practitioners now is to watch and nurture the plants as they continue to grow in the years ahead.

Bibliography

Agyeman, J. and Warner, K. (2002) Putting just sustainability into place: from paradigm to policy to practice, *Policy and Management Review*, 2(1), pp. 8–40.

Aldrich, B. C. and Sandhu, R. S. (eds) (1995). *Housing the Urban Poor: Policy and Practice in Developing Countries*. London/Atlantic Heights, NJ: Zed Books.

Andrelini, J. (2008) Olympic water diversion threatens millions, *Financial Times*, 26 February 2008, http://www.ft.com/cms/s/0/40b3e66a-e49d-11dc-a495-0000779fd2ac.html?nclick_check=1 [accessed March 2008].

Angel, S. (2000) *Housing Policy Matters: A Global Analysis*. Oxford: Oxford University Press.

Anheier, H., Glasius, M. and Kaldor, M. (eds) (2001) *Global Civil Society*. Oxford: Oxford University Press.

Aranya, R. (2003) *Globalization and Urban Restructuring of Bangalore, India*. Paper presented at 39th ISOCARP Congress, Cairo, 17–22 October.

Arimah, B. (2005) What drives infrastructure spending in cities of developing countries?, *Urban Studies*, 42(8), pp. 1345–1368.

Atkinson, A. (2007) Cities after oil – "Sustainable development" and energy futures, *City*, 11(2), pp. 201–213.

Atkinson, R. and Moon, G. (1994) *Urban Policy in Britain: The City, the State and the Market*. Basingstoke: Macmillan.

Azizi, M. H. (1995) The provision of urban infrastructure in Iran: an empirical evaluation, *Urban Studies*, 32(3), pp. 507–522.

Azizi, M. H. (2000) The user-pays system in the provision of urban infrastructure: effectiveness and equity criteria, *Urban Studies*, 37(8), pp. 1345–1357.

Baken, R. J. and Van der Linden, J. (1993) Getting the incentives right: banking on the formal private sector, *Third World Planning Review*, 15(1), pp. 1–22.

Baker, M. (2007) Corporate Social Responsibility – what does it mean? Mallen Baker website: http://www.mallenbaker.net/csr.

Ball, M. and Maginn, P. (2005) Urban change and conflict: evaluating the role of partnerships in urban regeneration in the UK, *Housing Studies*, 20(1), pp. 9–28.

Barrett, S. with Murphy, D. F. (1997) Final report of the ESRC-funded research on the implementation of Corporate Social Responsibility policies. School for Policy Studies, University of Bristol, Bristol.

Batley, R. (1994) *The Role of Government in Adjusting Economies, Paper 1 – Literature Review*. Development Administration Group, School of Public Policy, The University of Birmingham, Birmingham.

Batley, R. (1996) Public-Private relationships and performance in service provision, *Urban Studies*, 33(4–5), pp. 723–751.

Bendell, J. and Visser, W. (2004) *An Agenda for the Future of CSR: 2004 Lifeworth Annual Review of Corporate Responsibility*. Sheffield: Greenleaf.

Bendell, J. and Shah, S. (2006) Incredibly India, *The Lifeworth Review of 2006*, Lifeworth, first quarter, January to March 2006, http://www.lifeworth.com/2006review/qtr14-2006.htm [accessed February 2008].

Benjamin, S. (2000) Governance, economic settings and poverty in Bangalore, *Environment and Urbanization*, 12(1), pp. 35–58.
Bhalla, A. and Lapeyre, F. (1997) Social exclusion: towards an analytical and operational framework, *Development and Change*, 38(4), pp. 735–760.
Blowfield, M. and Frynas, J. G. (2005) Setting new agendas: critical perspectives on Corporate Social Responsibility in the developing world, *International Affairs*, 81(3), pp. 499–513.
Bowen, H. (1953) *Social Responsibility of the Businessman*. New York: Harper and Row.
Brindley, T. (2000) Community roles in urban regeneration, *City*, 4(3), pp. 363–377.
Bruno, K. (2002) *Greenwash +10: The UN's Global Compact, Corporate Accountability and the Johannesburg Earth Summit*, CorporateWatch and Tides Center, Oakland, CA, p. 6.
Buckley, R. M. and Kalarickal, J. (2004) *Shelter Strategies for the Urban Poor: Idiosyncratic and Successful, but Hardly Mysterious*. World Bank policy research working paper no. 3427.
Bull, B., Bøås, M. and McNeill, D. (2004) Private sector influence in the multilateral system: a changing structure of world governance?, *Global Governance*, No. 10, pp. 481–498.
Byrne, D. and Keithley, J. (1993) Housing and the health of the community, in: R. Burridge and D. Ormandy (eds) *Unhealthy Housing: Research, Remedies and Reform*. London: E & FN Spon.
Cao, A. and Keivani, R. (2007) *The Role of Property Markets in Supporting Economic and Social Development in China*, RICS Research Publication.
Carley, M. (2000) Urban partnerships, governance and the regeneration of Britain's cities, *International Planning Studies*, 5(3), pp. 273–297.
Cars, G., Healey, P., Madanipour, A. and De Magalhães, C. (eds) (2001) *Urban Governance, Institutional Capacity and Social Milieux*. Aldershot: Ashgate.
Castillo, H., Moobela, C., Price, A. D. F. and Mathur, V. N. (2007) Assessing urban social sustainability: current capabilities and opportunities for future research, *The International Journal of Environmental, Cultural, Economic and Social Sustainability*, 3(3), pp. 39–50.
Chahoud, T., Emmerling, J., Kolb, D., Kubina, I., Repinski, G. and Schlager, C. (2007) *Corporate Social and Environmental Responsibility in India: Assessing the UN Global Compact's Role*. Bonn: German Development Institute (GDI).
Cheney, H., Nheu, N. and Vecellio, L. (2004) *Sustainability as Social Change: Values and Power in Sustainability Discourse*. Sydney: Institute for Sustainable Futures, University of Technology.
Cherry, G. E. (1972) *Urban Change and Planning*. Henley-on-Thames: GT Foulis & Co. Ltd.
Chowdhury, F. J. and Nurul Amin, A. T. M. (2006) Environmental assessment in slum improvement programs: some evidence from a study of infrastructure projects in two Dhaka slums, *Environmental Impact Assessment Review*, 26, pp. 530–552.
Christensen, P. and O'Brien, M. (2003) Children in the city: introducing new perspectives, in: P. Christensen and M. O'Brien (eds) *Children in the City: Home, Neighbourhood and Community*. London: Routledge.
Clement-Jones, T. (2005) Corporate Social Responsibility – bottom-line issue or public relations exercise?, in: J. Hancock (ed.) *Investing in Corporate Social*

Responsibility: A Guide to Best Practice, Business Planning & the UK's Leading Companies. London: Kogan Page.

Colantonio, A. (2007) *Measuring Social Sustainability: Best Practice from Urban Renewal in the EU*. EIBURS Working Paper Series, http://www.brookes.ac.uk/schools/be/oisd/sustainable_communities/resources/SocialSustainability_Metrics_and_Tools.pdf [accessed February 2008].

Collignon, B. and Vezina, M. (2000) Independent water and sanitation providers in African cities, full report of ten country study. UNDP-World Bank, http://www-wds.worldbank.org/external/default/WDSContentServer/WDSP/IB/2001/07/28/000094946_01070704012185/RenderEd/PDF/multi0page.pdf [accessed October 2007].

Communities and Local Government (CLG) (2007) What is a sustainable community?, http://www.communities.gov.uk/communities/sustainablecommunities/whatis [accessed December 2007].

Conroy, M. E. (2007) *Branded! Branded!: How the "Certification Revolution" is Transforming Global Corporations*. Gabriola Island, BC, Canada: New Society Publishers.

Constructing Excellence (2007) Corporate Social Responsibility, http://www.constructingexcellence.org.uk/zones/sustainabilityzone/responsibility.jsp

Corporateregister.com (2007) Corporateregister.com Portal, http://www.corporateregister.com [accessed July 2007].

Crawford, P. and Vogl, B. (2006) Measuring productivity in the construction industry, *Building Research and Information*, 34(3), pp. 208–219, http://www.journalsonline.tandf.co.uk/mEdia/g275munwxgdqtvclpt6y/contributions/p/8/0/6/p80688180870m753.pdf [accessed July 2007].

Crinson, M. (1997) Abadan: planning and architecture under the Anglo-Iranian oil company, *Planning Perspectives*, 12(3), pp. 341–359.

Cullingworth, J. B. and Nadin, V. (1994) *Town and Country Planning in Britain*. London: Routledge.

Davey, K. J. (1992) *The Structure and Functions of Urban Government*, Development Administration Group, School of Public Policy, The University of Birmingham, Birmingham.

Davis, K. (1967) Understanding the social responsibility puzzle: what does the businessman owe to society?, *Business Horizons*, 10(4), pp. 45–50.

Davoudi, S. and Healey, P. (1995) City challenge – sustainable process or temporary gesture?, *Environment and Planning C*, 13, pp. 79–95.

De Haan, A. (1999) *Social Exclusion: Towards an Holistic Understanding of Deprivation*, Department for International Development (DFID), http://www.dfid.gov.uk/pubs/files/social developmentd9socex.pdf [accessed February 2008].

Deb, A. (1998) Sustainable cities in developing countries, *Building Research and Information*, 26(1), pp. 29–38.

Devas, N. (2001) Does city governance matter for the urban poor?, *International Planning Studies*, 6(4), pp. 393–408.

Devuyst, D., Hens, L. and Impens, R. (2001) *Neighbourhoods in Crisis and Sustainable Urban Development*. Brussels: VUB University Press.

Ding, D., Fields, D. and Akhtar, S. (1997) An empirical study of human resource management policies and practices in foreign-invested enterprises in China: the case of Shenzen Special Economic Zone, *International Journal of Human Resource Management*, 5(1), pp. 595–613.

Doane, D. and Holder, A. (2007) *Why Corporate Social Responsibility is Failing Children*. London: Corporate Responsibility Coalition & Save the Children.

Dokmeci, V., Altunbas, U. and Yagzi, B. (2007) Revitalisation of the main street of a distinguished old neighbourhood in Istanbul, *European Planning Studies*, 15(1), pp. 153–166.

Douglas, M. (2000) Mega-urban regions and world city formation: globalization, the economic crisis and urban policy issues in pacific Asia, *Urban Studies*, 37(12), pp. 2315–2335.

Drakakis-Smith, D. (1995) Third world cities: sustainable urban development, *Urban Studies*, 32(4–5), pp. 659–677.

Durand-Lasserve, A. (2002) Current changes and trends: Benin, Burkina Faso and Senegal, in: G. Payne (ed.) *Land, Rights and Innovation*. London: ITDG.

Edwards, M. and Hulme, D. (eds) (1992) *Making A Difference: NGOs and Development in a Changing World*. London: Earthscan.

El-Hefnawi, A. I. K. (2005) *"Protecting" agricultural land from urbanization or "managing" the conflict between informal urban growth while meeting the demands of the communities (Lessons learnt from the Egyptian policy reforms)*. Paper presented at *World Bank urban research symposium*, Brazil, April 4–6.

Elkington, J. (1998) *Cannibals with Forks: The Triple Bottom Line of the 21st Century*. Oxford: Capstone Publishing.

Elkington, J. (2004) Enter the triple bottom line, in: A. Henriques and J. Richardson (eds) *The Triple Bottom Line, Does It Add Up? Assessing the Sustainability of Business and CSR*. London: Earthscan.

Employer Supported Volunteering (2007) ESV Portal, http://www.volunteering.org.uk/WhatWeDo/Projects+and+initiatives/Employer+Supported+Volunteering/ [accessed June 2007].

Ennew, J. and Swart-Kruger, J. (2003) Introduction: homes, places and spaces in the construction of street children and street youth, *Children, Youth and Environments*, 13(1), http://www.colorado.Edu/journals/cye/13_1/Vol13_1 Articles/CYE_CurrentIssue_ArticleIntro_Kruger_Ennew.htm [accessed February 2008].

Fainstein, S. (1995) Urban development and public policy in London and New York, in: P. Healey, S. Cameron, S. Davoudi, S. Graham and A. Madani-Pour (eds) *Managing Cities: The New Urban Context*. Chichester: Wiley.

Falck, O. and Heblich, S. (2007) Corporate social responsibility: doing well by doing good, *Business Horizons*, 50(3), pp. 247–254.

Farrington, D. P. and Welsh, C. (2002) Improved street lighting and crime prevention, *Justice Quarterly*, 19(2), pp. 313–342.

Firman, T. (1998) The restructuring of Jakarta metropolitan area: a "global city" in Asia, *Cities: The International Journal of Urban Policy and Planning*, 15(4), pp. 229–243.

Friedman, F. (1962) *Capitalism and Freedom*. Chicago: University of Chicago Press.

Friedman, F. (1970) The social responsibility of business is to increase its profits, *The New York Times*, 3 September, 1970.

Gandy, M. (2006) Planning, anti-planning and the infrastructure crisis facing Metropolitan Lagos, *Urban Studies*, 43(2), pp. 371–396.

Ganesan, S. (1978) The building industry in Sri Lanka and problems of common interest to developing countries, in: D. H. Koenigsberger and S. Groak (eds) *Essays in Memory of Duccio Turin (1926–1976): Construction and Economic Development Planning of Human Settlements*. Oxford: Pergamon.

Garg, S. K. (1990) Reaching low-income families: a private sector approach, in: P. Baross and J. Van der Linden (eds) *The Transformation of Land Supply Systems in Third World Cities*. Aldershot: Avebury.

Globalideasbank (2008) Curitiba and its visionary mayor, www.globalideasbank. org/site/bank/idea.php?ideaId=2236 [accessed February 2008].

Gorynski, J. (1978) The role of construction in global social-economic development, in: D. H. Koenigsberger and S. Groak (eds) *Essays in Memory of Duccio Turin (1926–1976): Construction and Economic Development Planning of Human Settlements*. Oxford: Pergamon.

Graham, S. (1999) Global grids of glass: on global cities, telecommunications and planetary urban networks, *Urban Studies*, 36(5–6), pp. 929–949.

Graham, S. (2000) Introduction: cities and infrastructure networks, *International Journal of Urban and Regional Research*, 24(1), pp. 114–119.

Grant, R. and Nijman, J. (2002) Globalization and the corporate geography of cities in the less-developed world, *Annals of the Association of American Geographer*, 92(2), pp. 320–340.

Gray, R. and Milne, M. (2002) Towards reporting on the Triple Bottom Line: mirages, methods and myths, in: A. Henriques and J. Richardson (eds) *The Triple Bottom Line, Does it Add Up? Assessing the Sustainability of Business and CSR*. London: Earthscan.

Gulyani, M., Talukdar, D. and Mukami Kariuki, R. (2005) Universal (non)service? water markets, household demand and the poor in urban Kenya, *Urban Studies*, 42(8), pp. 1247–1274.

Habisch, A. and Jonker, J. (2005) Introduction, in: A. Habisch, J. Jonker, M. Wegner and R. Schmidpeter (eds) *Corporate Social Responsibility across Europe*. Berlin: Springer.

Hall, N., Hart, R. and Mitlin, D. (1996) *The Urban Opportunity: the Work of NGOs in Cities in the South*. London: Intermediate Technology Publications.

Hall, R. (1988) *Enterprise Welfare in Japan: Its Development and Role*. Discussion paper WSP/31, Welfare State Programme, Suntory-Toyota, International Centre for Economics and Related Disciplines, London School of Economics.

Harpham, T., Lusty, T. and Vaughan, P. (1988) *In the Shadow of the City – Community Health and the Urban Poor*. Oxford: Oxford University Press.

Harris, N. (2006) *City Development Strategies: A Training Course*. Unpublished paper presented at Ministry of Housing and Urban Development, Iran September.

Hatter, W. (2007) Mainstreaming sustainable development, *Local Economy*, 22(1), pp. 6–11.

Healey, P. (1992) The reorganisation of state and market in planning, *Urban Studies*, 29(8), pp. 769–776.

Healey, P. and Shaw, T. (1993) Planners, plans and sustainable development, *Regional Studies*, 27(8), pp. 769–776.

Healey, P., Davoudi, S., O'Toole, M., Tavsanoglu, S. and Usher, D. (1992) *Rebuilding the City: Property-led Urban Regeneration*. London: Spon.

Ho, K. C. and So, A. (1997) Semi-periphery and borderland integration: Singapore and Hong Kong experiences, *Political Geography*, 16(3), pp. 241–259.

Holmgren, P., Holmgren, A. and Ahlner, J. (2004) Alcohol and drugs in drivers fatally injured in traffic accidents in Sweden during the years 2000–2002, *Forensic Science International*, 151, pp. 11–17.

Hopkins, M. (2006) *Corporate Social Responsibility and International Development*. London: Earthscan.

Hoyle, B. (2002) Urban waterfront revitalization in developing countries: the example of Zanzibar's Stone Town, *The Geographical Journal*, 168(2), pp. 141–162.

http://www.indianngos.com/ngosection/newcomers/whatisanngo.htm "What is an NGO?", 5 January 2007.

International Labour Organisation (ILO) (2006) *A Strategy for Urban Employment and Decent Work*. Geneva: ILO.

International Labour Organisation (ILO) (2003) *Global Employment Trends 2003*. Geneva: ILO.

International Labour Organisation (ILO) (2004) *Global Employment Trends 2004*. Geneva: ILO.

International Labour Organisation (ILO) (2005) *Global Employment Trends 2005*. Geneva: ILO.

Ingram, G. K. (1998) Patterns of metropolitan development: what have we learned?, *Urban Studies*, 35(7), pp. 1019–1035.

Jeppesen, S. (2006) Strengthening corporate social and environmental responsibility in SMEs: strengthening developing countries, in: E. R. Pedersen and M. Huniche (eds) *Corporate Citizenship in Developing Countries*. Copenhagen: The Copenhagen Centre.

Jones, C. (1996) The theory of property-led local economic development policies, *Regional Studies*, 30(8), pp. 797–801.

Jones, G. W., Tsay, C. L. and Bajracharya, B. (2000) Demographic and employment change in the mega-cities of South-east and East Asia, *TWPR*, 22(2), pp. 119–146.

Jones, P. and Evans, J. (2006) Urban regeneration, governance and the state: exploring notions of distance and proximity, *Urban Studies*, 43(9), pp. 1491–1501.

Karim, M. (1996) NGOs in Bangladesh: issues of legitimacy and accountability, in: M. Edwards and D. Hulme (eds) *Beyond the Magic Bullet: NGO Performance and Accountability in the Post-Cold War World*. West Hartford: Kumarian Press Books, pp. 132–141.

Karnan, A. (2006) *Fortune at the Bottom of the Pyramid: a Mirage: How the Private Sector Can Help Alleviate Poverty*. University of Michigan, Ross school of business working paper no. 1035, November 2006 version.

Keivani, R. and Mattingly, M. (2007) The interface of globalisation and peripheral land in developing countries: implications for local economic development and urban governance, *International Journal of Urban and Regional Research*, 31(2), pp. 459–474.

Keivani, R. and Werna, E. (2001a) Modes of housing provision in developing countries, *Progress in Planning*, 55(II), pp. 65–118.

Keivani, R. and Werna, E. (2001b) Refocusing the housing debate in developing countries from a pluralist perspective, *Habitat International*, 25(2), pp. 191–208.

Keivani, R., Mattingly, M. and Majedi, H. (2005) *Enabling Housing Markets or Increasing Low Income Access to Urban Land: Lessons from Iran*. Paper presented at the World Bank/IPEA Urban Research Symposium 2005, Brasilia, 4–6 April.

Keivani, R., Parsa, A. and Younis, B. (2003) The role of ICTs in urban competitiveness: the case of Dubai, *Journal of Urban Technology*, 10(2), pp. 19–46.

Keivani, R., Parsa, A. and McGreal, S. (2001) Globalisation, institutional structures and real estate markets in central European cities, *Urban Studies*, 38(13), pp. 2457–2476.

Kell, G. and Levin, D. (2002) *The Evolution of the Global Compact Network: An Historic Experiment in Learning and Action*. Paper presented at *The Academy of Management Annual Conference "Building Effective Networks"*, Denver, August 11–14, 2002, p. 2.

Kessides, C. (1993) *The Contributions of Infrastructure to Economic Development: A Review of Experience and Policy Implications*. World Bank Discussion Paper no. 213. Washington, DC: The World Bank.

Khan, A. H. (1997) The sanitation gap: development's deadly menace, *Progress of Nations 1997*, UNICEF, http://www.unicef.org/pon97 [accessed November 2007].

Koenigsberger, D. H. and Groak, S. (eds) (1978) *Essays in Memory of Duccio Turin (1926–1976): Construction and Economic Development Planning of Human Settlement*. Oxford: Pergamon.

Kohler, N. (2006) A European perspective on the Pearce Report: policy and research, *Building Research and Information*, 34(3), pp. 287–294, http://www.journalsonline.tandf.co.uk/mEdia/99a0hgxqlk2xrxnxuq7p/contributions/x/6/4/7/x647245554q01635.pdf [accessed July 2007].

Kuhndt, M., Tunçer, B., Andersen, K. S. and Liedtka, C. (2004) *Responsible Corporate Governance: An Overview of Trends, Initiatives and State-of-the-Art Elements: What Sort of Globalisation is Sustainable?* Wuppertal Institute for Climate, Environment and Energy, paper no. 139, ISSN 0949-5266.

Kumar, R., Murphy, D. F. and Balsari, V. (2001) *Altered Images: The 2001 State of Corporate Responsibility in India Poll*. New Delhi: Tata Energy Research Institute.

Lee, K. (1994) *Awe and Humility: Intrinsic Value in Nature*. Cambridge: Cambridge University Press.

Lee, S. K. and Anas, A. (1992) Costs of deficient infrastructure: the case of Nigerian manufacturing, *Urban Studies*, 29(7), pp. 1071–1092.

Littig, B. and Griessler, E. (2005) Social sustainability: a catchword between political pragmatism and social theory, *International Journal of Sustainable Development*, 18(1/2), pp. 65–79.

Llewellyn, G. (2005) Corporate governance, best practice, in: J. Hancock (ed.) *Investing in Corporate Social Responsibility: A Guide to Best Practice, Business Planning & the UK's Leading Companies*. London: Kogan Page.

Loftman, P. and Nevin, B. (1996) Going for growth: prestige projects in three British cities, *Urban Studies*, 33(6), pp. 991–1019.

Lund-Thomsen, P., Mansur, A. and Lotia, H. (2006) Corporate social responsibility and sustainability of donor-financed interventions in the South: the case of Pakistan, in: E. R. Pedersen and M. Huniche (eds) *Corporate Citizenship in Developing Countries*. Copenhagen: The Copenhagen Centre.

Lungo, M. (2000) Downtown San Salvador: housing, public spaces, and economic transformation, in: M. Polese and R. Stren (eds) *The Social Sustainability of Cities: Diversity and the Management of Change*, Toronto: University of Toronto Press.

Macleod, S. and McGee, T. (1996) The Singapore-Johore-Riau growth triangle: an emerging metropolitan region, in: F. Lo and Y. Yeung (eds) *Emerging World Cities in Pacific Asia*. Tokyo: United Nations Press.

Marsh, A., Gordon, D., Pantazis, C. and Heslop, P. (1999) *Home Sweet Home?: The Impact of Poor Housing on Health*. Bristol: The Policy Press.

Matten, D. and Moon, J. (2004) Corporate social responsibility education in Europe, *Journal of Business Ethics*, 54(4), pp. 323–337.

McAlister, D. T., Ferel, O. C. and Ferel, L. (2005) *Business and Society: A Strategic Approach to Corporate Citizenship*. Boston: Houghton Mifflin Company.

McCarney, P., Halfani, M. and Rodriguez, A. (1994) Towards an understanding of governance, in: R. Stren (ed.) *Urban Research in the Developing World*. Toronto: University of Toronto Press.

McGreal, S., Parsa, A. and Keivani, R. (2002) Evolution of property investment markets in central Europe: opportunities and constraints, *Journal of Property Research*, 19(3), pp. 213–230.

McGuirk, P. (2000) Power and policy networks in urban governance: local government and property-led regeneration in Dublin, *Urban Studies*, 37(4), pp. 651–672.

McIntosh, M., Leipziger, D., Jones, K. and Coleman, G. (1998) *Corporate Citizenship: Successful Strategies for Responsible Companies*. London: Financial times/Pitman.

Meikle, J. and Dickson, M. (2006) Understanding the social and economic value of construction, *Building Research and Information*, 34(3), pp. 191–196, http://www.journalsonline.tandf.co.uk/mEdia/3l93gqewxgdxxm54rye0/contributions/r/x/3/0/rx30h20q600x2311.pdf [accessed July 2007].

Meirelles, H. L. (1996) *Direito Municipal Brasileiro*, 8th ed. São Paulo: Malheiros Editores.

Meng, B. (2006) *Collective Action and Community Participation in the Delivery of Urban Services and Infrastructure*. Research publication, Department of Urban and Regional Planning, University of Hawaii at Manoa.

Milliken, M. (2000) Brazil's 'Valley of Death' breathes again, barely, http://forests.org/archive/brazil/brvallde.htm [accessed February 2008].

Moatazed-Keivani, R. (1993) *The Role of Formal Private Building Firms in Low Income Housing Provision in Developing Countries: The Case of Tehran*. Unpublished PhD thesis, Development Planning Unit, University College London.

Monaghan, P. (2002) Put up or shut up, in: A. Henriques and J. Richardson (eds) *The Triple Bottom Line, Does It Add Up? Assessing the Sustainability of Business and CSR*. London: Earthscan.

Montgomery, M. R. (2008) *The Health of Urban Populations in Developing Countries*. United Nations expert group meeting on population distribution, urbanization, internal migration and development, Population Division, Department of Economic and Social Affairs, United Nations Secretariat, New York, 21–23 January 2008.

Morshidi, S. (2000) Globalising Kuala Lumpur and the strategic role of the producer services sector, *Urban Studies*, 371(2), pp. 2217–2240.

Mukami Kariuki, R. (2002) Water and sanitation utilities and the urban poor, *Waterlines*, 21(2), p. 1.

Mukhija, V. (2002) An analytical framework for urban upgrading: property rights, property values and physical attributes, *Habitat International*, 26, pp. 553–570.

Mukhija, V. (2004) The contradictions in enabling private developers of affordable housing: a cautionary case from Ahmedabad, India, *Urban Studies*, 41(11), pp. 2231–2244.

Murphy, D. F. and Bendell, J. (1997) *In the Company of Partners: Business, Environmental Groups and Sustainable Development Post-Rio*. Bristol: The Policy Press.

Mutter, M. (2006) Foreword, in: A. Brown (ed.) *Contested Space: Street Trading, Public Space, and Livelihoods in Developing Cities*. Warwickshire: ITDG Publishing.

NC State University (2007) *Mayday 23: World Population Becomes More Urban Than Rural*, http://news.ncsu.Edu/releases/2007/may/104.html [accessed February 2008].

New Academy of Business and UNV (2004) *Global Report on Enhancing Business-Community Relations: The Role of Volunteers in Promoting Global Corporate Citizenship*. Bath and Bonn: New Academy of Business and United Nations Volunteers.

Nickson, A. (2001) *Cochabamba: Victory or Fiasco?*, id21, http://www.id21.org/insights/insights37/insights-iss37-cochabamba.html [accessed November 2007].

Nickson, A. and Franceys, R. (2003) *Tapping the Market: The Challenge of Institutional Reform in the Urban Water Sector*. Basingstoke: Palgrave Macmillan.

Nickson, A. and Vargas, C. (2002) The limitations of water regulation: the failure of the Cochabamba Concession in Bolivia, *Bulletin of Latin American Research*, 21(1), pp. 99–120.

O'Brien, R. and Williams, M. (2004) *Global Political Economy: Evaluation and Dynamics*. Basingstoke: Palgrave Macmillan.

ODPM (2006) *Securing the Future: Delivering UK Sustainable Development Strategy*, Office of the Deputy Prime Minister, http://www.communities.gov.uk/documents/planningandbuilding/pdf/144563 [accessed March 2008].

Paredes, M., Lawrence, R., Fluckiger, Y., Lambert, C., Mbiba, B., Wells, J. and Werna, E. (2007) *Promoting Decent Work in Construction and Related Services: The Key Role of Local Authorities*. Final report of project funded by the Geneva International Academic Network, University of Geneva and International Labour Office.

Parkin, S. (2000) *Context and Drivers for Operationalizing Sustainable Development*, Proceedings of ICE, 138, pp. 9–15.

Parsa, A. and Keivani, R (2002) The Hormuz Corridor: building a cross-border region between Iran and UAE, in: S. Sassen (ed.) *Global Networks, Linked Cities: Urban Connections in a Globalizing World*. London: Routledge.

Parsa, A., Keivani, R., Sim, L. L., Ong, S. E., Agarwal, A. and Younis, B. (2004) *Emerging Global Cities – Comparison of Singapore and the Cities of UAE*. RICS research publication.

Pearce, D. (2006a) Do we understand sustainable development? *Building Research and Information*, 33(5), 481–483, http://www.journalsonline.tandf.co.uk/ mEdia/hbmpyvwryhqn1dkt9t0m/contributions/h/8/5/j/h85j53p303t6506j.pdf [accessed July 2007].

Pearce, D. (2006b) Is the construction sector sustainable? Definitions and reflection, *Building Research and Information*, 34(3), 201–207, http://www.journalsonline.tandf.co.uk/mEdia/9h0b3q31qk4jyjfbfl1y/contributions/p/6/8/3/ p68328u401055656.pdf [accessed July 2007].

Pearce, D. (2003) *The Social and Economic Value of Construction*. London: nCRISP.

People and Planet (2007) Urban population trends, 29 January, http://peopleandplanet.net [accessed February 2008].

Pheng, L. S. (1995) *Synthesizing Construction and Marketing in Economic Development*. Hants: Avebury.

Plessis-Fraissard, M. (2007) Safety in the city, *Habitat Debate*, 13(3), p. 8.
Porritt, J. (2005) *Capitalism as if the World Matters*. London: Earthscan.
Porter, M. E. and Kramer, M. R. (2006) Strategy and society: the link between competitive advantage and corporate social responsibility, *Harvard Business Review*, 84(12), pp. 78–92.
Prahalad, C. K. and Hart, S. L. (2002) The fortune at the bottom of the pyramid, *Strategy+Business*, Issue 26, first quarter 2002.
Pugh, C. (1994) Housing policy development in developing countries: the World Bank and internationalisation, 1972–93, *Cities*, 11(3), pp. 159–180.
Pugh, C. (1996) Olympia and York, Canary wharf and what may be learned, *Property Management*, 14(2), pp. 5–18.
Rakodi, C. (2004) Representation and responsiveness – urban politics and the poor in ten cities in the South, *Community Development Journal*, 39(3), pp. 252–265.
Razzu, G. (2005) Urban redevelopment, cultural heritage, poverty and redistribution: the case of Old Accra and Adawso House, *Habitat International*, 29, pp. 399–419.
Richter, J. (2002) *Holding Corporations Accountable: Corporate Conduct, International Codes, and Citizen Action*. London: Zed Books.
Ricz, J. (2007) *Urbanisation Crisis in Developing Countries: The Case of Brazil*. Paper presented at *Regional Studies Association conference*, Lisbon, 2–5 April, http://www.regional-studies-assoc.ac.uk/events/lisbon07/papers/Ricz.pdf [accessed February 2008].
Robinson, P. B. (2002) "All for some": water inequity in Zambia and Zimbabwe, *Physics and Chemistry of the Earth*, 27, pp. 851–857.
Rodriguez, P. (2004) The debate on privatization of water utilities: a commentary, *Urban Studies*, 20(1), pp. 107–112.
Sassen, S. (2001) *The Global City: New York, London, Tokyo*. Princeton, NJ: Princeton University Press.
Savenje, H. H. G. (2002) Why water is not an ordinary economic good, or why the girl is special, *Physics and Chemistry of the Earth*, 27, pp. 741–744.
Sddirect (2008) *Corporate Social Responsibility: How Social Development Adds Value?* Social Development Direct portal, http://www.sddirect.org.uk/index.php?m=page&o=78 [accessed February 2008].
Sennett, J., Simmie, J., Wood, P. and Hart, D. (2002) Space, linkages, and successful urban regions: a cross-national comparison, *Journal of Urban Technology*, 9(3), pp. 49–68.
Sexty, R. W. (2004) *Corporate Social Responsibility: The Concept*, http://www.ucs.mun.ca/~rsexty/business8107/CSocialR.htm [accessed July 2007].
Sexty, R. W. (2008) *Canadian Business and Society: Ethics & Responsibilities*, Toronto: McGraw-Hill Ryerson.
Shatkin, G. (2004) Planning to forget: informal settlements as "forgotten places" in globalising metro Manila, *Urban Studies*, 41(12), pp. 2469–2484.
Shatkin, G. (2000) Obstacles to empowerment: local politics and civil society in metropolitan Manila, the Philippines, *Urban Studies*, 37(12), pp. 2357–2375.
Shell Briefing Service (1969) Environmental conservation, a management information brief for the staff of the companies of the Royal Dutch/Shell Group, September, London: Shell Briefing Service.

Sim, L. L., Ong, S. E., Agarwal, A., Parsa, A. and Keivani, R. (2003) Singapore's competitiveness as a global city: development strategy, institutions and business environment, *Cities: The International Journal of Urban Policy and Planning*, 20(2), pp. 115–127.

Sims, D. (2002) What is secure tenure in urban Egypt?, in: G. Payne (ed.) *Land, Rights and Innovation*. London: ITDG.

Sisulu, N. L. (2007) Keynote address to the United Nations World Habitat Day Conference, 1 October 2007, The Hague, Netherlands file:///H:/2nd%20book/Chapters/Utility%20chapter/Sisulu%202007.htm [accessed November 2007].

Sivaramakrishnan, K. C. (1996) Urban governance: changing realities, in: M. Cohen, B. Ruble, J. Tulchin and A. Garland (eds) *Preparing for the Urban Future: Global Pressures and Local Forces*. Washington, D.C.: Woodrow Wilson Centre Press.

Sørensen, M. B. and Petersen, S. M. (2006) *Partnering for Development – Making it Happen*. Copenhagen: United Nations Development Programme.

Soumare, M. (2002) Local initiatives and poverty reduction in urban areas: the example of Yeumbeul in Senegal, *International Social Science Journal*, 54(172), pp. 261–266.

Spence, R., Wells, J. and Dudley, E (1993) *Jobs from Housing: Employment, Building Materials and Enabling Strategies for Urban Development*. London: IT/ODA.

Stanley, B (2003) Going Global and Wannabe World Cities: (Re)conceptualizing Regionalism in the Middle East, in W. A. Dunaway (ed.) *Emerging Issues in the 21st Century World-System Vol I, Crisis and Resistance in the 21st Century World-System*, Westport, CN: Praeger, pp. 151–70.

Stren, R. and Polese, M. (2000) Understanding the new sociocultural dynamics of cities: comparative urban policy in a global context, in: M. Polese and R. Stren (eds) *The Social Sustainability of Cities: Diversity and the Management of Change*. Toronto, Buffalo, London: University of Toronto Press.

Swyngedouw, E., Moulaert, F. and Rodriguez, A. (2002) Neoliberal urbanization in Europe: large-scale urban development projects and the new urban policy, *Antipode*, 34(3), pp. 542–577.

Tennyson, R. (2005) *The Brokering Guidebook: Navigating Effective Sustainable Development Partnerships*. London: The International Business Leaders Forum.

Terradaily (2007) *Tehran pollution kills 3,600 in a month*, http://www.terradaily.com/reports/Tehran_Pollution_Kills_3600 [accessed February 2008].

Tessner, S. (2000) *The United Nations and Business: A Partnership Recovered*. New York: St. Martin's Press.

Tewdwr-Jones, M. (1994) The development plan in policy implementation, *Environment and Planning C*, 12, pp. 145–163.

Tichy, N. M., McGill, A. R. and St. Clair, L. (1997) *Corporate Global Citizenship: Doing Business in the Public Eye*. San Francisco: The New Lexington Press.

Tipple, G. (1994) Employment from housing: a resource for rapidly growing urban populations, *Cities*, 11(6), pp. 372–376.

Tipple, G. (2000) *Extending Themselves: User-initiated Transformation of Government-built Housing in Developing Countries*. Liverpool: Liverpool University Press.

Tremolet, S. (2001) *Power to Choose: Is pro-poor Privatisation Possible?*, id21, http://www.id21.org/insights/insights37/insights-iss37-choice.html [accessed October 2007].

Turin, D. (1978) Construction and development, in: D. H. Koenigsberger and S. Groak (eds) *Essays in Memory of Duccio Turin (1926–1976): Construction and Economic Development Planning of Human Settlements*. Oxford: Pergamon.

Turner, J. (1967) "Barriers and Channels for Housing in Modernizing Countries", in the *Journal of the American Institute of Planners*, Washington DC.

Turner, J. (1968) The squatter settlement, architecture that works, (illustrated), in: M. Pidgeon and G. Bell (eds) *The Architecture of Democracy. A Special Issue of Architectural Design*, 8(38).

Turner, J. (1977) *Housing by People: Towards Autonomy in Building Environments*. New York: Pantheon Books.

Turner, J. and Fichter, R. (1972) *Freedom to Build*. New York: Macmillan.

United Kingdom Government (2004) CSR government report, http://www.csr.gov.uk/pdf/dti_csr_final.pdf [accessed June 2007].

United Kingdom Government (2007) The UK government CSR Portal, http://www.csr.gov.uk/whatiscsr.shtml [accessed June 2007].

United Nations (UN) (2007) CSR and developing countries: what scope for government action? Sustainable developments, *Innovation brief*, issue 1, February 2007. New York: United Nations Department of Economic and Social Affairs.

United Nations (UN) (1992). *Report of the United Nations Conference on Environment and Development*, A/CONF.151/26 (Vol. I), Annex I, Rio Declaration on Environment and Development, http://www.un.org/documents/ga/conf151/aconf15126-1annex1.htm. [accessed December 2007].

United Nations Centre for Human Settlements (UNCHS) (1996a) *An Urbanizing World: Global Report on Human Settlements, 1996*. Oxford: Oxford University Press.

United Nations Centre for Human Settlements (UNCHS) (1996b) *The Istanbul Declaration and Habitat II Agenda*, Istanbul.

United Nations Centre for Human Settlements (UNCHS)/International Labour Organisation (ILO) (1995) *Shelter Provision and Employment Generation*. Nairobi and Geneva: UNCHS/ILO.

United Nations Children's Fund (UNICEF) (2007) *The State of the World's Children 2007: Women and Children – the Double Dividend of Gender Equality*. New York: UNICEF.

United Nations Development Programme (UNDP) (1999) *Cities and Sustainable Human Development*, UNDP: Policy Paper.

United Nations Development Programme (UNDP) (2004) *Unleashing Entrepreneurship: Making Business Work for the Poor*. New York: United Nations Development Programme, Commission of the private sector for development.

United Nations Human Settlements Programme (UN-Habitat) (2005) *Financing Urban Shelter: Global Report on Human Settlements*. London: Earthscan.

United Nations Human Settlements Programme (UN-Habitat) (2006a) *State of the World's Cities 2006/7*. London: Earthscan.

United Nations Human Settlements Programme (UN-Habitat) (2006b) Nairobi urban sector profile, www.unhabitat.org/pmss/getElectronicVersion.asp?nr=2079&alt=1 [accessed November 2007].

United Nations Human Settlements Programme (UN-Habitat) (2007a) *Business partnership for sustainable urbanisation – a strategic alliance of business companies, foundations, civil society organizations and the UN working towards sustainable urbanization*, http://www.unhabitat.org/downloads/docs/4228_32301_ BPSU%20brochure.pdf [accessed February 2008].

United Nations Human Settlements Programme (UN-Habitat) (2007b) *Poverty mapping a situation analysis of poverty pockets in Jabalpur*, www.unhabitat.org/pmss/getElectronicVersion.asp?nr=2394&alt=1 [accessed November 2007].

United Nations Human Settlements Programme (UN-Habitat) (2007c) *Poverty mapping a situation analysis of poverty pockets in Gwailor*, http://www.unhabitat.org/pmss/getPage.asp?page=bookView&book=2393 [accessed November 2007].

United Nations Industrial Development Organization (UNIDO) (2002) *Report on Corporate Social Responsibility: Implications for Small and Medium Sized Enterprises in Developing Countries*. Vienna: UNIDO.

United Nations Population Fund (UNFPA) (2007) *State of World Population 2007*, http://www.unfpa.org/swp [accessed February 2008].

United Nations Programme on HIV/AIDS (UNAIDS) (2006) Overview of the global AIDS epidemic, *2006 Report on the Global AIDS Epidemic*. Joint United Nations Programme on HIV/AIDS, Geneva.

United Nations Programme on HIV/AIDS (UNAIDS) (2007) Global HIV prevalence has levelled off; AIDS is among the leading causes of death globally and remains the primary cause of death in Africa. Press release, 20 November 2007, Joint United Nations Programme on HIV/AIDS, Geneva.

United Nations Volunteers (UNV) (2001) *Caring Cities – Volunteerism in Urban Development and the Role of the United Nations Volunteer Programme*. UNV: Policy Paper.

van Vliet, W. (2002) Cities in a globalizing world: from engines of growth to agents of change, *Environment and Urbanization*, 14(1), pp. 31–40.

Viloria-Williams, J. (2006) *Urban Community Upgrading – Lessons from the Past, Prospects for the Future*. Washington, D.C.: World Bank Institute.

Visser, W. (2003) Exploring the myths of corporate responsibility in a developing country context. *Ethical Corporation*, 20, pp. 32–34.

Visser, W. (2006a) Research on corporate citizenship in Africa, in: W. Visser, M. McIntosh and C. Middleton (eds) *Corporate Citizenship in Africa: Lessons from the Past; Paths to the Future*. Sheffield: Greenleaf.

Visser, W. (2006b) Revisiting Carroll's CSR pyramid: an African perspective, in: E. R. Pedersen and M. Huniche (eds) *Corporate Citizenship in Developing Countries*. Copenhagen: The Copenhagen Centre.

Visser, W., Matten, D. Pohl, M. and Tolhurst, N. (eds) (2007) *The A–Z of Corporate Social Responsibility*. Chichester: John Wiley & Sons, Ltd.

Vogel, D. (2005) *Market for Virtue: The Potential and Limitations of Corporate Social Responsibility*. Washington, D.C.: Brookings Institution.

Wallace, M. (2001) A new approach to neighbourhood renewal in England, *Urban Studies*, 38(12), pp. 2163–2166.

Wallman, S. (1984) *Eight London Households*. London: Tavistock.

Wanderley, L. O. (2002) *Sen's Capability Approach: A Meaningful Framework for Corporate Social Responsibility?* Working paper which was to be presented in the seminar: "*Justice and poverty: examining Sen's capability approach*", Von Hügel Institute, Cambridge, 5–7 June 2001.

Warner, K. and Negrete, J. (2005) The urban growth machine goes South: conditions and capacities for more sustainable place-building, *Local Environment*, 10(6), pp. 571–593.

WCED (1987) *Our Common Future*. Oxford: Oxford University Press.

Wen, D. (2005) *China Copes with Globalization: A Mixed Review*, International Forum on globalization, San Francisco, http://www.ifg.org/pdf/FinalChina Report.pdf [accessed January 2008].

Werna, E. (1996) *Business as Usual – Small-scale Builders and the Production of Low-income Housing in Developing Countries*. Avebury: Ashgate.

Werna, E. (1997) *Shelter, Employment and the Informal City in the Context of the Present Economic Scene: Implications for Participatory Governance*. Paper presented at the conference *Governance and Participation: Practical Approaches to Urban Poverty Reduction: Towards Cities for the New Generation*, Florence, 9–13 November 1997.

Werna, E. (2000) *Combating Urban Inequalities: Challenges for Managing Cities in the Developing World*. Aldershot: Edward Elgar Publishing.

Werna, E., Abiko, A., Keivani, R., Coelho, L., Simas, R., Hamburger, S. and Anastasia, M. (2004) *Pluralism in Housing Provision in Developing Countries – Lessons from Brazil*. New York: Nova Science Publishers.

Werna, E., Dzikus, A., Ochola, L. and Kumarasuriyar, M. (1999) *Implementing the Habitat Agenda: Towards Child-centred Human Settlement Development in Developing Countries*. Aldershot: Ashgate.

Wheeler, D. (2000) Racing to the bottom? Foreign investment and air quality in developing countries, The World Bank, http://econ.worldbank.org/external/default/main?pagePK=64165259&piPK=64165421&theSitePK=469372&menuPK=64216926&entityID=000094946_01012705513587 [accessed February 2008].

Wikipedia (2008) *Social Development Theory*, http://en.wikipedia.org/wiki/Social_development_theory [accessed February 2008].

Wilks-Heeg, S. (1996) Urban Experiments Limited revisited: urban policy comes full circle?, *Urban Studies*, 33(8), pp. 1263–1279.

Wilks-Heeg, S. (2000) *Mainstreaming Regeneration: A Review of Policy over the Last Thirty Years*. London: Local Government Association.

Witte, J. M. and Reinicke, W. (2005) *Business Unusual: Facilitating UN Reform Through Partnerships*, New York: UN Global Compact Office.

Wong, T. (1999) The transition from physical infrastructure to infostructure: infrastructure as a modernizing agent in Singapore, *GeoJournal*, 49, pp. 279–288.

World Bank (1994) *Governance – The World Bank's Experience*. Washington, D.C.: World Bank.

World Bank (1999) *A Strategic View of Urban and Local Government Issues: Implications for the Bank*, March, mimeo.

World Bank (2004a) *The World Bank and the Copenhagen Declaration: Ten Years After*. Washington, D.C.: The World Bank.

World Bank (2004b) *Social Development in World Bank Operations: Results and Way Forward, Discussion Draft*. Washington, D.C.: The World Bank.

World Bank (2004c) *A History of the Social Development Network in the World Bank, 1973–2002*. Social Development paper No. 56/March 2004. Washington, D.C.: The World Bank.

World Business Council for Sustainable Development (WBCSD) (1999) *Corporate Social Responsibility*, World Council for Sustainable Development Publications, ISBN No. 2-94-0240-03-5.

World Commission on Environment and Development (WCED) (1987) *Our Common Future*. Oxford: Oxford University Press.

World Health Organisation (WHO) (2004) Water, sanitation hygiene links to health, facts and figures, http://www.who.int/water_sanitation_health/facts figures2005.pdf [accessed November 2007].

World Health Organisation /UNICEF (2006) *Meeting the MDG drinking water and sanitation target*, http://www.wssinfo.org/pdf/JMP_06.pdf [accessed November 2007].

Wu, V. (1998) The Pudong development zone and China's economic reforms, *Planning Perspectives*, 13, pp. 133–165.

Wu, F. (2000) The global and local dimensions of place-making: remaking Shanghai as a world city, *Urban Studies*, 37(8), pp. 1359–1377.

Wu, F. (2003) Globalization, place promotion and urban development in Shanghai, *Journal of Urban Affairs*, 25(1), pp. 55–78.

WUP (2005) World Urbanization Prospects: The 2005 Revision, http://www.un.org/esa/population/publications/WUP2005/2005wup.htm [accessed February 2008].

WUP (2007) World Urbanization Prospects: The 2007 Revision Population Database, http://esa.un.org/unup/p2k0data.asp [accessed April 2008].

Xu, J. and Yeh, A. G. O. (2005) City repositioning and competitiveness building in regional development: new development strategies in Guangzhou, China, *International Journal of Urban and Regional Research*, 29(2), pp. 283–308.

Yap, K. S. and Shrestha, M. (1998) The development of housing for women factory workers in Bangkok – a documentary assessment, *Habitat International*, 22(3), pp. 313–326.

Yin, R. (1989) *Case Study Research: Design and methods*. Newbury Park: Sage.

You, N. (2007) Sustainable for whom? The urban millennium and challenges for redefining the global development planning agenda, *City*, 11(2), pp. 214–220.

Zammit, A. (2003) *Development at Risk: Rethinking UN-Business Partnerships*. Geneva: The South Centre and UN Research Institute for Social Development, p. 8.

Zhu, J. (2004) Local developmental state and order in China's urban development during transition, *International Journal of Urban and Regional Research*, 28(2), pp. 424–447.

Author Index

Agyeman, J.   56
Aldrich, B. C.   111
Andrelini, J.   80
Angel, S.   109
Anheier, H.   45
Aranya, R.   66
Arimah, B.   144, 145, 146
Atkinson, A.   79
Atkinson, R.   61
Azizi, M. H.   144

Baken, R. J.   119
Baker, M.   12, 13
Ball, M.   61, 62
Barrett, S.   8, 9
Batley, R.   41, 42, 161
Bendell, J.   9, 27, 33
Benjamin, S.   66, 67, 70
Bhalla, A.   180, 182, 185
Blowfield, M.   29, 32
Bowen, H.   8, 9
Brindley, T.   63
Bruno, K.   24, 25
Buckley, R. M.   109
Bull, B.   24
Byrne, D.   111

Cao, A.   65, 80, 82
Carley, M.   63
Cars, G.   77
Castillo, H.   175, 180, 182
Chahoud, T.   29, 31, 32
Cheney, H.   181
Cherry, G. E.   8
Chowdhury, F. J.   74
Christensen, P.   188
Clement-Jones, T.   8, 19
CLG (Communities and Local Government)   57
Colantonio, A.   53, 55, 56–58
Collignon, B.   146, 151, 155, 163
Conroy, M. E.   8

Constructing Excellence   13
Corporateregister.com   14, 15, 28
Crawford, P.   107
Crinson, M.   120
Cullingworth, J. B.   61

Davey, K. J.   42
Davis, K.   9
Davoudi, S.   62
De Haan, A.   181
Deb, A.   79
Devas, N.   77
Devuyst, D.   182
Dickson, M.   106, 108
Ding, D.   120
Doane, D.   29
Dokmeci, V.   68, 69
Douglas, M.   66, 67
Drakakis-Smith, D.   58, 81–83
Durand-Lasserve, A.   70

Edwards, M.   47
El-Hefnawi, A. I. K.   81, 82
Elkington, J.   10, 14, 32, 53
Employer Supported Volunteering   19
Ennew, J.   190
Evans, J.   60, 76, 77

Fainstein, S.   60
Falck, O.   9
Farrington, D. P.   160
Fichter, R.   48
Firman, T.   66
Franceys, R.   146–149, 151, 152, 156, 162, 164, 165
Friedman, F.   19
Frynas, J. G.   29, 32

Gandy, M.   145, 146, 158, 160, 165
Ganesan, S.   108

Garg, S. K.   119
Globalideasbank   82
Gorynski, J.   106
Graham, S.   65, 143
Grant, R.   66
Gray, R.   12
Griessler, E.   54, 55
Groak, S.   107
Gulyani, M.   146, 148–151, 155

Habisch, A.   12, 18
Hall, N.   47
Hall, R.   8, 194
Harpham, T.   38
Harris, N.   61
Hart, S. L.   30, 43
Hatter, W.   54, 57
Healey, P.   56, 60, 62, 63
Heblich, S.   9
Ho, K. C.   64
Holder, A.   29
Holmgren, P.   190
Hopkins, M.   31
Hoyle, B.   71
Hulme, D.   47

Ingram, G. K.   65
International Labour Organisation (ILO)   109, 110, 186, 189

Jeppesen, S.   29, 30
Jones, C.   60–62, 119
Jones, G. W.   66
Jones, P.   60, 76, 77
Jonker, J.   12, 18

Kalarickal, J.   109
Karnan, A.   29, 30
Keithley, J.   111
Keivani, R.   40, 64–66, 68, 80, 82, 109, 113, 118–120, 143, 166
Kell, G.   22
Kessides, C.   143
Khan, A. H.   71, 156, 157
Koenigsberger, D. H.   107
Kohler, N.   107
Kramer, M. R.   17, 206

Kuhndt, M.   18
Kumar, R.   29, 31

Lapeyre, F.   180, 185
Lee, K.   53
Lee, S. K.   145, 157, 158, 164
Levin, D.   22
Littig, B.   54, 55
Llewellyn, G.   18
Loftman, P.   62, 63
Lund-Thomsen, P.   29
Lungo, M.   68

Macleod, S.   64
Maginn, P.   61, 62, 76
Marsh, A.   110, 111
Matten, D.   12
Mattingly, M.   64, 66
McAlister, D. T.   17
McCarney, P.   77
McGee, T.   64
McGreal, S.   35
McGuirk, P.   77
McIntosh, M.   17, 212
Meikle, J.   106, 108
Meirelles, H. L.   164
Meng, B.   40
Milliken, M.   82
Milne, M.   12
Moatazed-Keivani, R.   68
Monaghan, P.   194
Montgomery, M. R.   187
Moon, G.   61
Moon, J.   12
Morshidi, S.   66
Mukami Kariuki, R.   147
Mukhija, V.   40, 74, 75, 120
Murphy, D. F.   9
Mutter, M.   180, 183

Nadin, V.   61
NC State University   35
Negrete, J.   53, 77
Nevin, B.   62, 63
New Academy of Business   4, 16, 50
Nickson, A.   146–149, 151, 152, 156, 162, 164, 165
Nijman, J.   66
Nurul Amin, A. T. M.   74

O'Brien, R. 107
ODPM (Office of the Deputy Prime Minister) 58

Paredes, M. 4
Parkin, S. 52
Parsa, A. 35, 64
Pearce, D. 106–109
People and Planet 35
Petersen, S. M. 24
Pheng, L. S. 106–108
Plessis-Fraissard, M. 160
Polese, M. 55, 59, 65, 66, 68, 82, 83, 181
Porritt, J. 53
Porter, M. E. 17, 206
Prahalad, C. K. 30, 43
Pugh, C. 61, 110

Rakodi, C. 77
Razzu, G. 71–73
Reinicke, W. 24
Richter, J. 24
Ricz, J. 24
Robinson, P. B. 148, 151, 155
Rodriguez, P. 165

Sandhu R. S. 111
Sassen, S. 61, 62
Savenje, H. H. G. 164
Sddirect 183, 185
Sennett, J. 143
Sexty, R. W. 11, 12, 14
Shah, S. 33
Shatkin, G. 66, 67, 70
Shaw, T. 63
Shell Briefing Service 9
Shrestha, M. 120
Sim, L. L. 64
Sims, D. 70
Sisulu, N. L. 160
Sivaramakrishnan, K. C. 77
So, A. 11, 39, 64
Sørensen, M. B. 24
Soumare, M. 73
Spence, R. 107–111
Stanley, B. 64
Stren, R. 55, 59, 65, 66, 68, 82, 83, 181

Swart-Kruger, J. 190
Swyngedouw, E. 61–63

Tennyson, R. 207
Terradaily 81
Tessner, S. 20
Tewdwr-Jones, M. 61
Tichy, N. M. 212
Tipple, G. 106–112
Tremolet, S. 165
Turin, D. 107
Turner, J. 48

UN (United Nations) 53
UNAIDS (United Nations Programme on HIV/AIDS) 191
UNCHS (United Nations Centre for Human Settlements) 42, 109, 110, 112, 144
UNDP (United Nations Development Programme) 30, 31, 34
UNFPA (United Nations Population Fund) 35
UN-Habitat (United Nations Human Settlements Programme) 35–37, 44, 106, 107, 109–112, 159–161, 189, 214
UNICEF (United Nations Children's Fund) 146, 153–155, 186, 191
UNIDO (United Nations Industrial Development Organization) 29, 31, 33
UNV (United Nations Volunteers) 3, 4, 16, 17, 45, 49, 50, 133, 187, 188, 190, 194, 195, 206

Van der Linden, J. 119
Van Vliet, W. 78
Vargas, C. 165
Vezina, M. 146, 151, 155, 156, 163
Viloria-Williams, J. 48
Visser, W. 11–15, 27–31, 33
Vogel, D. 29
Vogl, B. 107

Wallace, M. 57
Wallman, S. 4
Wanderley, L. O. 12, 13

Author Index

Warner, K. 53, 56, 77
WBCSD (World Business Council for Sustainable Development) 12
WCED (World Commission on Environment and Development) 53, 180
Welsh, C. 160
Wen, D. 80
Werna, E. 4, 36, 37, 39, 40, 41, 45, 75, 77, 106, 109–111, 113, 118–120, 166, 188, 190
Wheeler, D. 81
WHO (World Health Organisation) 146, 153–155
Wikipedia 182
Wilks-Heeg, S. 61–63
Williams, M. 48, 107

Witte, J. M. 24
Wong, T. 143
World Bank 34, 55, 77, 143, 181–184
Wu, F. 66
Wu, V. 65
WUP (World Urbanization Prospects) 35, 145

Xu, J. 65

Yap, K. S. 120
Yeh, A. G. O. 65
Yin, R. 4
You, N. 37, 38

Zammit, A. 25
Zhu, J. 65

Subject Index

Abidjan   146, 156, 163, 164
ABN Amro Bank   89
Accountability   9, 17, 19, 25, 182, 212, 213
Accra   71–73, 128, 135
Ache Laboratarios Farmaceuticos   94
Achrafieh   88, 89
adolescents   189, 190
adult illiteracy   186
advocacy   24, 49, 63, 73, 83, 84
Afghanistan   153
Africa   4, 20, 28, 35, 37, 71, 111, 112, 120, 128, 144, 147, 148, 150, 153–156, 159, 160, 164, 178, 183, 191, 192, 194, 205, 209, 210
African Oxygen   192, 200
Aga Khan Trust   71
Agency for the Development of Guarulhos   93
AGENDE   93, 95
Agua e Cidade   121–125, 141, 167, 170–173, 179, 205, 207, 211
Al-Bustan Festival   87, 92
Allianz   86, 87, 92
Aluminium Company   196–198, 202, 205
Alvaro Mesquita Companhia   94
Amartya Sen   185
American Chocolate Manufacturers Association   192
Amnesty International   10
Anambara   158
anti-corruption   23
Antoine Wakim   88
Antonio Carlos de Almeida   97
Antonio Carlos Koch   94
ANPEZ Centre for Environment and Development (ACFED)   199–201
Aprendiz   195, 201
  Agencia   195, 201
  Café   195, 201
architecture   110
Argentina   153

Ashanti Kingdom   135
Ashfoam (Ashanti Foam Factory Limited)   122, 135, 136–139, 142, 205, 207
Asia   4, 20, 64, 120, 144, 149, 151, 153, 155, 156, 158, 178, 191
Association of Guarulhos Citizens for the Defence of Citizenship (AGDC)   93, 95
Assurances General de France (AGF)   86, 87
audit   19, 199
Austria   8

Bahrain   64
Bamako   156, 163
Bangalore   64, 66, 67, 70
Bangkok   65, 67, 120, 166
Bangladesh   46, 147, 149
Bank Boston Foundation   195
Banque Audi   89
Banque Nationale de Paris Intercontinatale (*BNPI*)   89
Banque Saradar   89
Battle of Seattle   11
Beijing   79, 149
Beirut   86, 88
Belize   153
Benin   153
Beyoglu   68–70
Birmingham   63
Bogota   65, 149, 157
Bolivia   153
bottom of the pyramid   13, 30
brand image   47, 131
Brasilia   79, 149, 170
Brazil   4, 10
Bristol Accord   57, 58
British   8, 9, 193
British Oxygen Company Group   193
Brown Agenda   83
Brundtland's Report   10

235

Subject Index

building solidarity   1
building standards   113–117
Bumbanani Day   192
Business   2–17, 19–27, 29, 30, 32,
   33, 39, 43, 50, 53, 61, 63–67, 69,
   77, 84, 85, 91–97, 99, 101, 102,
   104, 109, 110, 119, 120, 125,
   133–136, 138–141, 143, 146, 167,
   169–171, 174, 177, 178, 185,
   192–195, 198–200, 202, 203,
   206–210, 212–214
   and society   12, 19
   ethics   10, 12
   sustainability   12
Business Community Relations (BCR)
   2, 3, 16, 39, 44, 91, 92, 99, 102,
   109, 119, 120, 125, 135, 138, 140,
   141, 207, 210–212, 214

Cable and Wireless Company   71
Cadburys   8
Calcutta   41, 79, 118
Cambodia   153
capital   41, 55, 61, 70, 77, 78, 86,
   100, 104, 107–110, 135, 143–146,
   148, 149, 156, 158, 164
   asset   110
   formation   109, 110
   markets   144, 164
capitalism   9, 11
Caribbean   144, 153, 154, 191, 197
Carnegie   8
cause-related marketing   14, 134
Central Business District (CBD)
   65–68
Centro das Industrias do Estado de
   Sao Paulo   9
Chandigarh   79
charities   134
Charles Dickens   9
child labour   10, 23, 29, 189, 192
children   38, 86–88, 110, 156, 161,
   180, 186, 188–193, 195–202
Chile   77, 149
China   30, 79, 80–82, 149, 153, 154
Cholera   111
Cities   1–4, 9, 34–39, 41, 48, 50, 52,
   56–62, 64–69, 74, 75, 77, 79–83,
   85, 93–95, 99, 103–107, 120, 122,
   123, 125, 139, 143–149, 151, 152,
   155–159, 163, 166, 168, 172, 173,
   178, 186–190
citizenship   12, 16, 17, 19, 22, 93,
   182, 194, 206, 211, 212
city regeneration   52, 60
citywide interventions   35, 52–105
civil service   46
civil society   22, 26, 28, 31, 32, 45,
   47, 59, 77, 85, 93, 94, 99, 105,
   141, 142, 165, 181, 194, 195, 212
   organisations   26, 31, 32, 212
Clark Family   8
climate change   11, 27, 78
Coca-Cola   99
Cochabamba   165
Colombo   147, 149
Commercialisation   70
Commission for Social Development
   182
Commission on Transnational
   Corporations (TNCs)   21, 25
community development   2, 20, 52,
   60, 63, 73, 76, 78, 83–85, 97, 132,
   168, 209, 211
Community Involvement Process
   193
Community-Based Organisations
   (CBOs)   45, 48, 51, 211
community-driven development
   184
competition   41, 42, 61, 125, 128,
   134, 135, 143, 152, 162
competitive advantage   11, 17
Conakry   164
conservation   9, 53, 69, 71–73, 87,
   121, 173, 187, 225
construction   1, 4, 5, 13, 62, 74, 75,
   106–142, 152, 156, 162, 167, 173,
   179, 195, 202, 204, 205
   companies   204
   excellence   13
   industry   1, 4, 62, 106–110, 113,
   120, 140
   industry association   1
Copenhagen   182–184
   Commitments   183, 184
   Declaration   182, 183
   Summit   182

corporate
  citizenship   12, 16, 17, 22, 206, 211, 212
  environmental management   12
  governance   11, 12, 16, 18
  philanthropy   10, 205, 206
  responsibility   12, 16, 134, 211, 215, 219, 222, 228
  social responsibility (CSR)   1–6, 7–33, 34, 39, 43, 44, 47–52, 84–86, 90–92, 98, 99, 104–106, 109, 113, 119–123, 139, 141, 142, 166–168, 176, 178–180, 192, 194–208, 210, 211, 213–215
  sustainability   12
  world   11
corruption   23, 27, 29, 93, 145, 184
Costa Rica   149
Cote d'Ivoire   151
Cotonou   156, 163
credit   33, 42, 72, 73, 119, 129, 131
crime   22, 37, 39, 55, 57, 145, 159, 160, 174–176, 181, 188, 189
CSR Projects   1, 2, 31, 203
Cubatao   81, 82
culture   58, 86, 87, 94, 98, 102, 145, 180, 183–185, 187, 194, 195, 200
customers   16, 74, 90, 131, 133, 134, 136, 156, 173, 177, 178

Dakar   73, 146, 156, 163, 164
Davao   167, 173–179, 205, 207, 209
Davao Light & Power Company   167, 173, 174, 209
David Pearce   108
DECA   170, 171
Delhi   67, 79, 149, 156
demand   19, 28, 41, 42, 43, 49, 68, 70, 75, 81, 97, 103, 111, 119, 135, 148, 150, 168, 172, 179, 201
Democratic Republic of Congo   153
deregulation   61
developing countries   1, 3–5, 8, 27, 28, 30, 31, 33–37, 41–43, 45–48, 50, 56, 58, 60, 65, 66, 69, 71, 74, 76–80, 82–84, 101, 103, 106–108, 110–119, 121, 140–147, 149, 152, 154–156, 160, 162, 164–166, 168, 178, 179, 186–188, 190–192, 200, 210, 214–215
Development Plans   63, 207
Dhaka   74, 147, 149, 152
Diamond Cement Ghana Limited (DCGL)   121, 125, 127–131
disease   27, 37, 38, 111, 145, 147, 187, 191, 131, 132
District Assemblies   131, 132
DOCOL Sanitary Metals Ltd   168
donations   10, 90, 98, 105, 127, 198, 201, 202
drainage   144
drug abuse   186, 190, 191
Dubai   64, 221
Duccio Turin   107

Earth Summit   10, 53, 63, 180
East Africa   71
economic
  development   12, 13, 30, 31, 35, 57, 60, 62, 69, 71, 77, 81–83, 86, 104, 107, 143, 150, 159, 178, 197
  growth   35, 62, 81, 107, 113, 143, 186–188, 196
  prosperity   13, 14, 53
Ecuador   153
education   3, 4, 12, 29, 40, 41, 52, 59, 87, 88, 97, 99, 102, 104, 108, 122, 127, 134, 140, 161, 168, 176, 180–186, 188, 194–196, 198, 200, 202
Education for All   186
Egypt   70, 82, 86, 153, 226
electricity   33, 36, 40–42, 50, 73, 86, 123, 144, 157, 166, 175, 196, 197
employee involvement   194, 200, 205, 209, 210
employee volunteering   17, 24, 209
Employer Supported Volunteering   19
employment   23, 30, 36, 57, 59, 61, 67, 68, 83, 90, 103, 108, 120, 140, 157, 158, 176, 180–183, 185, 186, 200
engagement   18, 22, 24, 25, 31, 50, 85, 87, 91, 122, 135, 138, 141, 184, 208–210, 215

English Partnerships 61
entrepreneurship 12, 184
environment 9–11, 13, 16, 21–23, 27, 29, 31, 53, 57–59, 72–74, 78, 79, 82, 83, 89, 92, 98, 99, 100, 103, 106, 108, 111, 123, 125, 130, 131, 134, 135, 143, 160, 164, 167, 169–172, 178, 180, 181, 183, 199, 201, 213
environmental
  quality 13, 14, 53
  pollution 29, 80, 81
Environmental Impact Assessment (EIA) 180
equity 14, 53, 55, 56, 58, 183, 184
estate agency 110
ethical 12–15, 17, 30, 91, 192, 212, 213
  entrepreneurship 12
Ethiopia 153
Ethnic minorities Business Initiative 61
Europe 8, 12, 28, 63, 64, 66, 76, 78, 148, 196
European Union 57

family 8, 38, 86, 157, 189, 190
farming 39
favelas 75
Fiji 149
Florianopolis 149
forced labour 10
formal finance 113, 114
Framework Convention on Tobacco Control 26
France 8, 86
Frederick Engels 9
Friends of the Earth 10

garbage 17, 36, 48, 50, 74, 87
  disposal 48, 74
Garden Festivals 61
gender 181, 183, 184
General Electric 20
gentrification 70
George Cadbury's Bourneville 120
George Wilson 8
Germany 8

Ghana 4, 24, 121, 122, 125, 127, 128, 131, 133, 135, 139, 141, 142, 196–198, 202, 205
  Education Service 198, 202
Gilberto Dimenstein 195, 201
Global Campaign for Secure Tenure 78
Global Compact Society (GCS) 32
Global Reporting Initiative (GRI) 32
globalisation 11, 22, 25, 27, 35, 61, 66, 79, 187
Go Green Partnership 98, 101, 205, 209
good citizen 17
Gordon Brown 16
governance 11, 12, 16, 18, 19, 27, 59, 76, 77, 78, 84, 85, 104, 106, 181
government agencies 2, 20, 110, 121
Grass Roots Organisations (GROs) 48, 78
green 10, 68, 82, 83, 85, 98–102, 123, 205, 207–209, 212
greenhouse gases 78
Greenpeace 10
Gross Domestic Product (GDP) 36, 107, 108, 109, 144, 145
Gross National Product (GNP) 36, 107
Guangdong 80
Guarulhos 85, 93–97, 104
Guatemala 152
Guinea-Bissau 153

Haiti 153
health 4, 8, 9, 17, 36, 38, 40, 52, 57–59, 78, 87, 108, 110, 111, 122, 126, 127, 134, 140, 143, 147, 152, 154, 161, 162, 180–182, 187, 190, 200, 210
Healthy Cities Project 38
healthcare 29, 193
Help Lebanon 85, 86, 88–90, 92, 104
Hersheys 8
HIV/AIDS 29, 184, 188, 189, 191, 193, 201
Holland 8

Subject Index 239

homelessness 39, 111, 188, 190
Hong Kong 28, 64, 149
hospitals 8, 36, 60, 170, 192, 193
housing 8, 29, 37, 40, 52, 55, 57,
  59–62, 64–66, 68, 69, 70, 72, 74,
  75, 78, 106, 109–125, 140–142,
  162, 166–168, 173, 185, 188
  shortage 111, 112
  provision 74, 112–122, 125, 141,
    166, 167
  informal 117, 120, 166
  low income 40, 114, 119–121
  squatter 117, 118
human capital 110
human rights 10, 11, 14, 22, 23, 26,
  27, 58, 67, 191, 200

inclusivity 78
income generating activity 73, 110,
  111, 196
India 24, 31, 32, 33, 41, 45, 119,
  146, 149, 153, 154, 156, 161
India Partnership Forum 32
indigenous peoples 21
Indonesia 144, 153
industrialisation 29, 81, 103, 107,
  158
industrialised countries 27, 28, 34,
  212, 215
infant mortality 37
informal finance 113, 115–118
information and communication
  technology (ICT) 11, 32
infrastructure 24, 29, 36, 40, 41, 60,
  61, 64, 65, 67, 69, 73, 74, 81, 86,
  106, 121, 124, 126, 142–145, 148,
  157–159, 174, 187
in-kind support 24
Intergovernmental Panel on Climate
  Change (IPCC) 78
International Alliance of
  Inhabitants 2
International Chamber of
  Commerce 20
International Convention Centre 63
International Council of
  Monuments & Sites 72
international development 2, 20,
  27, 47, 107, 183

International Labour Office iii, 186
International Monetary Fund
  (IMF) 20
International Organisations 1, 2, 7,
  84, 85, 99, 100, 103, 104
International Sculpture Forum 87
internet 32, 33, 199, 202
investment 2, 12, 17, 21, 24, 27, 36,
  41–43, 46, 51, 57, 59, 61, 62,
  67–69, 72–74, 84, 91, 94, 96, 97,
  133, 143–145, 148, 152, 158, 177,
  179, 197, 200, 205–207, 213
Iran 120, 153, 166
Islamabad 79, 183
Istanbul 68, 69, 72
Italy 8

Jamaica 153
Japan 8, 28, 66, 78
Jakarta 66, 151
John Elkington 10
Jordan 86
just sustainability 56
justice 13, 14, 53, 55, 56, 58, 59,
  181, 182, 208

Kakamega 146
Karl Marx 9
Kathmandu 149
Kenya 146, 150, 151, 194
kinship 38
Kofi Annan 21
Korea 28, 149, 153, 154
Kpone 198
Kuala Lumpur 66, 149
Kumasi 135, 136, 139, 140
Kwame Nkrumah 196
Kyoto Agreement 78

labour 31, 49, 59, 63, 64, 73, 108,
  110, 118, 124, 127, 130, 143, 156,
  157, 177, 186, 188, 189, 192
Lagos 79, 145, 158, 160, 165
land 35, 60–62, 65–67, 70, 74, 75,
  80–82, 103, 114, 116–120, 161,
  174
  markets 35
  use control 62
Las Vegas 79

Latex Foam   137, 138
Latin America   4, 45, 144, 149, 153, 154, 156, 158, 159
latrines   74, 154–157
Learner Cyber Café   195, 201
Learner School City   194, 201, 205, 211
Lebanese Broadcasting Corporation International (LBCI)   90
Lebanon   4, 85–92, 98, 99, 101, 102, 104, 205, 207
liberalisation   61, 62
license to operate   17, 194, 197
Lilianne Tyan   88
limits   10
Living Waters Programme   124
Local Agenda 21   54
Local Authorities   21, 54, 57, 59, 60, 62, 63, 82, 110, 125, 131, 148, 172
Local Governments   47, 61, 62, 65
Local Strategic Partnerships   76
London   61, 62, 66, 79, 92
London Docklands Corporation   61
Los Angeles   79
low income communities   1, 2, 43, 44, 48, 166, 204, 211, 213, 214
low income housing *see* housing
Luis Roberto Mesquita   94

malaria   29
Malawi   194
Malaysia   41, 149
malnutrition   37, 38, 187
Manama   64
Mandalay   149
Manila   66, 67, 70, 78, 149, 174, 177
Mark Kramer   17
Markandeya slum   74
markets   24, 35, 42, 43, 56, 61, 62, 64, 68, 110, 119, 141, 144, 164–166, 186, 190
Mauritania   153
mega-cities   35, 221
merit goods   40, 164
Mexico   35, 41, 65, 81, 82, 153
Mexico City   35, 65, 81, 82
Michael Porter   17
Middle East   4, 64, 79, 144

Millennium Declaration   26
Millennium Development Declaration   182
Millennium Development Goals (MDGs)   25, 26, 27, 28, 147, 180, 186, 188, 192, 200, 203, 206
Minas   149
Mombasa   146
monopolies   42, 162
Moscow   79
Mozambique   194
Mumbai   66, 74, 75
Myanmar   149

Nairobi   146, 150, 151, 156, 160, 163
Namibia   194
neighbourhood upgrading   52, 60
neoliberal   25, 42
Nepal   149
Networking   65, 90, 100, 102
New Academy of Business   3, 4, 16, 17, 50, 133, 194, 195, 206
New Delhi   79, 156
New York   iv, 35, 62
New Zealand   28
Newton   198
Nigeria   4, 28, 144, 148, 153, 155, 157, 158, 199, 201, 205, 212
Non-Governmental Organisations (NGOs)   2, 20, 21, 28, 31, 32, 39, 45–49, 51, 72, 78, 83, 84, 87, 90, 92, 102, 103, 105, 107, 118, 119, 121, 142, 152, 153, 156, 164, 166, 199, 212, 214
Norms on the Responsibility of Transnational Corporations and other Business Entities   26
North   8, 28–31, 58, 66, 77, 103, 144
North America   8, 28
North-South divide   28
Norway   128
Notaries   110
Nouakchott   156
NWASCO (National Water & Sanitation Supply Council)   148

Office of the High Commissioner for Human Rights (OHCHR)   22

Subject Index 241

Organisation for Economic Co-operation & Development (OECD) 20, 53
olympic games 80
Omani fort 71
Omar Sakr 99
Organização da Sociedade Civil 85, 93, 205, 207, 208, 211
Ouagadougou 146, 156
Our Common Future 53, 180
Our Water Programme 168
overcrowding 39, 190

Pakistan 120, 166, 183
Paraguay 152
Parrainages et Actions Civiques SNA 90
participation 20, 31, 41, 42, 47–49, 55, 58, 69, 72, 73, 87, 94, 95, 125, 162, 173, 179, 181, 184, 202
partnerships 2, 7, 20, 25, 26, 43, 47, 48, 57, 61, 76, 77, 86, 88, 94, 96–98, 105, 125, 164, 165, 167, 179, 195, 200–202, 208, 209, 212
Pearce Schema 108, 109
Persian Gulf 64
Peru 153
philanthropy 8, 10, 14, 16, 17, 49, 103, 205, 206, 207
Philippines vii, 4, 144, 149, 153, 173, 174, 179, 205
physical upgrading 60
planning regulations 113–117
political parties 45, 78, 97, 116, 117
pollution 29, 39, 57, 68, 80–82, 108
Port Harcourt 199
poverty 3, 11, 16, 25, 27, 29, 30, 33, 34, 36–39, 46, 50, 51, 58, 59, 72, 73, 79, 83, 84, 103, 158, 159, 174, 180, 181–186, 189, 190, 202
Poverty Reduction Strategy Papers (PRSPs) 184
power (electric) 143, 146, 156, 157–158, 159, 161, 167, 173, 174, 178, 179, 196, 197, 205, 207, 209
pressure waves 10
Prima Woods 122, 139, 140, 142, 205, 207

Prime Minister's Grant Project (PMGP) 74
private companies 1, 2, 4, 20, 47, 49, 50, 93, 94, 96, 97, 121–123, 192, 213
private contractors 114, 156
private developers 74, 75, 116, 117, 119, 120, 223
private sector 2, 3, 20–22, 24–26, 28–30, 39–46, 48, 51, 59, 61–63, 76, 84, 89, 91, 96, 97, 99, 104, 121, 141, 164–166, 179, 187, 196, 212
private suppliers 162
privatisation 40, 42, 43, 62, 165, 167
product stewardship 12
production 10, 35, 38, 40–42, 64, 79, 81, 112, 124, 128–130, 135, 143, 150, 158, 162, 169, 178, 186, 196
productivity 32, 108, 110, 111, 123, 143, 218
profit 1, 12, 14, 25, 40, 49, 75, 96, 122, 133, 151, 156, 187, 193, 213
property management 110
property-led urban development 60, 62, 63
prostitution 186, 200
Protestant work ethic 8, 9
public policy 7
Public Private Partnership (PPP) 43, 44, 84, 164, 167, 179, 200
Public Private Partnerships for Service delivery (PPP-SD) 43
Public Private Partnership Programme for the Urban Environment (PPP-UE) 43
public sector 40, 41, 48, 49, 60, 72, 77, 83, 84, 85, 96, 97, 101, 103, 104, 141, 142, 145, 152, 155, 162
public spaces 55, 66, 85, 112
publicity 87, 89–91, 102, 105, 196
Pullman 8

Quality of life 12, 13, 15, 57, 69, 81, 93–97, 108, 143, 145, 181
quantity surveying 110

Subject Index

Rachana 87
Rafik Hariri 88
Rashana forum 92
real estate 62, 69, 70
recreation 37, 177
redevelopment 52, 60–62, 64, 67, 71, 74, 75, 103, 104
Refurbishment 68
refuse collection 73, 144, 145
regeneration 52, 56, 60, 64, 68, 70, 76, 83–85, 104, 212
Republic of Korea 28, 153, 154
reputation 19, 87, 91, 99, 102, 131, 174, 175
responsible corporate governance (RCG) 18
Rio de Janeiro 10, 21, 170
Rio Earth Summit (earth summit) 53, 63, 180
roads 36, 41, 73, 106, 136, 160, 161, 166, 174
Robert Bosch 8
Robert Owen 8
Rockefeller 8
Rowntrees 8
rural 17, 35, 37–39, 69, 127, 139, 155, 186, 187, 189, 191
  population 35
  poverty 37–39

Safer Cities 61, 189
San Salvador 67, 68
Sanitation 29, 72, 73, 123, 124, 146, 148, 153–156, 159, 166, 168, 172, 173, 185
  facilities 154, 155
Santiago 149
Sao Paulo 75, 93, 94, 122, 149, 170–172
Sassine Tunnel 89, 90
Schlumberger 199–201, 205, 212
Schlumberger Excellence in Educational Development (SEED) 199–202
Schlumberger Oil services 199
Schlumberger Marcel 199
Schlumberger Conrad 199
schools 12, 36, 58, 60, 121, 169, 170, 193, 198, 199, 202

Schtroumpf 85, 98, 99, 101, 102, 212
Science World 199, 202
security of tenure 118
self build 114, 118
Senegal 73
Seoul 67, 149, 157
septic tanks 155, 156
settlement upgrading 81, 115
sewerage 48, 50, 73, 74, 144, 145, 155–157, 161, 166, 167
Shanghai 65, 66, 149
shareholders 16, 18, 32, 213
Shell Group 9
shelter 58, 59, 66, 88, 109, 111, 112, 141, 190, 193
Shenzen 120, 166
Singapore 64, 82, 149, 177
sites and services 114
Skyscrapers 66
slum 1, 36, 37, 66–68, 74, 75, 78, 111, 112, 149, 150, 156, 159, 161, 165, 202, 204
  dwellers 37, 74, 75, 112
  redevelopment 74, 75
Slum Redevelopment Scheme (SRD) 74
Slum Upgrading 74
Slum/Shacks Dwellers International (SDI) 1, 2, 204
small, medium & micro enterprises (SMMEs) 28, 30, 31, 33
social
  capital 55, 77, 78, 100, 108, 109
  Charter 183
  Development 5, 25, 52, 55, 76, 84, 93–97, 133, 139, 180–200, 202, 203
  Development Direct 185
  Equity 14
  Exclusion 159, 181
  investment 3, 17, 27, 94, 97, 201, 205–207
  investment programmes 2
  justice 13, 14, 53, 55, 56, 58
  networks 55
  protection 184
  protection schemes 181

Subject Index 243

responsibility 8, 17, 27, 133
sciences 6
sustainability 53, 55, 59, 103
Socially Responsible Investment (SRI) 12
welfare 8, 143
Societe Nationale D' Assurances (SNA) 85, 86, 104
solid waste 144
South 4, 25, 28–33, 45, 48, 64, 66, 68, 75, 77, 103, 146, 153, 157, 160, 174, 183, 191, 192, 194, 205, 215
   Africa 4, 28, 153, 160, 192, 194, 205
   Asian Association for Regional Cooperation 183
Spitalfields 66
Squatter 39, 74, 111, 117, 118, 157
   Housing 118
Sri Lanka 146, 149
stakeholders 1, 2, 5, 11, 13, 16, 17, 19, 20, 26, 31–33, 50, 51, 99–102, 125, 173, 175, 177, 178, 185, 198, 201, 208, 212
Stone Town 71
street 17, 38, 40, 68–70, 74, 88, 89, 145, 146, 159–162, 167, 175–179, 186, 189–191, 193, 201, 202
   children 38, 186, 190, 193, 201
   lighting 40, 69, 74, 145, 159–161, 167, 175–179
sub-Sahara 37, 144, 155, 156, 164, 178, 191, 192
supply 10, 11, 40–43, 48, 61, 74, 89, 119, 144, 146–148, 150, 151, 153, 159, 164–168, 175, 190, 192, 196, 213
sustainability 3, 12, 15, 33, 52–59, 72, 77, 79, 83, 86, 91, 92, 96, 100–103, 106, 109, 122, 140, 141, 168, 180, 185, 195, 199, 201, 202, 212, 214
sustainable communities 57, 58
sustainable development ii, vi, 10–13, 21, 33, 44, 47, 53, 54, 56, 63, 76, 92, 108, 109, 142, 180, 206, 208, 212

sustainable urban development 52, 58, 59, 67, 78, 83, 85, 86, 103, 104, 182, 203
Suva 149
synergies 98

Tabaris 88, 89
Taipei 66
Tanzania 150, 153, 154
Tehran 68, 72, 79, 81, 82
telecommunications 40
Tema 130, 198, 202
   Municipal Assembly 198, 202
tenure 70, 74, 78, 118
Tetra Pak East Med 99
Thatcher period 60
TIGRE S/A 168, 170
Titus Salt 8
Togo 128, 129
Tokyo 35, 65
tourism 63, 64, 71, 72, 167, 177
Town and Country Planning Act 63
trade 15, 21, 31, 167, 177, 184, 189, 212
transparency ii, 26, 47, 184, 198
transport 36, 37, 41, 58, 64, 65, 79, 82, 112, 125, 158, 177
triple bottom line 14, 31, 53, 212
Tunis 86

Ulan Baator 79
unemployment 29, 39, 57, 61, 158, 159, 182
United Arab Emirates (UAE) 79
United Nations 1, 2, 7, 16, 20–23, 25, 27, 33, 50, 53, 99, 107, 112, 180, 182, 183, 188, 204
United Nations Children's Fund (UNICEF) 24, 146, 153–155, 186, 188, 190, 191
United Nations Code (UN-Code) 21
United Nations Convention on the Rights of the Child (UNCRC) 188, 192
United Nations Development Programme (UNDP) 22, 30, 31, 34, 43, 50, 85, 99, 101, 214
United Nations Economic and Social Council (ECOSOC) 182

United Nations Education, Scientific
  & Cultural Organisation
  (UNESCO)   71, 73
United Nations Environment
  Programme (UNEP)   22, 26
United Nations General Assembly
  25
United Nations Global Compact
  22–24, 32
United Nations Habitat (UN-Habitat)
  35–37, 44, 50, 106, 107, 109–112,
  159–161, 189, 214
United Nations Industrial
  Development Organisation
  (UNIDO)   22, 29, 31, 33
United Nations Office on Drugs and
  Crime (UNODC)   22
United Nations Research Institute for
  Social Development   (UNRISD)
  25
United Nations Volunteers (UNV)   1,
  2, 3, 4, 16, 17, 22, 45, 49, 50, 99,
  101, 133, 187, 188, 190, 194, 195,
  204, 206, 214
United States   8, 160
urban children   180, 188–192, 202
urban design   55
urban development   1–6, 8, 33,
  34–51, 52, 56, 58–63, 66, 67,
  76–78, 82–86, 103, 104, 106, 112,
  113, 139, 140, 162, 180, 182, 185,
  188, 200, 203, 204, 212–214
Urban Development Corporations &
  Enterprise Zones   61
urban employment   186
urban housing   112, 140
urban infrastructure   73, 74,
  143–145, 216
urban policy   56, 57, 60, 61, 63, 76,
  103
urban poor   37, 38, 152, 186, 187,
  189, 203
urban populations   3, 35
urban poverty   3, 34, 36–39, 46, 50,
  51, 83, 103
urban problems   3, 39, 50, 51, 57,
  186
urban regeneration   52, 57, 60, 76,
  83, 84, 104, 212

urban renewal   94
urban settlements   38, 187, 189
urbanisation   34–37, 44, 58, 67,
  79–81, 84, 103, 111, 147, 178,
  189, 190
utilities   4, 27, 42, 52, 58–60, 72, 80,
  81, 86, 103, 123, 139, 143–179,
  205

Valparaiso   77
Venezuela   153
Victor Siaulys   94
Victorian period   8
Vietnam   24
violence   37, 41, 159, 165, 181, 188,
  189
visibility   90, 96, 102, 196, 203
viva guarulhos   85, 93–97, 104
Viviane Alves Machado   93
Volta River   196, 202
  Project   196
volunteerism   3, 39, 45, 49, 50, 194,
  195, 205, 208, 210, 211, 214
vulnerability   38, 81, 181, 189

Wakif Takkilak   87
waste management   29, 99, 144
Walls Project   196
water   29, 36, 37, 40, 42, 48, 50, 61,
  71, 73, 74, 79, 80, 86, 121–125,
  138, 143, 145–154, 156, 158,
  161–173, 178
  consumption   149, 150
  kiosks   151
wealth   36, 62, 64, 110, 131, 145
well being   40, 54, 55, 57
West Africa Cement   128
Western Europe   8
William Morris   8
worker housing   8
World Bank   11, 20, 34, 55, 77, 107,
  119, 143, 157, 181–185, 197
World Business Council for
  Sustainable Development
  (WBCSD)   12, 13
World Commission on Environment
  & Development (WCED)   53,
  180
World Conservation Strategy   53

World Health Organisation (WHO) 24, 38, 146, 153, 154, 155
World Summit for Social Development 182
Worldwide Fund for Nature (WWF) 10

Yemen 153
Yeumbeul 73, 74

Zambia 148, 150, 155
Zanzibar 71, 72
zoning 78